"The book by John Eterno discusses a root problem in our contemporary world: how is it possible to police a democratic society? It has been the subject of extensive debate in academia, the practitioners' field, and public opinion. Departing from the Stop and Frisk at the New York Police Department, the book traces the contextual factors that led to its implementation, the political injunctions that underpinned its measures, and its questionable results. It stresses the fine balance between protecting the community and respecting human rights, and how miscalculation can lead to negative outcomes. Despite its focus on the New York experience, the book provides an insightful perspective for all those interested in democratic police reform in distinct contexts across the globe."

Vicente Riccio, *Law and Graduate Program, Federal University of Juiz de Fora, Brazil and Visiting Scholar at the Professional Graduate Program on Human Rights, Citizenship, and Public Security at the State University of Amazonas, Brazil*

"*Cops and Stops* is an important resource for leaders committed to reform-oriented policing. It is a constructive contribution to contemporary policing debates, supporting informed, lawful, and sustainable approaches to crime control in democratic societies. Drawing on decades of scholarship, judicial analysis, and empirical evidence, John A. Eterno illuminates how police stop practices—particularly stop-and-frisk—can simultaneously reduce crime and erode constitutional rights, legitimacy, and community trust. With exceptional clarity, the book traces the evolution of aggressive policing strategies, performance management systems, and their unintended consequences, situating the New York City experience within a broader global and comparative framework. This work is not an argument against policing, but a compelling call for evidence-based, rights-respecting, and legitimacy-centered law enforcement. Essential reading for scholars, police leaders, policymakers, and students of criminal justice, *Cops and Stops* sets a benchmark for thoughtful, data-driven reflection on the future of democratic policing."

Dr. Richa Mishra, *Parul University, India*

"Policing in democracies demands a delicate balance between reducing crime and upholding civil rights. This book traces how New York City's policing strategies—from community policing, problem-oriented policing, to CompStat and the rise of stop-and-frisk—reshaped police culture, often at the expense of legitimacy and public trust. Through landmark court cases, shifting political leadership, and global comparisons, it reveals how aggressive, numbers-driven tactics resulted in dramatic crime drops and deep constitutional concerns. Examining racial disparities, oversight efforts, and international practices, the book offers a clear-eyed roadmap for democratic policing, grounded in accountability, data, and respect for the communities officers serve."

Gorazd Meško, *Professor of Criminology, University of Maribor, Slovenia*

"Eterno provides a unique and expert analysis of the origins, variations, dimensions, and dilemmas of police stops in a democratic society. As such, this study could not be more pertinent to policing in the United States today as it explores the ramifications of this practice in terms of racial/ethnic disparity, police legitimacy, large-scale top-down management and the proper role and practice of policing.

The value of this volume exceeds all others in exploring the multi dimensions of stop and frisks since the author possesses a unique blending of extensive high ranking police experience and incisive academic research of this practice. While the bulk of this work centers on the NYPD, Eterno's familiarity with and research of other democracies provides a much-needed context in examining the key dimensions of stops and frisks.

Cops and Stops is a 'Must Read' book."

Eli B. Silverman, *Ph.D. Professor Emeritus, John Jay College of Criminal Justice and Graduate Center, City University of New York, United States; co-author of* The Crime Numbers Game: Management by Manipulation

COPS AND STOPS

This book focuses on the controversial aggressive police practices employed to control crime by the New York City Police Department (NYPD) and the harm that has resulted and may further be produced if not checked. Informed by the author's personal experience as a retired NYPD Captain, as well as by his research in the field, this book explains the broad influence of stop and frisk as well as other aggressive policies.

In the mid-1990s, with the election of Mayor Rudolph Giuliani, a new era of aggressive policing began in New York City. While apparently helping lead to a decline in crime, the side effects of tactics such as stop and frisk led to powerful repercussions. A new Inspector General was appointed, the department came under federal review for racist and unconstitutional stops, and officers were required to record almost every citizen interaction. Names of individuals affected by these tactics, including Amadou Diallo, Eric Garner, and Abner Louima, among others, remain in the public consciousness. Practices such as stop and frisk in part fueled social justice movements like Black Lives Matter, and their use erodes public trust in the police, with many calling for increased scrutiny of police power, reduced police budgets, and even abolishment.

Designed for students in criminal justice programs as well as recruits in police training, this book explains and critiques stop and frisk and related tactics and recommends paths to a better future.

John A. Eterno, Ph.D., is Professor and Chair of the Criminal Justice and Legal Studies Department at Molloy University. He is also Director of Graduate Studies in Criminal Justice and a retired NYPD Captain. He is a Fulbright scholar and President of the American Academy for Law Enforcement, Long Island. He has penned numerous books, chapters, articles, and editorials on various criminal justice topics. His research has appeared on the front page of *The New York Times* and op-eds published in *The New York Times*, *The Atlantic*, and *The Guardian*. Among his books is *The Crime Numbers Game: Management by Manipulation* (with Eli Silverman).

COPS AND STOPS

An Analysis of NYPD's Stop, Question, and Frisk Practices

John A. Eterno

Routledge
Taylor & Francis Group
NEW YORK AND LONDON

Designed cover image: Getty Images

First published 2027
by Routledge
605 Third Avenue, New York, NY 10158

and by Routledge
4 Park Square, Milton Park, Abingdon, Oxon, OX14 4RN

Routledge is an imprint of the Taylor & Francis Group, an informa business

Library of Congress Cataloging-in-Publication Data
Names: Eterno, John, 1959- author
Title: Cops and stops : an analysis of NYPD's stop, question, and frisk program / John A. Eterno.
Description: New York, NY : Routledge, 2026. | Includes bibliographical references and index. |
Identifiers: LCCN 2026009458 (print) | LCCN 2026009459 (ebook) |
ISBN 9781032973272 paperback | ISBN 9781032973289 hardback |
ISBN 9781003593256 ebook
Subjects: LCSH: New York (N.Y.). Police Department | Stop and frisk (Law enforcement)—New York (State)—New York | Police-community relations—New York (State)—New York | Police misconduct—New York (State)—New York
Classification: LCC HV8148.N5 E8368 2026 (print) | LCC HV8148.N5 (ebook)
LC record available at https://lccn.loc.gov/2026009458
LC ebook record available at https://lccn.loc.gov/2026009459

ISBN: 978-1-032-97328-9 (hbk)
ISBN: 978-1-032-97327-2 (pbk)
ISBN: 978-1-003-59325-6 (ebk)

DOI: 10.4324/9781003593256

Typeset in Galliard
by codeMantra

CONTENTS

PREFACE

Noted sociologist Max Weber informs us that social scientists need to be value-neutral (Hammersley, 2017). That is, researchers in discussing their findings must be evidence-based, or as objective as possible, not politically biased or overly subjective. Indeed, one of the most important errors of inquiry is placing one's ideology and politics onto the research (Maxfield & Babbie, 2017). This type of error especially occurs when answers are suggested based on one's point of view rather than the data.

Such arguments are made by legal scholars with regard to court decisions. For example, the attitudinal model argues that the United States Supreme Court makes decisions based on the political positions of the judges rather than on the meaning of the law. This is why so many are concerned when a position opens on the high court. Each political wing is looking not for the greatest legal mind who can interpret the law, but rather for the person who will most likely vote on a case nearest to their political point of view. Thus, a conservative president picks a conservative jurist, and conversely, a liberal president picks a liberal judge. A study by Segal and Spaeth confirms this ideological bent (Segal & Spaeth, 2002). Judges on the high court vote according to their political ideology rather than the meaning of the law. As an example, when Dwight D. Eisenhower was President, he appointed Earl Warren as Chief Justice, thinking he would be a conservative. Mr. Eisenhower later remarked that this pick was one of the worst decisions of his life, as Mr. Warren became one of the most liberal judges in the history of the court (*Time*, 1974).

In the present-day United States, we are highly polarized. Remaining value-neutral is a rare quality, perhaps a luxury. Is Weber simply too idealistic? Perhaps. But attempting, at a minimum, to extricate oneself from the political fray and examining the facts without that albatross around one's neck would seem a valuable exercise. While we all have some level of bias, limiting those biases and examining the evidence are likely the most productive ways to get meaningful results.

Recall in the early part of the Enlightenment, when Galileo was challenged by the Church for speaking the truth. The heliocentric (sun-centered) system is clearly and demonstrably (even at his time) accurate. When minds become so closed to ideas, we fail miserably. The New York City Police Department (NYPD), and its highly touted crime decrease in the mid-1990s until today, is certainly astounding. However, when we link such crime decreases to a particular program, such as stop and frisk, we falsely take our politics and join it to a program. The NYPD did exactly this with stop and frisk. They argued, over and over again, despite mountains of evidence to the contrary, that huge increases in stop and frisk were necessary to prevent the "bad old days." Rather than engaging in evidence-based policing, they engaged in policy-based evidence making. They strained to find evidence to support the policy. They would point to high crime figures in minority communities, suggesting that stop and frisk is the answer. Pay no attention to the fact that crime was already down 60 percent before stop-and-frisk numbers went to "infinity and beyond."

This book will outline what occurred in New York City over many years. It will also examine other countries' laws and actions with respect to police stops. It will cover some general patterns that can be gleaned from all of this information. It will attempt to be value-neutral and based on specific evidence. Nevertheless, I do take the position that the police must obey the law while enforcing it. This is not completely value-neutral, as some might argue that other governments are superior. Rather, I admittedly take the position that democracy is the worst form of government except for all the others (Churchill, 1947). That is, I do take the framework of democratic principles as necessary for police in free society. This, it seems to me, is, by definition, critical to understanding this book.

Definitions are important. When I talk about democracy, I talk about representative democracy or a republic. The term democracy, then, is not a pure democracy as in Athens. Rather, I am talking about a representative democracy, a constitutional democracy, or a republic. So, for purists who prefer the term republic, I will use the term democracy simply for ease of understanding. That is, it is the term most associated with Western society. Nevertheless, I understand the nuances but feel it is important to note how I use the terms in this book. With respect to definitions, readers need to be cautious with associating terms in other materials with those here. For example, the name of the country the People's Republic of China has little to do with the people or a republic. It is a communist regime that does not recognize checks and balances, representative government, or even police following due process. This book focuses on democracies as discussed above. The police, as part of the executive branch, are checked and balanced by the other branches. Thus, in the United States, for example, court cases such as *Terry v. Ohio* (1968) carry meaning to both the public and the police. Furthermore, legislators (representatives elected by the people) make laws and budgetary decisions that deeply influence police behavior.

In the book, I discuss police stops and numerous terms that are used to describe these activities by the police. Some purists prefer stop, question, and frisk, Terry stops, or numerous other terms. I will use the terms police stops or stop and frisk in a general sense that includes all these other terms. I understand the nuances, but, for the purposes of this book, they are interchangeable. Many countries will be discussed, and if I were to get into various definitional issues, the book would be impossible to decipher. In this book, I use the terms discussed above throughout; however, please do not pick up another publication and expect the same clarity. Social scientists need to have a healthy skepticism. That is, look for evidence, replication, and reputation to help guide you.

To be value-neutral, scientists need to be free from unwarranted pressures. To that end, I would also like to point out that the current vogue against tenure at universities is something I abhor. University education and research are part of the democratic process. Ideas flourish, and, with a liberal education, we debate ideas. We focus on scholarship, not merely opinion. That is, one must be able to defend one's position in an academic way. To that end, tenure promotes free thinking and research without the worry of having one's position threatened. Researchers need to be free to study topics they wish to. In this way, new ideas can flourish. This is the essence of democracy. When we threaten tenure, we are also threatening free thinking and, yes, democracy. My research on the NYPD is a good example. When Dr. Eli Silverman (John Jay College of Criminal Justice, City University of New York) and I published critical materials on the NYPD based on very specific and clear evidence, we were subject to a wide variety of attacks by the NYPD and their sycophants. Such attacks are to be expected, but we have tenure. That is, our jobs cannot be threatened. This protection was critical to us being able to defend our work in both public and academic settings. We did not have to worry about our positions. While we had a difficult fight before us, we were able to defend ourselves from such critique through continued scholarship. Our positions have held up to wide-ranging scrutiny. At this point, I can confidently state our research is highly respected. Although not all will agree with every position, that too is part of the academic process. It must be understood that tenure and the university system of the United States needs to be protected. While I do not agree with every position taken by the American Association for University Professors (AAUP), I am an active member who was President and on the Board of my local chapter. Organizations like AAUP are important and even critical to the University system. We must cherish this system and understand that it is part of the power of democracy. Academics must be allowed to conduct research as they see fit. This is part of the democratic process, allowing for scholarly debate and the defense of ideas. University administrators, politicians, and others who threaten this process are threatening our way of life, our democracy.

With this in mind, I use evidence and experience to defend my positions. While no one can be completely value-neutral, I attempt to do just that. As a former police captain with the NYPD, I try to use my experiences to help guide my notions of police stops. I had an excellent career with the police department and am proud of that. At the same time, I allow that experience to inform me, not adversely affect my ideas. I endeavor to base my thoughts on evidence and not conjecture or opinion. This should be seen throughout the book.

References

Churchill, W. (1947, November 11). Speech delivered in the House of Commons [Speech]. House of Commons, London, England.

Hammersley, M. (2017). On the role of values in social research: Weber vindicated? *Sociological Research Online*, *22*(1), 130–141. https://doi.org/10.5153/sro.4197

Maxfield, M. G., & Babbie, E. (2017). *Basics of research methods for criminal justice and criminology* (8th ed.). Cengage Learning.

Segal, J. A., & Spaeth, H. J. (2002). *The Supreme Court and the attitudinal model revisited.* Cambridge University Press.

Time. (1974, July 22). *The law: Earl Warren's way: Is it fair?* Time. https://time.com/archive/6876037/the-law-earl-warrens-way-is-it-fair/

ACKNOWLEDGMENTS

First and foremost, I want to thank my God, Lord, and Savior Jesus Christ for everything. Importantly, He has sent many people to help me. This is only a short list. There are many others not mentioned here. Graduate assistants Carly Howell and Sean Michael Ronan have been outstanding researchers and editors for me. Other graduate assistants, Jessica Gruenfelder and Logan Dexter, also assisted. I must thank Dr. Eli B. Silverman, professor emeritus John Jay College of Criminal Justice, City University of New York. Our many works together have helped me to understand these issues. The synergy of our efforts is amazing. Without his input, this work would not be possible. My administrative assistant Regina Gorney was a tremendous help. She freed me up to work on the book and assisted in countless other ways. My colleagues at Molloy University, especially Dr. Christine Barrow, Dr. Deniese Kennedy-Kollar, Wilson Marrero, James Dean, Stephen McAllister, Joy Watson, Robert Von Werne, and many others have made my life easier with all the work they do. I would also like to thank Don Horn, my vocational and rehabilitation counselor for the New York State Commission for the Blind. His guidance has been an invaluable help. My wife and children (adults now) have been awesome support. JoAnn, my wife, Julia, and Lauren have been a constant source of inspiration. I have tested ideas on them, and they always give me honest feedback. Thanks for all you do. I love all of you and may God bless you all abundantly.

1

POLICING IN DEMOCRACIES

Introduction

We often think of a democratic society as peaceful. We may have thoughts of people strolling through places like Central Park in New York City or perhaps running along the FDR Drive with the East River, the Brooklyn Bridge, and South Street Seaport as scenery. Yet, in terms of crime, democracies will, in the traditional sense (e.g., burglary, robbery, assault, etc. by members of the public) tend to have more crime. Why is this so? In a police state, everyone lives in fear of law enforcement. In Romania after World War II during communist times, for example, the police role was once of protecting the Communist Party (Cofăn & Băloi, 2019). The police were very intrusive and had no need for proof or evidence. Essentially, the police were unbridled. They were unlimited in power—a police state. When people live in fear of the police, street crime is much less likely.

As Romania became more democratic, a shift in how police do their work took place. Police had to find evidence for illegal behavior. They became less intrusive. Additionally, perpetrators had far more freedom and, therefore, access to transportation. They could more easily flee from police. Similar experiences have been documented in new democracies. For example, Frantz (2019, p. 404) writes,

> The transition from dictatorship to democracy is a challenging moment for all polities. Amid the turbulence, new governments face an urgent and pressing need to create order. The police—the critical state organization tasked with combating crime—are at the core of such societal changes (Marenin, 1996). They must adjust to changing times and work to restore order, while continuing to fight crime. This results in many observers citing spikes in violent crime following democratization (Moran, 2011). Notable examples include post-Apartheid South Africa and much of Eastern and Central Europe following the collapse of communism.

By necessity, processes based on free principles must be developed by new democracies. For example, a new closeness with other democratic societies has to be established in order to

DOI: 10.4324/9781003593256-1

legally extradite criminals. Furthermore, modern intelligence analysis was employed and developed to deal with the issues that democracy brings. Democratic society develops a wide range of sophisticated tools such as mapping and other computer software. Court cases have to be built and evidence that can be used in courts must be properly collected. Decision-making is also more complicated. Since democratic policing has many legal guidelines, police are constrained far more in their behaviors (e.g., respecting rights, obeying legal guidelines, and following the restrictions of civilian complaint review boards and inspectors general).

This is not to say that police in democratic society cannot be aggressive and proactive. However, when they become overly militaristic and blatantly disregard the basic tenets of democracy, their work becomes a focal point for debate, controversy, possible outright disobedience, lawsuits, complaints, and other repercussions. The founders of the United States, for example, had numerous grievances against the totalitarian British. The American Declaration of Independence outlines many of those issues:

> We hold these truths to be self-evident, that all men are created equal, that they are endowed by their Creator with certain unalienable Rights, that among these are Life, Liberty and the pursuit of Happiness—That to secure these rights, Governments are instituted among Men, deriving their just powers from the consent of the governed—That whenever any Form of Government becomes destructive of these ends, it is the Right of the People to alter or to abolish it, and to institute new Government.
>
> *(National Archives, 2025)*

These are not shallow words but the opening volley of war. The Declaration discusses many issues with an abusive government. Totalitarian regimes, then, abuse their powers and commit what is worse than street crimes on its own citizens. Street crimes, in such a society, are less important to the populace because the government itself has become the main criminal—abusing its power and, in general, minimizing human dignity and rights.

Police in a democracy must work within the law to enforce the law. As Madison (1788) writes in *Federalist No. 48*,

> An elective despotism is not the government we fought for but one which should not only be founded on free principles but in which the powers of government should be so divided and balanced among several bodies … as that no one can transcend their legal limits without being checked and restrained by the others.

The police, then, as agents of the executive branch, are checked and balanced by the other equal branches of government. That is, the legislative and judicial branches of government. An additional check is, of course, the people. Further, a free press and educational system should also serve to check and balance government power.

The police must work within the law, and they also must serve the people as citizens themselves. A staple of this service is having an understanding of the social contract. We need one another to survive. For example, if attacked by another country, we rely on one another to defend ourselves. Yet, at the same time, we want to remain free. There is a need for some compromise. We defer to the government willingly giving up some freedoms to allow the general will to rule. In our democratic society, the importance of the rule of law and submitting to it are critical. We give up some freedoms willingly to benefit from the whole. This means we agree to follow the laws but, as free people, we only give up so much of our freedoms as to allow the functioning of the whole (Rousseau, 1968). The United States Constitution can be seen as a written document that represents this social contract. While the social contract is generally not written, the Constitution is a close example of what we agree to. Thus, we gain freedoms and rights under the Constitution but, at the same time, we agree to uphold the limitations this puts on us and agree to uphold the rules. We get freedom of speech, but we cannot yell "fire" in a theater. Further, we agree to follow due process of law. That is, the government cannot take life, liberty, or property without some level of due process. You are entitled to that. For example, if you are arrested, you are entitled to a jury trial. We agree to these laws voluntarily to benefit from the country and what it gives to all.

Police are the focal point of all of this. How they operate is akin to looking under a microscope to determine the health of a democracy (Bouza, 1990). If the police are brutal, militaristic, or abusive, the democracy is not functioning well. If the police are respectful, following the rule of law, and enforcing the law while respecting it, then democracy is healthy. By analyzing police behavior, we are able to determine the function or dysfunction (or something in between) of government.

The father of modern-day sociology, Emile Durkheim, discusses this using different terms. He argues that we must understand that all of us are dependent on one another. We are not truly independent. That is, we rely on others for food, shelter, and numerous other items. In this industrial age, division of labor makes us reliant. He argues that we develop what he terms organic solidarity as compared with mechanical solidarity, which is what occurs in agricultural society. That is, in an agrarian society, one can be more independent. However, in a modern society, we are more dependent on one another.

Without modern conveniences, we all are essentially helpless. Division of labor makes us very efficient but, at the same time, creates dependency. Once we realize this, either consciously or subconsciously, we can develop what Durkheim (1964) calls a collective conscience. If the conscience is strong, we all understand the rules or norms of the society in which we live. If it is weak, then we are more likely to have crime, as the rules are not understood.

What does all this mean? Police must have a keen understanding of the rules. As society changes, the police, as agents of the government, must be enforcing the rules. Fundamental fairness needs to be seen by all such that people generally obey *willingly*. The role of the police, then, is to understand the social contract and to enforce the rules while at the same time following those rules. The police are citizens too. They cannot lose sight of their key obligations under the social contract. There are other aspects to these basic principles. We can visualize this by developing an understanding of two models of the criminal justice system. That is, crime control and due process.

Crime Control versus Due Process

The crime control and due process models of the criminal justice system can be seen as extremes. Both work together in a push–pull sort of way. As one pushes, the other pulls, and neither ever completely wins the tug-of-war. Additionally, some seem predisposed to one model or the other but neither works without the other. One model emphasizes stopping crime. That becomes the focal point of the system. The other model sees protecting the rights of processes of the system as key. Since both models are critically important to a functioning democracy, neither can operate without the other. As we shall see, there are times, however, where one model seems to have an advantage over the other.

Packer's Description

Packer (1964) explains these models in detail in a classic article, "Two Models of the Criminal Process." He describes the crime control model as an assembly-line. Police and prosecutors efficiently determine the likelihood of guilt. If the evidence is strong, then the alleged perpetrator must quickly be brought through the system with little to no interruptions. In this way, there is a presumption of guilt. Packer advises, however, this is not the opposite of presumption of innocence but rather instructs those in the system how to act. Fact-finding and plea bargaining become critical as the system must be operating at peak efficiency.

Those who see crime control as most important believe that law-abiding citizens will lose their freedom if the criminals are not removed from the streets. There must be fewer challenges and a more uniform system. The image of an assembly line, and even the term assembly line justice, seem apropos to this model. If this model is allowed to run wild or without any check and balance, there will, of course, be government overreach. As I have discussed, our founding fathers built within the systems of our government checks and balances to prevent overreach and abuse by government authority. Various court cases interpret the Bill of Rights to prevent too much intrusion.

Packer's due process model represents a critically important flip side to crime control. He likens this model to an obstacle course. That is, in order to convict someone, various challenges must be met by the prosecution. The accused must have full adjudication. This model strives to limit errors in the system and prevent the innocent from going to prison. Even more, it holds high the idea of legal guilt. That is, if the system does not follow the rules, the criminal, guilty or not, must go free. The system itself must be free from corruption. So, obstacles in the form of challenges must be pursued in order to be sure that the system is not abused. *Miranda*, *Mapp*, and many other challenges could lead to, for example, exclusion of illegally attained evidence. Some, such as Justice Benjamin Cardozo, have argued that the criminal goes free because the constable has blundered. This means the guilty should not go free due to a technicality. However, those who tend to argue for the due process model would say the person must go free, not because of the constable, but because the system cannot lose its integrity (Kamisar, 1979).

In the real world, neither of these models exists. They are ideal types or models for comparison purposes. Some lean one way or the other but, in practice, both models are essential to the functioning of the criminal justice system. That is, they are both important and work in tandem. Police leaders tend to suggest that the crime control model is critical, while those in the New York Civil Liberties Union of the Center for Constitutional Rights will argue that controlling government abuse is more important. Striking the balance becomes an issue.

Times of Peril

When the society itself is dealing with an immediate threat, by necessity, the power of the executive branch expands—sometimes enormously. The balance shifts toward control as opposed to due process. For example, during 9/11, the power of the executive expanded enormously with the consent of Congress, as the USA PATRIOT Act (2001) and the Authorization for the Use of Military Force Act (AUMF) (2001) were passed. Another example is seen by understanding the history of the writ of habeas corpus in the United States. Habeas corpus allows those who are detained by the government to petition for their release. That is, you go before a court of law to argue for your freedom, while the government must explain the reasons for your imprisonment. The American Constitution does not allow habeas corpus to be suspended except in times of rebellion or invasion.

Remarkably, there are only three times in American history in which the writ of habeas corpus was suspended. The first time was under Abraham Lincoln during the Civil War, which was, obviously, a time of insurrection by the Confederate States. Suspected Southern spies and so forth had to be detained. The second time was during World War II. After the bombing of Pearl Harbor, war hysteria took the country by storm. Franklin Delano Roosevelt suspended habeas corpus with Executive Order 9066. The Japanese Americans on the West Coast were forcibly interred. They had no choice. Years later, under President Reagan, the nation apologized and paid token reparations to the families affected by this. The third and final time to date that habeas corpus was suspended was by George W. Bush after 9/11. Suspected terrorists were held without the benefit of having typical due process. As one can see, during emergencies such as war and terrorism, the powers of the executive branch expand. After the emergency is over, the powers tend to return to normal.

These difficult times seem quite obvious to us, looking back. However, there are those who will advocate for crime control or due process and try to convince the people to sway one way or the other. For example, police leaders are more likely to try to convince us that there is a major issue with crime and/or terrorism that must be dealt with immediately. We will see this later on with Commissioner Kelly in New York City. The police leader advised how crime must be stopped and so forth. Conversely, some argue that government abuse of power is our main concern, such as police officers not respecting citizens' rights. Examples of these types of groups are the American Civil Liberties Union, the Center for Constitutional Rights, and police reform organizations such as the Police Reform Organizing Project. We can categorize them as "law and order" groups on the one side versus "abuse of power brokers" on the other. Both see themselves as being critically important. Both have powerful allies, and both are important, but neither is accurate alone. It is the balance between them that is important. This will ebb and flow with the times. As stated, in times of peril, police power or the executive branch expands. However, when police corruption or abuse of authority is exposed, the reformers' powers expand, as seen in the Knapp Commission and the Mollen Commission, which will be discussed in more detail later in the book. The stop-and-frisk controversy in New York City and throughout the world is an excellent example of the push–pull between these two sides.

What Is Stop and Frisk?

Stop and frisk is a police practice that is known by many names, such as: *Terry* stops; forcible stops; stop, question, and frisk; temporary stops; investigative stops; short detention; among other names. The commonality among these names is they have their legal foundation based on the United States Supreme Court case, *Terry v. Ohio* (1968).

The United States Supreme Court Case

The landmark case of *Terry v. Ohio* (1968) empowers police officers to detain those suspected of criminal activity for a short period of time. Sometimes, officers may frisk, and at times they may also search. These actions or inactions are based on a level of proof known as reasonable suspicion.

Levels of Proof

Reasonable suspicion means that officers must be able to articulate a reasonable level of suspicion that the person they are dealing with is committing, has committed, or is about to commit a crime. It is a level of proof below probable cause or reasonable cause to believe. Probable cause is a higher level than reasonable suspicion and is the level needed for officers to make a legal arrest throughout the United States. We can think of this as officers being about 50 percent sure the suspect is guilty of criminal activity. The level below probable cause is generally known as reasonable suspicion. We can think of this as being 20–25 percent sure that the suspect is guilty of a crime. The officer must be able to articulate why they are suspicious. For example, the suspect may be in a high-crime area, fits the description of a known robbery suspect whose modus operandi includes using a gun, is constantly glancing back and forth, and hides when a uniformed officer goes near. This is not enough for an arrest (probable cause) but is enough to forcibly stop, ask questions, and frisk the person to check for weapons (since a robbery suspect is known to carry weapons). The frisk is a pat-down of the outer garments to determine if a weapon may be concealed below. A search would be permitted if something were felt. The search is limited to the area where the possible weapon was felt. So, frisks, and especially searches, are limited in scope.

An even lower level of proof is mere suspicion. This level is based on a hunch. That is, the officer is only about 10 percent sure there is criminality afoot. In this case, the officer cannot yet articulate reasonable suspicion. The officer might approach but, at this lower level, the suspect can simply leave. Nevertheless, an officer may ask some questions such as, "What are you doing here?" and so forth to try to raise the level. If the person becomes very evasive and makes some sort of admission such as, "You got me, you know I have worked this corner before," the officer may then proceed with the forcible stop and attempt to gain probable cause. If probable cause is not achieved, the person is free to go. However, upon further questioning, if the person admits to the suspected behavior or other elements, the level of proof is elevated to probable cause, allowing the officer to make an arrest. At each level, the officer's behavior is circumscribed to certain actions and no more. I note that I have seen videos on the internet advising people how to act in certain situations. I caution readers, however, that one does not know the level of proof that an officer is at when being stopped or questioned. For example, the officer may have a detailed description of a rapist and you fit that description. That alone will give the officer a minimum level of reasonable suspicion. One should never assume that the officer is "fishing" for information. Officers are keenly aware, trained in the law, and know their limits. Later in this chapter, further complications of this within New York State will be explained.

Notable Issues from Terry v. Ohio

Terry indicates that stop and frisk as a practice is already known, but has not yet been decided by the United States Supreme Court. This case makes the practice of stopping suspects on less than probable cause official: "Reflective of the tensions involved are the practical and constitutional arguments pressed with great vigor on both sides of the public debate over the power of the police to 'stop and frisk'—as it is sometimes euphemistically termed—suspicious persons" (*Terry v. Ohio*, 1968).

There are some critically important facts in the case. Officer McFadden is a plainclothes officer observing three suspects who, based on his expertise and over 30 years' experience, are casing a store to commit robbery. He is able to articulate his suspicions. They are nervous, walking back and forth past a store window over a dozen times, and so forth. The officer eventually approaches and identifies himself as a police officer. He pats them down over the outside of their clothing and reaches in only after suspecting a weapon. Based on these facts, the court finds the officer's actions reasonable. The Supreme Court notes, however, that such behavior by an officer "must surely be an annoying, frightening, and perhaps humiliating experience" (*Terry v. Ohio*, 1968, 1882).

The Supreme Court allows the intrusion based on these facts. Further, the Court recognizes the intrusion will be a serious one that will affect those stopped. At this early stage in this work, it must be pointed out that the hundreds of thousands of stops made in New York City over the past few years were often conducted by rookie officers, sometimes with heavy quotas on them. Many of these officers were not yet fully trained and assigned to what the New York City Police Department called Impact Zones. The pressure on these officers came from their supervisors who were, in turn, influenced by their superiors due to a performance management system known as CompStat (compare statistics) (Eterno & Silverman, 2012). Later in this work, I will discuss the evidence for the practices of the New York City Police Department (NYPD). One cannot help but recognize the stark contrast between what the Supreme Court authorized and the over-aggressive tactics of the NYPD that include inexperienced officers, quotas, and enormous pressures from supervisors, as opposed to the professional, experienced officers who recognize robbery suspects based on clear, articulable evidence.

People State of New York v. Louis De Bour *and* People State of New York v. Milton La Pene

I have already explained the essentials of *Terry*. New York City was sued for its stop-and-frisk practices. In the seminal federal case on stop and frisk in New York City, *Floyd v. City of New York* (2013), understanding New York case law, especially in *People v. De Bour* (1976), becomes critical. Without an understanding of *De Bour*, one cannot understand stop and frisk as it is practiced in New York City. For example, the initial stop in *Floyd* is justified as a Level 1 *De Bour* stop. This means the officers did not yet have reasonable suspicion. In New York, officers cannot even approach a person without some level of proof. In New York, this is called an objective reason (or Level 1 stop). Without an objective reason, the officers may not approach. Training in the City police academy specifically teaches all levels of proof, including the complications of *De Bour*. Level 1 stops can increase to a full-fledged *Terry* stop, but only if the initial inquiry elevates to reasonable suspicion.

The two cases were decided together by New York's highest court. They are cited as *People v. De Bour* (1976). It is important to note that officers in New York State during the time of the most aggressive stop-and-frisk practices (i.e., 2003 to 2011) were actually under more restrictive legal limitations compared with the national standard explained previously in *Terry*, as cited by New York's highest court—the Court of Appeals. That Court created a confusing four-tiered system for officers in New York State. The legal opinion joins two separate cases—*De Bour* and *La Pene*—which were adjudicated in 1976 by New York's high court. Therefore, this was, and is, well-established law in New York. However, this case, including the dissent, shows a confusing array of levels that requires the wisdom of Solomon to decipher. As Justice Harold Rothwax (1996, pp. 40–41) advised:

> The problem is, the law is so muddy that the police can't find out what they are allowed to do even if they wanted to. If a street cop took a sabbatical and holed himself up in a library for six months doing nothing but studying the law on search and seizure, he wouldn't know any more than he did before he started. The law is totally confusing, yet we expect cops to always know at every moment what the proper action is. It's no wonder that police officers are somewhat edgy—especially when they are pursuing cases involving vicious murderers and rapists.

In any discussion of stop and frisk in New York, this case must be noted.

The four-tiered system created by the Court of Appeals attempts to explain to practitioners the behaviors officers may or may not do. Even the high State Court is divided on what should happen to the defendants in these two cases.

The facts of the two cases are not in dispute. The facts in *De Bour* follow:

> At 12:15 a.m. on the morning of October 15, 1972, Kenneth Steck, a police officer assigned to the Tactical Patrol Force of the New York Police Department, was working the 6:00 p.m. to 2:00 a.m. tour of duty, assigned to patrol by foot a certain section of Brooklyn. While walking his beat on a street illuminated by ordinary streetlamps and devoid of pedestrian traffic, he and his partner noticed someone walking on the same side of the street in their direction. When the solitary figure of the defendant, Louis De Bour, was within 30 or 40 feet of the uniformed officers he crossed the street. The two policemen followed suit and when De Bour reached them Officer Steck inquired as to what he was doing in the neighborhood. De Bour, clearly but nervously, answered that he had just parked his car and was going to a friend's house.
>
> The patrolman then asked De Bour for identification. As he was answering that he had none, Officer Steck noticed a slight waist-high bulge in the defendant's jacket. At this point, the policeman asked De Bour to unzip his coat. When De Bour complied with this request Officer Steck observed a revolver protruding from his waistband. The loaded weapon was removed [*214] from behind his waistband and he was arrested for possession of the gun.
>
> At the suppression hearing Officer Steck testified to the above facts noting that the encounter lasted "a few minutes". On cross-examination, Officer Steck stated that at the time he believed defendant might have been involved with narcotics and crossed the street to avoid apprehension. On the other hand, the defendant testified that he never saw the police until they crossed the street in front of him and that he continued walking straight ahead. He stated that the police asked him where he was going and also whether he had any dope in his pockets. He answered that he had been visiting his mother's home with relatives. De Bour further testified that during this encounter, Steck's partner proceeded to pat his clothing and two or three minutes later Steck found the gun and fired it in order to see whether it was operable. At the conclusion of this hearing the court found Officer Steck's testimony to be credible and denied the motion to suppress. Subsequently De

Bour pleaded guilty to felonious attempted possession of a weapon and was sentenced to a conditional discharge. The Appellate Division unanimously affirmed, without opinion.

(People v. De Bour, 1976, p. 375)

The Court holds that the actions of the police are lawful. This is true even though the suspect simply crossed the street—probably to avoid the officers. Reasonable suspicion was not yet achieved, but the officers, according to the Court, had enough evidence to approach. The suspect willingly opened his jacket when the officers asked. In this case, the intrusion was considered minimal.

Let us compare this with the facts of *La Pene* from the opinion of the Court:

> This case presents a counterpoint to *De Bour*. Here too, the police had a suitable predicate, an anonymous phone tip, to approach the defendant and make an inquiry. However, neither that predicate nor ensuing events or exigencies amounted to reasonable suspicion so as to justify the precipitate frisk of this defendant. Consequently, the weapon seized as a result of that search should have been suppressed.
>
> The evidence adduced at the suppression hearing reveals [*222] that on the morning of December 4, 1971, Officer Dennis Sheeran and his partner were assigned to uniformed radio motor patrol in Queens, New York. At about 1:45 a.m. they received a radio message from central communications that there was a male Negro with a gun, wearing a red shirt, in a place called Jean's Bar. This information was the result of an anonymous phone call. The policemen responded and arrived at the scene simultaneously with another radio patrol unit. After noticing no unusual conditions outside, the four uniformed officers entered the bar. One officer stationed himself at the front, another at the side. Officer Sheeran and his partner went directly to the rear of the bar as soon as they saw the defendant, Milton La Pene, who was wearing a red shirt. At this time, La Pene was standing in the back of the establishment with his hands in his pockets and was apparently engaged in conversation with some other patrons. La Pene was wearing a red shirt or overblouse which was worn outside his trousers and draped to a point below his waist.
>
> An examination of the record reveals that the policemen did nothing to verify or substantiate the information received over the radio. Neither the patrons nor the bartender were approached or questioned. Officer Sheeran conceded on cross-examination that on entering the bar he made no attempt to ascertain whether or not there were other Black men present wearing red shirts. He further testified that La Pene's conduct was neither suspicious nor furtive and that he did not see a bulge at the defendant's waist or any other indication that La Pene was armed. Nevertheless, without asking a single question Officer Sheeran ordered the defendant to "freeze" and raise his hands. The policeman then frisked defendant and discovered a.25 caliber Titan automatic pistol containing seven live rounds. La Pene was immediately handcuffed and arrested for felonious possession of a weapon.
>
> After his motion to suppress the handgun was denied, Le Pene pleaded guilty to attempted felonious possession of a weapon and was sentenced to probation. A divided Appellate Division affirmed. The issue before our court is whether or not the anonymous telephone tip which was received in this instance was sufficient to justify the ensuing police conduct.
>
> *(People v. De Bour, 1976, p. 213)*

In *La Pene*, the court does not find the actions of the police lawful. The majority advises that the officers needed reasonable suspicion to search. The anonymous tip, although somewhat specific, did not rise to reasonable suspicion. The officers should have done more of an investigation to raise the level.

Interestingly, the dissent shows how convoluted this can get. Two of the seven justices argued that in both cases, the officers' actions were not supported. They write, "There was no reason for the police to confront De Bour. They lacked 'probable cause,' reasonable cause,' or, for that matter, any cause for his detention as he walked along the street, so to speak, minding his own business" (*People v. De Bour*, 1976, p. 228).

Thus, in *De Bour*, the Court determined that the police actions were lawful, but, in *La Pene*, the Court held that the officers' actions were not justified. Additionally, the dissent argues vehemently, with the same set of facts, that the police actions were not lawful in this situation. In this case, New York's highest court creates a four-tiered system that officers must obey.

The Court comes to this system by balancing civil liberties and the need to fight crime. The high court writes in *People v. De Bour* (1976, p. 227), "A balance needs to be, and long ago was, struck, a balance between society's interest in encouraging law enforcement and society's interest in fostering individual privacy and personal inviolability." They further explicate the powers that officers have at various levels of evidence:

> We bear in mind that any inquiry into the propriety of police conduct must weigh the interference it entails against the precipitating and attending conditions. By this approach various intensities of police action are justifiable as the precipitating and attendant factors increase in weight and competence. The minimal intrusion of approaching to request information is permissible when there is some objective credible reason for that interference not necessarily indicative of criminality *People v. De Bour* (1976). The next degree, the common-law right to inquire, is activated by a founded suspicion that criminal activity is afoot and permits a somewhat greater intrusion in that a policeman is entitled to interfere with a citizen to the extent necessary to gain explanatory information, but short of a forcible seizure (*People v. Cantor*, 1975, p. 114; *People v. Rosemond*, 1970; *People v. Rivera*, 1964, p. 446; and authorities cited therein). Where a police officer entertains a reasonable suspicion that a particular person has committed, is committing or is about to commit a felony or misdemeanor, the New York State Criminal Procedure Law (CPL) authorizes a forcible stop and detention of that person (New York Criminal Procedure Law § 140.50[1]); *Terry v. Ohio*, 1968; *People v. Cantor*, 1975). A corollary of the statutory right to temporarily detain for questioning is the authority to frisk if the officer reasonably suspects that he is in danger of physical injury by virtue of the detainee being armed (New York Criminal Procedure Law § 140.50[3]). Finally, a police officer may arrest and take into custody a person when he has probable cause to believe that person has committed a crime, or offense in his presence (New York Criminal Procedure Law § 140.50[10]). This synopsis represents the gradation of permissible police authority with respect to encounters with citizens in public places and directly correlates the degree of objectively credible belief with the permissible scope of interference.
>
> *(People v. De Bour, 1976, p. 223)*

Explaining the Four-Tiered *De Bour*

I mentioned earlier various levels of proof for which officers have varying powers. In New York State there are four levels based on *De Bour*. The NYPD Patrol Guide Procedure 212-11 entitled, ***Investigative Encounters: Requests for Information, Common Law Right of Inquiry, and Level 3 Stops***, attempts to explain to officers their duties in this area (New York City Police Department, 2016). At the first level (or a Level 1 Intrusion) the officer must have an objective credible reason to approach. At this level, the officer may approach to request information. Interestingly, this reason may have nothing to do with criminality; for example, the person is slowing pedestrian traffic due to where they are standing. The officer can ask basic non-threatening questions. However, the officer cannot forcibly detain or ask consent to search. At times, if the officer is concerned for his or her own safety, the officer can take some protective measures such as asking the person to remove their hands from their pockets. This should only occur in unusual situations.

A Level 2 Intrusion is based on the common-law right of inquiry. At this level, the officer must have a founded suspicion that criminality is afoot. This is a lower level than reasonable suspicion required for a forcible *Terry* stop. The officer at this level may have reliable hearsay information about the person being approached. The officer cannot forcibly stop and seize the person but can ask for the consent of the person to be searched. I have already described Level 3 *Terry* forcible stops.

Thus, police officers operating in New York State work under a different set of guidelines compared with the United States Supreme Court. While *Terry* is still the law, people in New York State have more protection due to *De Bour*. Any discussion of stop and frisk in New York must have this understanding. Without this background, one cannot hope to understand what police must do in New York, including New York City. Of course, I will talk about other restrictions on New York City officers as I explain more about what has occurred and is occurring there.

Police Policy versus Law

With police work there is an important distinction between police policy and law. In general terms, the law is created by a government legislature. These laws can be outward facing to citizens such as murder, rape, or robbery. However, the law also applies to officials who are in the government. Some laws specifically restrict or limit government officials' authority. These laws are inward facing (e.g., when officers may arrest, use force, or stop suspects). Those government officials who ensure its proper application, which include law enforcement officers such as the police, must apply the law based on their discretion to the public, obey the law themselves, and follow agency policy.

In their role as enforcers of the law, the police are the gatekeepers of the criminal justice system. Once an arrest is made, which, as we already discussed, must be based on probable cause that the suspect did the act, other parts of the system are now invoked. This includes district attorneys, courts, defense counsel, court officers, correction officers, judges, and many others. These officials make sure the defendant is properly given due process. This includes, but is not limited to, a proper trial. The person arrested and going to trial must receive a proper defense. In the United States and many other democratic countries, one is innocent until proven guilty (also called a presumption of innocence). However, this is not true in some other democratic countries such as France, Romania, Brazil, and many others. Without the presumption, the burden is shifted to the defendant to prove his or her innocence.

Police discretion to arrest starts the process. Note that in some countries the judiciary can be more active than in others. Nevertheless, the police have a key role in initiating the criminal justice process regardless of country. Thus, various pressures on police are important.

These pressures are quite varied but there are critically important aspects. A short list of some of these pressures includes political, media, community, supervisors, peers, unions, oversight agencies, and more (Eterno, 2023). Under "political," police will feel varying pressures from mayors and legislators who may, for example, demand reductions in crime. Police pay attention to news media as well. Well-publicized events such as police brutality, stop and frisk, car pursuits, and so forth affect their behaviors. Community pressures demanding action on various issues ranging from something simple such as double-parking to preventing violent assaults and murders are commonplace. Supervisors may demand arrests and summonses, and require officers to act in a certain way, such as being polite and not getting complaints. Officers' peers have an enormous effect on officers, especially evident in countless studies (Drummond, 1976; Crank, 1995; Eterno, 2003). The police culture is based on the dangerousness of the work environment. Since officers are required to rely on other officers for protection, officers must be sure not to damage their reputation among other officers or face the consequences. Whistleblowers such as Adrian Schoolcraft are particularly vulnerable (This American Life, n.d.). Nevertheless, all officers are cognizant of this and, importantly, it affects their behavior. Research on the attitude effect (police must maintain respect in the streets) is particularly apropos (Worden & Shepard, 1996; Lundman, 1994, 1980, 1974; Klinger, 1994). Unions can add to these pressures, requiring slowdowns or officers to do or not do certain acts. Of course, numerous oversight agencies such as civilian complaint review boards, inspectors general, district attorneys, and much more have an influence on officers' behaviors as well. Overall, police are bombarded with varying pressures that each officer must sort through to determine how he or she will act.

While enforcing the law, police must also obey the law and agency policy. To that end, training is particularly important and highly influences officer behavior. Training will involve, at a minimum, a combination of police policy specific to that agency and the proscriptions of the law. I have discussed some of the legal aspects in the court cases *Terry v. Ohio* (1968) and *People v. De Bour* (1976). It is beyond the scope of this chapter to fully outline every aspect of these weighty rules. However, the chapter aims to show how complicated this is for officers.

Some of the nuances between law and policy can best be explained by example. The NYPD has very specific rules that do not have the force of law. If officers do not obey these policies, then they are subject to disciplinary action, which may include losing their jobs. Additionally, if they are sued civilly, the City may elect not to support them in court. The law, of course, must also be obeyed. However, if officers disobey the law, then the courts can deal with officers as they would any defendant. Officers, just like any citizens, are entitled to due process with both policy and law.

A further example of the differences between policy and law can be demonstrated through the chokehold death of Mr. Eric Garner. In that case, Officer Daniel Pantaleo used an unauthorized chokehold to arrest Mr. Garner. The chokehold, at the time, was not illegal. That is, the law allowed the use of a chokehold, if necessary, by police officers who needed to use force. Mr. Garner, based on available evidence, appeared to resist arrest. Therefore, Mr. Pantaleo could, under then-New York State law, use appropriate force to effect the arrest, including a chokehold. Both the District Attorney in Staten Island and the United States Attorney's office for the Southern District of New York determined that the officer did not violate any laws. That is, he used necessary force and did not violate the civil rights of Mr. Garner. As far as the law is concerned, Officer Pantaleo was not charged and was not guilty of any crimes on the basis of his actions in this case. However, the NYPD had a strict policy against the use of chokeholds. Thus, while the officer did not face legal charges of criminality, he still had to deal with the guidelines described in the NYPD policy (Eterno & Verma, 2024). Ultimately, after receiving due process through a police department trial, the officer received the penultimate penalty of being fired by the Department. While the officer did not violate any laws, he was found to have violated NYPD policy. After this incident, the New York State legislature made a law that now bans chokeholds in New York State. The law is named after this incident and is called The Eric Garner Anti-Chokehold Act (2020). It reads in part,

> Under our law, a person is guilty of aggravated strangulation when, being a police officer or a peace officer, he or she, uses a chokehold or similar restraint 1 that applies pressure to the throat or windpipe of a person in a manner that may hinder breathing or reduce intake of air, 2 and thereby causes serious physical injury or death to that person.
>
> *(pp. 1–3)*

What was once a NYPD policy now has the force of law.

It is not that unusual for policy to become law. Another example is NYPD shooting policy. In *Tennessee v. Garner* (1985), the United States Supreme Court determined that it violates the Fourth Amendment to shoot an unarmed, non-dangerous fleeing felon. This was already a part of NYPD's shooting policy. Courts can also have the force of law in interpreting statutes or, importantly, the Constitution (or other courts have similar interpretation powers which carry the force of law depending on the court).

Overall, then, police must follow both the law and policy. Laws are generally enacted by legislators but can also arise from court cases. Police policy, on the other hand, comes from the administration of a particular agency. Many examples of model policies can be found based on organizations with expertise in law enforcement such as the International Association of Chiefs of Police. Law and policy are both critically important to officers' roles and behaviors in the field.

Introduction to Stop and Frisk in New York City

The many pressures on officers previously discussed are particularly salient to the practice of stop and frisk. Stop and frisk is a very controversial topic in New York City. In 1994, the police became extremely aggressive at reducing crime. Under the tenure of Police Commissioner William Bratton, the NYPD reduced crime enormously. By 2002, the Department had reduced crime by 60 percent.

A variety of tactics were responsible for this, including a new performance management system known as CompStat (compare statistics). This held middle-ranking officers at the rank of captain (or slightly above captain—these higher ranks in NYPD are titled deputy inspectors or inspectors) responsible for their precinct's crime. These commanding officers were under tremendous pressure to reduce crime, especially index crime (i.e., murder/non-negligent manslaughter, forcible rape, robbery, felony assault, burglary, grand larceny, and motor vehicle theft [arson is also an index crime, but the NYPD does not include that crime]). The Federal Bureau of Investigation (FBI) uses these crimes to gauge how crime is trending, or the crime rate. The police are aware of this, and, therefore, choose to focus on these crimes.

Crime went down precipitously. However, there were concerns that citizens' rights were also being impacted. During this period, Abner Louima, an African immigrant prisoner, had a stick placed in his rectum by an NYPD officer. Communities were also concerned about the level of stop and frisk. Initially, at least, research indicates that the NYPD was actually obeying legal restrictions in this area. However, after 2002, with crime already down 60 percent, the NYPD ramped up its stop-and-frisk practices enormously. They went from approximately 100,000 stops to nearly 700,000 by 2011. Research during this time period (to be discussed in more detail later in this book) shows that the NYPD abused its powers—disobeying the law and department policy. As we shall see, a department myopically focused on one goal—crime control—can have a very deleterious influence.

Summary

Policing in democracies is no simple matter. The police must enforce the law while, at the same time, obeying the law. Police leaders will often forcefully proclaim that their main objective is to reduce crime. This is a misapplication of their mission. Rather, they should bring down crime *while at the same time protecting basic rights and respecting communities.* This is what makes policing in democracies such a high calling. Aggressive crime-fighting strategies will, at times, leave service, rights, community needs, and other key policing duties behind. Sometimes the marginalized (minorities, women, poor, homeless, etc.) become the targets of misunderstandings by police who focus exclusively on crime-fighting. Stop and frisk is one controversial tactic to reduce crime. This is a legal approach used by police who, having met the legal level of proof known as reasonable suspicion, may stop suspects. The tactic has been abused by police in the past. Two key court cases are especially important to understanding stop and frisk as practiced in New York: *Terry v. Ohio* (1968) and *People v. De Bour* (1976). Both must be understood to recognize what New York City officers do with respect to stops. It is also important to understand the difference between police policy and law. In brief, New York City police leaders saw enormous crime reductions. However, simultaneously, research and courts indicate that they abused their positions, thereby reducing the legitimacy of these findings. This same pattern was evidenced worldwide. This chapter briefly examined both issues.

Discussion Questions

1. Explain the difference between crime control and due process.
2. What are some issues of concern if an agency focuses too much on crime control?
3. Explain what stop and frisk is. Is it called any other name?
4. In the two key court cases, *Terry v. Ohio* and *People State of New York v. De Bour*, is police power restricted or increased? Explain.
5. What is the difference between police policy and law? Why is this difference important?
6. Briefly describe what happened between 1995 and 2011.
7. What is CompStat?

References

Authorization for Use of Military Force, Pub. L. No. 107–40, 115 Stat. 224 (2001)

Bouza, A. V. (1990). *The police mystique: An insider's look at cops, crime, and the criminal justice system*. Plenum Press.

Cofăn, S.-M., & Băloi, A.-M. (2019). Intelligence analysis: A key tool for modern police management—The Romanian perspective. In J. A. Eterno, A. Verma, A. Mintie-Das, & D. K. Das (Eds.), *Global issues in contemporary policing*. Routledge.

Crank, J. P. (1995, March 7–11). Understanding police culture. Paper presented at the Annual Meeting of the Academy of Criminal Justice Sciences, Boston, MA.

Drummond, D. S. (1976). *Police culture*. Sage.

Durkheim, E. (1964). *The division of labor in society*. Free Press. (Original work published 1893.)

Eterno, J. (2003). *Policing within the law: A case study of the New York City Police Department*. Praeger.

Eterno, J. A. (2023, October). *Extent of influence (if any) of policy and law on public opinion*. Paper presented at the Annual Meeting of the New York State Criminal Justice Educators Association, New York, NY.

Eterno, J. A., & Silverman, E. B. (2012). *The crime numbers game: Management by manipulation*. Routledge.

Eterno, J. A., & Verma, A. (2024). Does educating students influence their views about a sensational criminal justice event? An experiment on the chokehold death of Mr. Eric Garner. *Journal of Criminal Justice Education*, 1–19. https://doi.org/10.1080/10511253.2024.2418571

Floyd v. City of New York, 959 F.Supp.2d 540 (2013)

Frantz, E. (2019). The legacy of military dictatorship: Explaining violent crime in democracies. *International Political Science Review*, *40*(3), 404–418. https://doi.org/10.1177/0192512118769079

Kamisar, Y. (1979). The exclusionary rule in historical perspective: The struggle to make the Fourth Amendment more than "an empty blessing." *Judicature*, *62*(7), 337–350.

Klinger, D. A. (1994). Demeanor or crime? Why "hostile" citizens are more likely to be arrested. *Criminology*, *32*(3), 475–493. https://doi.org/10.1111/j.1745-9125.1994.tb01162.x

Lundman, R. J. (1974). Routine police arrest practices: A commonweal prospect. *Social Problems*, *22*(1), 127–141. https://doi.org/10.2307/799572

Lundman, R. J. (1980). Police behavior: A sociological perspective. *The Journal of Criminal Law and Criminology*, *71*(4), 657. https://doi.org/10.2307/1142832

Lundman, R. J. (1994). Demeanor or crime? The Midwest City police-citizen encounters study. *Criminology*, *32*(4), 631–656. https://doi.org/10.1111/j.1745-9125.1994.tb01168.x

Madison, J. (1788). *Federalist No. 48*. https://www.gutenberg.org/files/1404/1404-h/1404-h.htm#link2H_4_0048

Marenin, O. (Ed.). (1996). *Policing change, changing police: International perspectives (Current Issues in criminal justice)*. Routledge.

Moran, J. (2011). *Crime and corruption in new democracies: The politics of (in)security*. Palgrave Macmillan.

National Archives. (2025, August 7). *Declaration of Independence: A transcription*. https://www.archives.gov/founding-docs/declaration-transcript

New York City Police Department. (2016, October 15). *Investigative encounters: Requests for information, common law right of inquiry and Level 3 stops* (Procedure No. 212-11). https://www.nyc.gov/html/nypd/downloads/pdf/analysis_and_planning/212-11.pdf

New York Criminal Procedure Law §§ 140.50[1], 140.50[3], 140.50[10] (2024). In *McKinney's Consolidated Laws of New York Annotated*. Thomson Reuters.

Packer, H. L. (1964). Two models of the criminal process. *University of Pennsylvania Law Review*, *113*(1), 1. https://doi.org/10.2307/3310562

People v. Cantor, 36 N.Y.2d 106, 324 N.E.2d 872, 365 N.Y.S.2d 509 (1975)

People v. De Bour, 40 N.Y.2d 210, 352 N.E.2d 562, 386 N.Y.S.2d 375 (1976)

People v. Rivera, 14 NY2d 441 (1964)

People v. Rosemond, 26 NY2d 101 (1970)
Rothwax, H. J. (1996). *Guilty: The collapse of criminal justice*. Random House.
Rousseau, J.-J. (1968). *The social contract and discourses* (G. D. H. Cole, Trans. & Intro.). Everyman's Library. (Original work published 1762.)
Tennessee v. Garner, 471 U.S. 1, 105 S.Ct. 1694, 85 L.Ed.2d 1, 53 USLW 4410 (1985)
Terry v. Ohio, 392 U.S. 1, 88 S. Ct. 1868, 20 L. Ed. 2d 889 (1968)
The Eric Garner Anti-Chokehold Act, N.Y. Penal Law § 121.11 (2020); § 121.13-a (2020). https://www.nycourts.gov/judges/cji/2-PenalLaw/121/121.13-a%5B2%5D.pdf
This American Life. (n.d.). *Is that a tape recorder in your pocket, or are you just unhappy to see me? (Season 414)*. https://www.thisamericanlife.org/414/right-to-remain-silent/act-two-0
Uniting and Strengthening America by Providing Appropriate Tools Required to Intercept and Obstruct Terrorism (USA PATRIOT ACT) Act of 2001, Pub. L. No. 107–56, 115 Stat. 272 (2001).
Worden, R. E., & Shepard, R. L. (1996). Demeanor, crime, and police behavior: A reexamination of the Police Services Study data. *Criminology*, *34*(1), 83–105. https://doi.org/10.1111/j.1745-9125.1996.tb01196.x

2

THE COMMUNITY POLICING ERA—1980S TO EARLY 1990S

What Is Community Policing?

Before stop and frisk was abused in the super-charged performance management era of the early 2000s, other policing models were more common. From the 1980s to the mid-1990s, law enforcement was enamored with "community policing." This was the most popular "program" adopted by the vast majority of administrators and higher-ranking officials.

The community policing movement began with policing stalwarts such as Herman Goldstein, Robert Trojanowicz, and David Bayley. Bayley (1994, p. 120) talks about how community policing should work: "Community policing represents a renegotiation of the social contract between the police and society." Thus, police must understand the local needs and develop problem-solving strategies to deal with those issues. However, Bayley was not optimistic about the state of policing at the time he wrote his book. He writes about four key issues that he sees as problematic with the police during the community policing era:

> First, police actions are not closely related to publicized objectives. Police promise one thing but do something else. Second, strategies are too generic and are not adaptable to different circumstances .... Third, police forces are preoccupied with one kind of activity: the delivery of a small set of services .... Fourth, the evaluation of police performance is narrow and superficial.
>
> *(Bayley, 1994, pp. 160–161)*

The community policing era is filled with lofty rhetoric but seems to fall into problems that are difficult to overcome. The concepts seem simple enough, but in actuality will wind up touching on one or more of the above issues. Nevertheless, this does not mean we throw the entire idea out; rather, we work to recognize concerns and solve them. Ultimately, minimizing crime by working with communities is important. In essence, the police need the community, and the community needs the police. Understanding the errors of the past, then, will guide us in the future.

DOI: 10.4324/9781003593256-2

In New York City, Police Commissioners Benjamin Ward and Lee P. Brown became synonymous with the community policing movement. This model and similar ones spread through the profession like wildfire. In part, this is because many law enforcement agencies simply, and sometimes with little thought about how this will influence their own agencies, follow the lead of the New York City Police Department (NYPD). As Bayley (1994) has noted, NYPD is a flagship department. For better or worse, agencies tend to simply emulate the NYPD. Note that many of the broad concepts still exist in some form today. However, during this early period, there were major errors that need to be explained.

NYPD's brand of community policing was called the *Community Patrol Officer Program* (CPOP). This began in the 1980s under Benjamin Ward and Mayor Koch. It was filled with wonderful slogans and, in fact, some innovative ideas but in reality was essentially, especially in its initial stages during the 1980s, ineffective at reducing crime.

The CPOP program had mixed reviews. One of the most comprehensive was conducted by the Vera Institute of Justice. They are a think tank that often studies the NYPD. McElroy, Cosgrove, and Sadd (1990), in their 190-page report with additional appendices, discuss strengths and weaknesses based on surveys and discussions with officers. While they find some worth to the program, such as beat officers (these were officers assigned to CPOP and given steady and specific small areas for which they were responsible) obtaining information that typical officers might not be aware of, there are critical weaknesses that stand out.

One is the lack of training in problem-solving skills. Although McElroy et al. (1990) advise that officers somehow manage, this lack of training would appear to be another major oversight. For example, they write, "Despite the fact that they had no experience with, or training in, the problem-solving method prior to becoming CPO's, the officers learned enough about it to identify problems, focus attention and resources on, and secure widespread commendation from community leaders" (McElroy et al., 1990, p. 64). Essentially, lower-ranking police officers muddled along as best they could. Additionally, resources available to a beat officer are vastly different from those available to higher-echelon commanders. Indeed, they go on to write, "The vast majority of the action elements contained in the problem-solving strategies were designed to be carried out by the CPO [the individual officer], or by the other [sic] member of the CPOP unit" (McElroy et al., 1990, p. 65).

The problems identified by local beat officers were clearly not higher-level issues requiring very extensive resources. They tended to identify issues that the individual officer could manage. This meant that profoundly serious crime issues that need much more attention and resources were never addressed. For example, the need for the Drug Enforcement Administration and/or the Organized Crime Control Bureau of NYPD to deal with sophisticated drug kingpins would rarely be identified by a local beat cop. So, the principle is sound, but the operationalization of the method is weak, at best. As shall be seen in the future performance management era, resources of the entire department are brought to bear on local issues with far more consequences such as taking out drug dealers permanently (not just moving them to another area), closing buildings in a targeted way with civil enforcement, getting extensive amounts of guns off the streets by mobilizing numerous units and federal and state authorities, and stopping major criminal activity in general. These require vast resources not available to local CPOP officers.

Everything done at the precinct level was done in a silo. That is, detectives did their work without informing or even collaborating with other officers. Anti-crime (aggressive crime-fighting, plainclothes officers) police also tended to work their jobs with little input from patrol. Officers who were tasked with crime prevention or highway safety simply did their work behind closed doors. CPOP severely exacerbated this silo effect. Through division of labor without a common link, each precinct became a microcosm of the entire department, lurching from key issue to key issue with no common mission. With all the good intentions of CPOP, it simply created another specialized unit working in its own silo. It was about as inefficient as you can get with little to no accountability except showing some activity. That activity, however, had no common mission or theme. That is, all units worked on their own with no common purpose. Commanding officers were either not held accountable, or held others accountable for making sure everyone was proceeding in a common purpose. Nor did they have to, since the agency itself was disjointed. The silo effect was a widespread problem with law enforcement at the time. After 9/11, for example, the Department of Homeland Security was formed, helping to alleviate this problem with the federal government. In 1994, CompStat, at the police agency level, was another example of an attempt to get the department to have a common purpose.

Another of the key weaknesses with the CPOP program was its failure to hold supervisors and commanders accountable. The program in its infancy took many officers off patrol and placed them in a highly specialized CPOP unit. Many officers thought themselves different from others. This was sometimes good and sometimes not. It gave a sense of pride, which was good, but also gave enormous independence to make decisions. One especially important and problematic issue was that CPOP officers would make their own hours. The reason behind this was that these officers needed to have the flexibility to handle issues pertaining to their beats (areas of responsibility). The idea was that by assigning officers to specific beats, they would feel some level of responsibility for what happened there. Invariably, however, without strict accountability, officers in the CPOP program began to drift away from their mission. Few officers, for example, would choose to work during times and days of high crime—late in the evenings and on weekends. Additionally, CPOP officers were mostly taken from patrol. Therefore, fewer and fewer officers remained to handle emergencies and crime at the times and days that they were most needed. The idea behind this was that officers were supposedly being proactive rather than reacting to 911 radio runs. That is, they could address problems that would ultimately lead to crime before crimes occurred. Officers, for example, might start a basketball team with local youth to keep them off the streets. On paper, this looked great. However, on the streets, the ultimate effect was minimal, as little dent was made in the crime in New York. While not a complete failure, it was certainly not the optimal use of personnel. As increasing numbers of officers were removed from their patrol duties, fewer officers remained to handle major crimes during peak hours. Ultimately, this morphed into an inefficient organizational practice that infected the entire agency. However, commanders found the unit successful. Why? Essentially, CPOP could be used by commanding officers in whatever way they might be needed. Thus, regardless of efficiency, supervisors tend to approve of the unit because of its flexibility.

However, the lack of direct supervision of the CPOs is problematic:

> CPO's generally work flexible hours. On any given day, the CPOP office would be open from twelve to 14 hours, with the CPO's working staggered tours. The CPOP sergeants work nine-hour tours, therefore, there are large blocks of time during which the officers

> are not under the direct supervision of their sergeants. Additionally, there are days when the CPOP sergeant is absent … to some extent the CPO's operated under the "honor principle."
>
> *(McElroy et al., 1990, p. 74)*

McElroy et al. (1990) make extremely specific recommendations to improve CPOP. I shall point out some of the more pertinent. First, they advise that there needs to be better training for officers. This is a staple of policing, and officers can always use more training. The deficits in training officers, especially in problem solving, are critical. Helping the community to participate is another key recommendation. In general, community outreach is something police can do a much better job of doing. Police need to be seen as partners with the community for any type of community policing to work. Another key recommendation is to strengthen the integration of CPOP into the precinct. The program was never truly accepted by the rank and file. They suggest the commanding officer needs to be more involved. They see the essence of this as the commanding officer being involved in the problem-solving process. One cannot help but see parallels with the CompStat innovation a few short years later that makes the commanding officer strictly accountable for crime and other aspects of what is happening at the precinct level. This requires a real change in NYPD that will be addressed later in this book. However, even in these early times, the lack of leadership bringing all parties together and working under a single rubric is seen. Developing additional ways to enact the principles of CPOP also seems instructive as a recommendation. Innovation is the way we advance techniques and better our methods. The last recommendation is also something that seems critical. That is, protecting officers from malicious complaints. While there must be ways for the community to hold officers accountable, the officers also need to be protected from sometimes overburdensome oversight. This shall also be discussed later but, with numerous internal and external agencies overseeing officers, this can not only depress morale but prevent the successful implementation of community policing as officers shy away from duties due to concerns, sometimes accurately, about the lack of ability to properly do their demanding work. These are just some of the lessons learned at the NYPD. Other lessons are critical as well.

Beyond New York, a key issue with community policing in general was defining what it meant. Everyone seemed to jump on the bandwagon, but few could explain what it was or how to implement its tenets in a practical way. Everyone used the buzzwords, but, with few exceptions, no one had a meaningful implementation plan. More recently the Department of Justice realized this was an issue and attempted to provide some level of clarity to police agencies. In their publication, they define community policing:

> Community policing is a philosophy that promotes organizational strategies that support the systematic use of partnerships and problem-solving techniques to proactively address the immediate conditions that give rise to public safety issues such as crime, social disorder, and fear of crime.
>
> *(Community Oriented Policing Services, 2014, p. 3)*

This more recent document does a fair job of explaining concepts. Unfortunately, during the prior period that I am talking about, there was little to no understanding of the most basic concepts. Other organizations, such as the Community Policing Consortium, also belatedly helped to better operationalize concepts that had little meaning to those in the field in this early era. Later in this book, we will explore how these relatively new definitions and more practical applications can be used today. For now, we must understand that the mistakes of the past helped inform these new more feasible community policing approaches.

There were some exceptions to this. For example, Judith Greene (1999) wrote about a successful community policing program in San Diego, where crime was effectively reduced. Although this is later in time, it had similar processes. This finding and others suggest that if community policing is better understood and more properly implemented, it can be more successfully applied. However, this can be contrasted with Hickman, Piquero, and Greene's (2000) study of Philadelphia and its community policing model. In this study, it can be seen that some of the issues that community policing should address, such as few civilian complaints, did not appear in Philadelphia (Hickman et al., 2000). It appears that the way in which leaders implement various aspects of community policing is critical to its success or failure.

Note that new types of community policing models that have been developed are often hybrids, adapting concepts that seem to work from several different areas. This shall be discussed in more detail in later chapters.

Safe Streets, Safe City

Under Mayor David Dinkins, New York City developed a program to reduce crime. It was called *Safe Streets, Safe City*. This was, in its essence, a community policing model with the expectation of numerous arrests being made. Importantly, as we shall see, it did reduce crime. While the CompStat process, which began in 1994, undoubtedly reduced crime as well, the performance management system clearly overshadowed what was another successful innovation just a few short years earlier. Indeed, it can be argued that the huge increase in officers budgeted under the *Safe Streets, Safe City* program helped to give CompStat an initial boost. The momentum was already there. While little credit is generally given to *Safe Streets, Safe City*, it deserves some coverage.

There was a joint proposal from both the Mayor and the City Council released on December 5, 1990 (New York City Bar Association, 1991). The City Council had an initial proposal—not nearly as innovative or substantial—on September 6 of that year, and Mayor Dinkins released his proposal about a month later, on October 2 (Blumenthal, 1990). *Safe Streets, Safe City* is largely the work of Mayor Dinkins that led to the revolutionary changes in the plan to reduce crime. Dinkins' plan was a monumental proposal to revamp the entire criminal justice system. Staffing at the police department, in particular, was greatly increased. Mayor Dinkins, with then-Police Commissioner Lee P. Brown, proposed colossal changes to vastly increase police on the streets and to essentially make community policing or problem-solving policing successful. The mayor at the time of the proposal was reeling from many highly publicized criminal events that later were, in part, responsible for the election of Rudolph Giuliani in 1993. This program, including the increase in staffing of the police department, was successful in reducing crime and helped the new mayor and his police commissioner, William Bratton, beginning in 1994. Giuliani and Bratton had the resources already in place when they took over. This should not be underestimated as it could have taken years, and possibly could have been blocked by the City Council (New York City's legislature).

Dinkins' proposal was a behemoth and should be remembered as such. It was like nothing seen before or since, in terms of resources and new taxes to fund it. The proposal included a 535-page police staffing study and a 57-page mayoral report. Staffing at the NYPD would go to its highest level in history at the time:

> The hiring of 3,416 new police officers in addition to 3,063 already budgeted would lift the department to its highest uniformed total of all time, 31,944, surpassing the 31,700 of 1970 [note: This was before the Housing and Transit police merged with NYPD in 1995]. The department now stands at 25,465.
>
> *(Blumenthal, 1990, p. 1)*

The new officers would be working in community patrol teams, especially in high-crime areas. Additionally, during late night hours, officers would be assigned to every subway train.

Other key aspects of the proposal were also ambitious. The Fire Department would pick up certain calls to free police officers for other duties. Extra jail beds were also anticipated and placed into the proposal. It also included increases in other aspects of the criminal justice system. The probation department, district attorneys, legal aid lawyers, and other aspects of the system were all seeing increases in their respective budgets. If nothing else, this was an ambitious proposal. New taxes were proposed to be levied to pay for it all. Indeed, the finalized plan was a staggering $1.8 billion.

If crime decreases were a measure of success, then the *Safe Streets, Safe City* initiative was a success. Crime under the program went down. In 1990, the drop started with a minuscule. 03 percent decline compared with 1989. However, in 1991 it went down 4.4 percent and then again in 1992 an additional 7.8 percent (Silverman, 1999). These are not trivial decreases, and they show modest success with a clear trend of decline. Unfortunately for Mayor Dinkins, in 1990, murders hit their high point at 2,245. However, they too went down 13 percent to 1,946 in his last year in office (Mays & Fitzsimmons, 2020). It is important to note that Raymond Kelly became Police Commissioner under Mayor Dinkins on October 16, 1992. He left on January 10, 1994, when Dinkins lost the election. Mr. Kelly, at the time, was dedicated to community-oriented policing. This, however, would drastically change when he was appointed again a few years later by Mayor Bloomberg in 2003.

By this point in Mayor Dinkins' term, the public was weary of high crime. Even the successful decreases were not enough to change the election of 1993. Nevertheless, Mayor Dinkins' legacy must include ushering in the crime drop. Later, overshadowed by the astounding crime decreases under Giuliani and Bratton, the turnaround actually started before they entered office. While Giuliani and Bratton are given wide credit for their contributions, Mayor Dinkins and his revolutionary proposal are rarely given a footnote. We will never know what would have happened if Mayor Dinkins had won, but we must at least give Mayor Dinkins some recognition for his robust initiative and setting the stage for what would come next.

The Mollen Commission

With respect to the community policing model, one tenet is developing community partnerships which have the two-fold advantage of community involvement with problem solving and increased public relations. As stated in Community Oriented Policing Services (2012, p. 4):

> Community policing, recognizing that police rarely can solve public safety problems alone, encourages interactive partnerships with relevant stakeholders. The range of potential partners is large, and these partnerships can be used to accomplish the two interrelated goals of developing solutions to problems through collaborative problem solving and improving public trust. The public should play a role in prioritizing and addressing public safety problems.

While these are lofty and ambitious ideas, there are significant dangers hidden in this statement. One of the major weaknesses comes from developing close relationships with the communities. The increased temptations that officers face when developing strong community relationships can lead to corruption. As one reads through community policing guidelines and pamphlets, the wording appears innocuous. Developing relationships, for example, especially when they are with either seen or unforeseen criminal elements in the community, can easily lead to corruption. Indeed, during this period, there were several major corruption scandals that erupted. One of the most important terminated with the Mollen Commission.

In June 1992, Mayor David Dinkins created the Mollen Commission. This commission was formed right after a major scandal was discovered in the 75 Precinct. Then-police officer Michael Dowd was the ringleader of officers who were dealing drugs, stealing money, and generally abusing their authority as law enforcement officers. Dowd was the key witness at the hearings. He gave riveting testimony describing blatant disregard for the law. In the film, *The Seven Five* (Russell, 2014), Officer Dowd describes his actions. He claims he felt like an officer and a criminal at the same time. He would drive expensive cars, take extravagant vacations, and was clearly living a lifestyle that no officer could afford. He was eventually caught by the Suffolk County police when dealing drugs. The film reveals that the federal government was well aware of Dowd's behavior for a lengthy period of time due to a wiretap in a local car stereo installation store. The store owner knew of many nefarious characters, especially those within the drug-dealing world in the 75. Dowd and his partner, among others, used these people to develop contacts in the underworld. Dowd offered protection and information to local drug kingpins that ultimately led to his downfall. The film is a reminder of a past NYPD scandal in which Frank Serpico tried to report corruption within the NYPD, but no one would listen until he went to the *New York Times*, which publicized the corruption especially in plainclothes units. This led to the Knapp Commission in the early 1970s. Officer Serpico, the whistleblower, was the key witness at the Knapp Commission. While Serpico is an honest, diligent police officer trying his best to remain candid, Dowd is just the opposite. Dowd is a corrupt police officer to his core and does everything to keep a lavish lifestyle, ultimately becoming hooked on the illegal drugs he is selling. The contrast between the two could not be greater. However, both commissions ultimately find some similar issues. Perhaps the main issue the two scandals have in common is the police culture.

Police Culture

The police culture is based on the dangerousness of the work environment. Officers must rely on one another for protection in the streets. Therefore, officers will not "rat-out" another officer. More explicitly, the police culture "emphasizes the danger and unpredictability of the work environment, the consequent dependence of officers on each other for assistance and protection, officers' autonomy in handling situations and the need to assert and maintain one's authority" (Westley, 1970; Brown, 1981; Skolnick, 1966; Worden, 1992). The police culture, like any other culture, has certain aspects to it that make it distinctive. Key elements involve its language, loyalty to officers, and the attitude test.

With respect to the language officers use, it tends to vary a bit by jurisdiction, but there are commonalities. Words such as "dirt-bag," "mope," and "asshole" are fairly common (Eterno, 2003). The language may be unspoken but simply understood.

Van Maanen (1978), for example, describes how officers stigmatize citizens as "assholes." He advises that there are three stages that generally occur quickly: 1) affront, 2) clarification, and 3) remedy. Affront involves a challenge to police authority, control, and definition of situation. Clarification involves having the means available. Was the person aware? What was the purpose of the person? An asshole is ultimately one deemed culpable. The remedy is the likely response based on the officer's assessment. Those individuals who know they were wrong and could have acted differently are most likely to be arrested and possibly receive extralegal punishment. This calculus that officers do is, in its essence, based on the police culture. The need to maintain respect is particularly important (Van Maanen, 1978).

Loyalty is a well-known aspect of the police culture as well. The Knapp Commission specifically writes:

> To understand these feelings, one must appreciate an important characteristic of any metropolitan police department, namely an extremely intense group loyalty. When properly understood, this group loyalty can be used in the fight against corruption .... Pressures that give rise to this group loyalty include the danger to which policemen are constantly exposed and the hostility they encounter from society at large.
>
> *(Commission to Investigate Allegations of Police Corruption and the Anti-Corruption Procedures of the Police Department, 1980, p. 264)*

Westley (1970) talks about loyalty and advises that it is often operationalized by police as secrecy. He writes, "Secrecy ... [is] a shield against the attacks of the outside world. ... Secrecy is loyalty" (Westley, 1970, pp. 111–112). The common euphemism of the "blue wall of silence" has its roots, then, in the police culture. As noted, corrupt officers such as Dowd take advantage of loyalty, knowing that other officers will never reveal his corrupt actions. The power of loyalty should not be underestimated. Officers will be loyal to one another due to the culture, and this may even transcend legal limitations (Alderson, 1979; Skolnick & Fyfe, 1993).

Another well-known aspect of the police culture is the attitude test. This is a particularly important part of the culture that is indicated by numerous policing experts and studies (Brown, 1981; Riksheim & Chermak, 1993; Black, 1970; Bayley, 1986; Lundman, 1974; Sykes & Clark, 1975; Westley, 1970). In essence, the attitude test is based on the demeanor of the suspect. If the suspect does not show respect for the officer, then the officer is more likely to take some sort of action such as arresting or summonsing the suspect. There is evidence to indicate that officers will even go beyond their legal limits to maintain that respect (Worden & Shepard, 1996; Lundman, 1994). However, there is some contrary work on this which suggests that officers will stay within their legal boundaries despite the attitude of the suspect (Klinger, 1994). As we will see in Chapter 5, this controversy is demonstrated in audiotapes taken by whistleblower officer Adrian Schoolcraft. His recordings indicate that the duty-captain demands that Officer Schoolcraft stop and question people sitting in front of their apartment even with little or no evidence of wrongdoing. Officer Schoolcraft questions the captain on the tapes. Yet, the captain continues to demand that Schoolcraft take some action in a hypothetical situation regardless of legality in order to maintain respect. The captain is clearly enforcing the demands of the police culture. He goes so far as to advise that maybe Officer Schoolcraft should find another job. Regardless, it is clear that maintaining respect is critical to officers (Eterno & Silverman, 2012).

The police culture, then, has an immensely powerful influence on officers (Manning, 1989). That influence can be good in the sense that officers support one another, especially when the job gets dangerous. However, that same culture has an extremely negative effect when officers remain silent even when other officers are doing corrupt or brutal actions. In addition, officers may treat suspects with illegal actions to maintain respect.

In the case of Dowd, he used the police culture to protect himself. That is, he was well aware that officers would never turn him in because the informal code of officers is extraordinarily strong. Dowd, then, took advantage of the culture. Serpico, on the other hand, became a victim of the same culture. He tried his best to work within the department's anti-corruption structure, but the police culture prevented any significant changes. Serpico went all the way to the police commissioner, and even to the mayor's office, but kept hitting dead-ends because the culture protected itself. All were unwilling to expose the corruption of which he was aware. In the case of Schoolcraft, supervision attempted to enforce the culture. We shall see more of Schoolcraft's story later in this book as his journey takes place in another decade—well into the future. His truth shows how culture is still a powerful influence even though it was exposed half a century earlier.

One of the main findings of the Knapp Commission was that corrupt officers could be categorized as "grass-eaters" and "meat-eaters." The meat-eaters were those who engaged in the worst types of corruption. The grass-eaters were not engaged in the serious corruption but took what came their way. They were aware of the corrupt activities and had taken part in some illegal doings. The Commission determined that it was the grass-eaters who were most responsible for the continued corruption. That is, because they tolerated the illegal activities and made no attempt to expose them:

> Corrupt policemen have been described as falling into two basic categories: "meat-eaters" and "grass-eaters" … meat-eaters are those policemen who … aggressively misuse their police powers for personal gain. The grass-eaters simply accept the payoffs that the happenstances of police work throw their way. … The truth is, the vast majority of policemen on the take don't deal in huge amounts of graft … grass-eaters are the heart of the problem …. They … tend to encourage the code of silence that brands anyone who exposes corruption a traitor.
>
> *(Commission to Investigate Allegations of Police Corruption and the Anti-Corruption Procedures of the Police Department, 1980, p. 261)*

The Mollen Commission also finds that the informal code (i.e., police culture) has a powerful influence on officers. The blue wall of silence based on loyalty to one another is particularly powerful. One of the results of the Mollen Commission is the creation of a permanent body to investigate corruption in NYPD outside the department: "Based upon their recommendation [the Mollen Commission], former Mayor Rudy Giuliani, with the support of the Police Commissioner, created the Commission to Combat Police Corruption (the 'Commission') on February 27, 1995, by Executive Order No. 18" (Commission to Combat Police Corruption. (n.d.).

Stop and Frisk Before CompStat

The Knapp and Mollen Commissions helped to expose corrupt acts by police in their respective times. Classic policing studies, essentially dating back to the 1960s and continuing to the present, shed light on police misconduct and helped inform oversight of police. In particular, works by Skolnick (1966), Chevigny (1969), and Westley (1970) are now required reading for students of police. Police working outside the law became a staple of study. This controversy continues to this day. Numerous questions are yet to be resolved. How much oversight, power, and training are necessary for professional police? What do we give to oversight agencies? Should they be able to administer punishment? Are the police not entitled to due process themselves? How much? Under what circumstances? Today we can argue that the main focal point of this controversy is stop and frisk. Are police operating within the boundaries of the law? With these weighty questions in mind, I now turn to those practices during the years discussed in this chapter.

In this community policing era, there was much less pressure on officers of all ranks to write stop-and-frisk reports. In a 2012 survey of retired uniformed officers of all ranks, only 9.1 percent of the 514 respondents who retired during the community policing era (before 1994) felt high pressure to write these reports. Additionally, a 2008 survey of retired captains and above showed comparable results, with a meager 5.4 percent of the 137 higher ranking officials who retired in that era feeling high pressure to write stop-and-frisk reports (Eterno, Barrow, & Silverman, 2017). With two separate scientific studies showing remarkably congruent results, one can be confident that there was relatively little pressure to write these reports during this time.

During the community policing era, these reports were used as an investigatory tool. They were not yet computerized, and officers were only mandated to write a report under limited circumstances, or would write them at their own discretion. There was little supervision of these activities (Eterno, 2003). The officers were supposed to attain a level of proof called reasonable suspicion in order to conduct a legal stop. They filled out the stop-and-frisk form (also called UF 250) under certain specific circumstances described in the NYPD Patrol Guide. According to the procedure (NYPD, 1986, p. 1), an officer only had to fill out the report if:

a. Person is stopped by use of force.
b. Person stopped is frisked or frisked and searched.
c. Person is arrested.
d. Person stopped or refused to identify himself.

Officers may also write a report at their own discretion. According to the New York State Office of the Attorney General's report (1999, p. 91), 75 percent of the reports reviewed by that office were mandated, leaving 25 percent as discretionary. However, it is highly likely that numerous stops (including mandated ones) were not completed due to the lack of focus on the issue at the time.

Lessons Learned

Overall, the community policing era was lax in its supervision. Officers were given wide latitude to do as they saw fit. This even went so far as officers making their own work hours. Additionally, supervisors, at times, were not even working when their officers were. Other supervisors knew little to nothing about units that CPOP had to supervise. At the same time, other supervisors were told that CPOP officers were generally not to be given other assignments—at the expense of patrol officers. This, at times, led to strained relationships among the rank and file. Lack of supervision was true throughout the department, and this is especially true with respect to stop and frisk. With fewer and fewer officers on patrol as CPOP expanded, cracks in the armor became evident. The need to simply answer the calls for service and do other, sometimes menial but time-consuming, tasks (e.g., guard prisoners at hospitals, watch dead human bodies, do required paperwork ...) became difficult, at best. Additionally, with the lack of supervision of CPOP, officers were focused on problems which were generally of little consequence. This is because the department had little direction in terms of crime-fighting or even its mission. Of course, many were concerned about the crime problem, but efforts at stopping crime were disaggregated, localized, and had no focus. The NYPD allowed too much discretion to local beat cops who were under-supervised. The ideas of the era were sound, such as being proactive and not reactive. However, the way the concepts were operationalized at the field level were weak, at best. Corruption scandals blind-sided the NYPD, and they failed to fully understand those practices. In particular, learning to properly deal with the police culture will haunt them going forward. Bayley (1994) describes some of the failures of the era, but suggests that community policing is still critical and must be used in the future of policing. The tenets of this era are solid but the failures are not trivial. As will be seen in the next few chapters, a failure to heed the lessons of the past will have lasting consequences for NYPD and for law enforcement in general.

Summary

Community policing or problem-solving policing became the mainstay of policing in the 1970s through the early 1990s. While its tenets are still viable, there were lessons learned from its early years. Some examples of issues are officers making their own hours, little supervision, and even precarious definitions. Some successes were seen, such as *Safe Streets, Safe City* in New York as well as a model in San Diego. Another key issue is the closeness officers are supposed to have with the communities they serve. Special oversight commissions on police must deal with these problems, as seen in the Knapp and Mollen Commissions. These commissions exposed key weaknesses that need attention. The police culture, including the blue wall of silence and the attitude effect, was uncovered during this era. Some successes, including crime decreases, were accomplished. However, those successes were overshadowed by performance management (CompStat) in later years.

Discussion Questions

1. Describe some of the issues with the CPOP program.
2. What lessons can we learn from CPOP's weaknesses?
3. Discuss the *Safe Streets, Safe City* program under Mayor Dinkins.
4. Why is *Safe Streets, Safe City* important?
5. What are the Knapp and Mollen Commissions?
6. Describe some of the critical lessons learned from those commissions.

References

Alderson, J. (1979). *Policing freedom: A commentary on the dilemmas of policing in Western democracies.* Macdonald & Evans.

Bayley, D. H. (1986). The tactical choices of police patrol officers. *Journal of Criminal Justice, 14*(4), 329–348. https://doi.org/10.1016/0047-2352(86)90126-1

Bayley, D. H. (1994). *Police for the future.* Oxford University Press.

Black, D. J. (1970). Production of crime rates. *American Sociological Review, 35*(4), 733–748. https://doi.org/10.2307/2093948

Blumenthal, R. (1990, October 3). Dinkins on crime; Dinkins proposes record expansion of police forces. *The New York Times.* https://www.nytimes.com/1990/10/03/nyregion/dinkins-on-crime-dinkins-proposes-record-expansion-of-police-forces.html

Brown, M. K. (1981). *Working the street: Police discretion and the dilemmas of reform.* Russell Sage Foundation.

Chevigny, P. (1969). *Police power: Police abuses in New York City.* Pantheon Books.

Commission to Combat Police Corruption. (n.d.). *About the commission.* City of New York. Retrieved March 14, 2025, from https://www.nyc.gov/site/ccpc/about/about.page

Commission to Investigate Allegations of Police Corruption and the Anti-Corruption Procedures of the Police Department. (1980). Police corruption in New York. In R. J. Lundman (Ed.), *Police behavior: A sociological perspective* (pp. 260–272). Oxford University Press. (Original work published 1972.)

Community Oriented Policing Services. (2014). *Community policing defined.* U.S. Department of Justice. https://cops.usdoj.gov/RIC/Publications/cops-p157-pub.pdf

Eterno, J. A. (2003). *Policing within the law: A case study of the New York City Police Department.* Praeger.

Eterno, J. A. & Silverman, E. B. (2012). *The crime numbers game: Management by manipulation.* CRC Press.

Eterno, J. A., Barrow, C. S., & Silverman, E. B. (2017). Forcible stops: Police and citizens speak out. *Public Administration Review, 77*(2), 181–192. https://doi.org/10.1111/puar.12644

Greene, J. A. (1999). Zero tolerance: A case study of police policies and practices in New York City. *Crime & Delinquency, 45*(2), 171–187. https://doi.org/10.1177/0011128799045002001

Hickman, M. J., Piquero, A. R., & Greene, J. R. (2000). Does community policing generate greater numbers of citizen complaints than traditional policing? *Police Quarterly, 3*(1), 70–84. https://doi.org/10.1177/1098611100003001004

Klinger, D. A. (1994). Demeanor or crime? Why "hostile" citizens are more likely to be arrested. *Criminology, 32*(3), 475–493. https://doi.org/10.1111/j.1745-9125.1994.tb01148.x

Lundman, R. J. (1974). Routine police arrest practices: A commonweal perspective. *Social Problems, 22*(1), 127–141. https://doi.org/10.2307/799572

Lundman, R. J. (1994). Demeanor or crime? The Midwest City police-citizen encounters study. *Criminology, 32*(4), 631–656.

Manning, P. K. (1989). Occupational culture. In W. G. Bailey (Ed.), *The encyclopedia of police science* (pp. 360–364). Garland Publishing.

Mays, J. C., & Fitzsimmons, E. G. (2020, November 24). 5 ways that Mayor Dinkins shaped New York City. *The New York Times*. https://www.nytimes.com/2020/11/24/nyregion/david-dinkins-legacy-nyc.html

McElroy, J. E., Cosgrove, C. A., & Sadd, S. (1990). *CPOP: The research: An evaluative study of the New York City Community Patrol Officer Program*. Vera Institute of Justice. https://www.vera.org/publications/cpop-the-research-an-evaluative-study-of-the-new-york-city-community-patrol-officer-program

New York City Bar Association. (1991). *Report on Safe Streets, Safe City: An analysis*. https://www.nycbar.org/reports/safe-streets-safe-city-an-analysis/

New York City Police Department. (NYPD). (1986). *Patrol guide procedure no. 116–33: Stop and frisk*.

New York State Office of the Attorney General. (1999). *The New York City Police Department's "stop & frisk" practices: A report to the people of the State of New York*. https://ur.ag.ny.gov/sites/default/files/reports/stp_frsk.pdf

Riksheim, E. C., & Chermak, S. M. (1993). Causes of police behavior revisited. *Journal of Criminal Justice*, *21*(4), 353–382. https://doi.org/10.1016/0047-2352(93)90019-J

Russell, T. (Director). (2014). *The seven five* [Film]. All3Media America; Belfor Entertainment; Waltz International Pictures.

Silverman, E. B. (1999). *NYPD battles crime: Innovative strategies in policing*. Northeastern University Press.

Skolnick, J. H. (1966). *Justice without trial: Law enforcement in democratic society*. John Wiley & Sons.

Skolnick, J. H., & Fyfe, J. J. (1993). *Above the law: Police and the excessive use of force*. The Free Press.

Sykes, R. E., & Clark, J. P. (1975). A theory of deference exchange in police-civilian encounters. *American Journal of Sociology*, *81*(3), 584–600. https://doi.org/10.1086/226115

Van Maanen, J. (1978). The asshole. In P. K. Manning & J. Van Maanen (Eds.), *Policing: A view from the street* (pp. 221–238). Goodyear Publishing.

Westley, W. A. (1970). *Violence and the police: A sociological study of law, custom, and morality*. MIT Press.

Worden, R. E. (1992, March). *Police officers' belief systems: A framework for analysis* [Paper presentation]. Annual Meeting of the Academy of Criminal Justice Sciences, Pittsburgh, PA, United States.

Worden, R. E., & Shepard, R. L. (1996). Demeanor, crime, and police behavior: A reexamination of the Police Services Study data. *Criminology*, *34*(1), 83–105.

3

WILLIAM BRATTON I—1994–1996

The Birth of CompStat

CompStat (compare statistics) was developed by William Bratton and his colleagues in early 1994 at the New York City Police Department (NYPD). Its introduction led to a revolution in policing methods. As we have seen, community policing was all the rage in the immediate past. CompStat would change this into performance management, zero tolerance, broken windows (that is, dealing with the lesser issues that will help prevent more serious ones), intelligence-led policing, and similar names. In essence, these names referred to Brattonesque, CompStat-like models. Indeed, Bratton's book, called *Turnaround*, is a compilation of his accomplishments especially in bringing down crime (Bratton & Knobler, 1998). During his tenure at NYPD, Bratton and his team were responsible for tremendous decreases in index crime. As discussed, these are the crimes used by the Federal Bureau of Investigation's Uniform Crime Reports (UCR) to determine the crime rate. The crimes included murder or non-negligent manslaughter, robbery, felonious assault, forcible rape, burglary, serious larcenies, and motor vehicle theft. The drop in crime in New York City for those two years was responsible for much of the crime decrease in the entire country (Silverman, 2001).

At the time, large decreases in crime were unthinkable. Such dynamic reductions ultimately led the law enforcement community to completely emulate the NYPD's mythical performance management system (CompStat). This was not only done by agencies in the United States but also by those across the globe (Eterno & Silverman, 2012). CompStat received an Innovations in American Government Award at the John F. Kennedy School of Government at Harvard University. Its crime reduction results drew countless agencies to observe its workings and copy the NYPD's practices. Many who came to observe simply went to a meeting or two and then went back to their own agencies and did precisely what they saw. Most had little, or no, understanding of its mechanisms. Indeed, often agencies simply did not care because the program controlled crime and it appeared to work. They simply wanted crime reductions. They completely overvalued the performance management system. As far as many police leaders were concerned, it was the answer to law enforcement's main mission.

DOI: 10.4324/9781003593256-3

With little to no concern about other aspects of police work, the CompStat model was copied around the globe. Ultimately, CompStat turned out to be both a blessing and a curse.

What Is CompStat?

CompStat was, and is, a performance management system. It took advantage of fairly new mapping and computer technologies that were burgeoning at the time. Jack Maple, one of Bratton's main confidants, was brought into the NYPD from the Transit Department. He was a lieutenant there and developed something similar to CompStat in that department, which was a separate agency at the time (the Transit and Housing Departments were merged into NYPD in 1995—April 2 and May 1 of that year, respectively).

Maple was assigned by Bratton as the Deputy Commissioner of Operations. He was one of the key architects of CompStat. His focus was almost exclusively on crime control. As a lieutenant in the Transit Department, he caught the eye of Bratton. When he was brought into the NYPD, he was concerned about the very slow process of the NYPD collecting crime and getting accurate crime statistics. He wanted them quickly so that commanders could develop strategies to combat them immediately. At the time there was about a six-month lag between a report being filed and it then being properly recorded. Maple initially approached the Office of Management Analysis and Planning's Crime Analysis and Program Planning Section to determine if they could get the crime numbers faster. That unit was responsible for the crime figures at the time. After being told no, Deputy Commissioner Maple set out to get "preliminary statistics" directly from precincts. He established his own collection process and, using an old software program, collected the figures in the program called CompStat (Silverman, 2001; Eterno & Silverman, 2012). Eventually, the entire collection system was automated, and preliminary statistics came right from the computerized systems at the precinct level. In this way, the entire Uniform Crime Reporting (UCR) collection system was subverted. This allowed for the quick centralization of collected information. It became the first part of CompStat's four-part mantra: accurate and timely information. This, it seemed, was the workaround needed by central headquarters to get at those numbers. Before this, most commanders of precincts were not nearly as aware of the crimes committed in their commands. Suddenly, these numbers were available almost immediately as the precinct signed off on the complaint. There were, of course, numerous issues with the accuracy of those numbers, especially since commanders soon became aware of the statistics going directly to headquarters (Eterno & Silverman, 2012). The CompStat report, to this day, indicates the numbers are preliminary. However, nearly everyone takes them as gospel.

A key aspect of CompStat, then, is getting the crime figures quickly. Commanders were then held strictly accountable for those numbers. At the time, they were brought in to twice-weekly CompStat meetings. Meetings were held at 7 a.m. after Maple began seeing numerous conflicts with other engagements when trying to do the CompStat meetings later in the day. The 7 a.m. formal gatherings involved commanding officers of precincts presenting their main issues mostly involving crime. Large electronic pin maps were displayed at the meeting behind the commander as he or she spoke about what was occurring in the command. Initially, Bratton replaced numerous precinct commanders and higher-level chiefs. Indeed, the City was sued and lost an age discrimination suit to four high-level chiefs who lost their jobs at the time (Kocieniewski, 1997). The commanders were at the podium and questioned by inquisitors (the high-ranking headquarters officials such as the Deputy Commissioner of Operations, Chief of Department, Police Commissioner, and others central figures depending on the meeting). The commanders were on the hot seat. They had to have answers. Why was index crime going up? What are you doing about it? For the first time, commanders of precincts were held strictly accountable. Commissioner Bratton brought all the key officials into one room focusing on crime control. There were many good aspects to this. By putting the key officials into one room, numerous resources could be brought to bear on a problem. For example, if drug sales and distribution were a problem, the Organized Crime Control Bureau was at the meeting, and discussions about what was being done and what could be done in the future would take place. These meetings, then, prevented the silo effect. That is, each unit working without others knowing what was going on. For an excellent history of NYPD including CompStat, see Silverman (2001).

During the initial years of CompStat, accolades were ubiquitous. Initial assessments portrayed CompStat as an effective managerial crime-reduction accountability device (Bratton, 1997; Bratton & Knobler, 1998; DeLorenzi, Shane, & Amendola, 2006; Geoghegan, 2006; Gurwitt, 1998; Kelling & Sousa, 2001; McDonald, 2002; Maple & Mitchell, 1999; Moore, 2003; O'Connell & Straub, 1999; Safir, 1988; Sanow, 2003; Schick, 2004; Silverman, 2001; Walsh, 2001; Walsh & Vito, 2004) (Eterno & Silverman, 2010, p. 427). In the practitioner world, CompStat was seen as a beacon of light showing the way to effectively reduce crime. In short, here is something that works. Setting aside, for now, the principal arguments about the harmful side effects of CompStat, one must understand that this was seen as the saving grace of the policing world and even society. It was emulated nearly everywhere—regardless of potential problems.

The NYPD widely advertised its new model of policing. They even had grant money to run conferences that many took advantage of. Countless agencies perceived this method, based on how the NYPD sold it, as one of using inquisitors to strictly hold commanders of precincts accountable for the crime that was committed in their areas of responsibility, using glitzy computerized pin mapping, following a four-part mantra, and, importantly, using the meetings to spread the word throughout the agency as well as bringing all resources to bear on the crime problem.

The four-part mantra included accurate and timely intelligence, which was the bedrock of CompStat; rapid deployment; effective tactics; and relentless follow-up and assessment. By getting those crime statistics in a timelier manner, commanders could now be questioned about what was currently happening in their commands. As well as the CompStat numbers, commander profiles, which contained other basic information about the commanders and the command, were also collected and distributed

Much of CompStat depends on the inquisitors. At many of these meetings commanders were grilled. At times, it was a game of "gotcha," as commanders were caught in mistakes by the inquisitors who had many more resources at their disposal. Some of this was incredibly good such as determining whether officers' hours comported with the crime that was occurring in the command. Robberies might be happening at midnight but few, if any, officers were assigned to attack that problem at that hour. The computer screens behind the commander presenting might visually display the times robberies took place and compare those with officers' working hours. One could easily see the issue. Commanders, then, would be asked, "What are you doing about these mismatched working hours?" Ultimately, the message quickly spread that commanders had better be prepared. There is no doubt that the method had success in reducing crime. Numerous agencies came to New York and followed what they thought was CompStat based on their short visits. They too wanted to reduce crime. Unfortunately, there were cracks in the armor, even in these initial stages. These included community unrest, manipulation of index crime reports, overzealous demand of summonses, arrests and stops, among other issues. Much of these side effects can be traced to the unrelenting pressures from higher-ranking officials at CompStat meetings.

Pressures

Initially, the pressures on commanders at CompStat may have been necessary. Bratton and his colleagues were trying to change a culture of malaise or, at least, somewhat ignoring the high crime. Up to this point, a commander's major concerns included preventing or minimizing corruption, dealing with communities, and generally responding to local needs, especially of the patrol borough or even divisions. The NYPD was divided into patrol boroughs such as Brooklyn South or Manhattan North. These were further broken down into divisions. Bratton eliminated the divisions so that more positions would be open to promote precinct commanders. This all made sense. Additionally, Bratton had numerous committees that advised him of changes needed in the department. Bratton also allowed officers to make low-level arrests for minor violations such as marijuana. Under him, these arrests began to widely increase. It is without a doubt that these changes led to rapid decreases in crime. The more sinister side of these changes, however, began to show.

One of the negative aspects was that the principal motivator of CompStat was fear. Initially, it was likely necessary. However, as we shall see, these pressures went too far. What pressures? Commanders at CompStat knew they had to present their crime information. However, commanders were never taught how to do this. They were never trained, at this point, to properly manage the intense pressure on them to reduce crime. Later, as the need became obvious, new captains were given some minimal instruction on how to manage CompStat meetings. In the initial stages, however, it was "baptism by fire." Some commanders eventually adapt. Others were simply not good at presenting. It was new to the job description. The pressures were so powerful that it was not unknown for commanders to vomit before they had to present (Silverman, 2001).

When commanders got back to precincts, the top-down leadership style was generally emulated. Lower-ranking officers now had to deal with commanders concerned about their next meetings. Commanders began to count every index crime. The message from CompStat was essentially the following: if crime goes down, you are golden; however, if crime increases, you have no career. This scientific management, top-down approach had consequences—both positive and negative. As we shall see, as time goes on, the negative side became far more apparent.

Crime Control Is Supreme

At this time, crime control was the key mission of police. There was little concern about due process rights. Henry (2002), in writing about CompStat, explains the reasoning of the time, arguing that police must get back to their original roots of crime-fighting. He goes even further to explain how broken windows theory is correct: "At some level of awareness, both the police and the public knew all along that the principles of Wilson and Kelling articulated in Broken Windows theory were accurate" (Henry, 2002, p. 118).

Many, however, would not agree with this anecdote. Maple and Mitchell (1999, p. 154, as cited in Eterno & Silverman, 2012, p. 199) write:

> The implication [of Broken Windows theory] is, if the police would take care of petty things, the more serious things would take care of themselves. How sad. That idea was tested in New York's subways in the late 1980s along with a strain of community policing. … The result was an 87 percent rise in subway robberies from 1987 to the middle of 1990. implementing quality-of-life tactics alone is like giving a facelift to a cancer patient: The patient may look better and even feel better, the killer disease hasn't been arrested.

Maple, the key architect of CompStat, clearly finds broken windows theory objectionable and even incorrect. His practical attitude was one of "make the dots go away," referring to the electronic pin maps seen behind commanders presenting at CompStat meetings. His focus, like that of most police managers of the time, was on stopping crime. There was little thought given to possible side effects. Using his analogy, they needed to save the patient, and that came first. The assumption being they would worry about side effects later, assuming the patient survived.

Going forward, Bratton does realize the issue of pressure. However, since he leaves on April 15, 1996, his short tenure as Police Commissioner leaves the unrelenting pressure of CompStat in its original state; namely, powerful enough to change a culture causing great anxiety in the rank and file. The pressure simply continued to rise. Ultimately, like a tea kettle, the steam comes out and the whistle of water boiling is key. However, the water continued to boil for years until Bratton returned to NYPD in 2014 (although the ebb and flow of pressures often depend on who the inquisitors are even today). Bratton discusses this as well. He believed in peace dividend long after leaving the NYPD. That is, once crime goes down, there needs to be a scaling back on the myopic focus on crime control.

> As Bratton has explained it, the peace dividend that his NYPD is yielding to the public is the use of more discretion—a less punitive approach to broken windows policing—even while staying vigilant about crime. It includes encouraging people committing low-level offenses to "move along," issuing summonses instead of arrests in some instances, fewer stop-and-frisks, coordinating mental health services, and NYPD officers taking a more friendly approach to interacting with the public. "We project that by the end of this year there will have been one million fewer what I would describe as negative interactions—enforcement actions by members of my department," Bratton said.
>
> *(Max, 2015)*

Bratton was way too late in returning to NYPD with this attitude. In the mid-1990s, when Bratton and Maple were in New York City, the idea of not arresting, stopping, and/or writing summonses was unthinkable. This was an all-out attack on crime. This peace dividend makes sense after knowing crime will drastically decrease. Yet, in the mid-1990s, no one was thinking that crime would decrease 80 percent. So, this peace dividend does not happen until Bratton returns in 2014 through 2016. I will discuss this more in later chapters. Until 2014, then, the overwhelming focus on crime control was supreme throughout law enforcement circles. For better or worse, the die was cast. The horses were out of the barn and running wildly. There was no stopping the craze. From the mid-1990s to at least 2012, it was full-speed ahead for crime control, regardless of obvious and pending dangers.

Strategies

With crime control firmly established as the goal, Bratton and the NYPD focused on that one goal. The entire organization moved from "service and the beat cop" to "crime and commanding officers." It was an incredible turnaround but one that would reveal its ugly side in a few short years. With newly elected Mayor Rudolph Giuliani looking to make a name for himself, it was a new game.

Initially when appointed in January 1994, Bratton was ready to pounce. He and his team developed specific strategies aimed entirely at crime control. Fresh from the corruption scandals leading to the Knapp and Mollen Commissions, the NYPD would be reinvigorated with a new focus. No longer would commanders lay awake worrying about a scandal. Now every single index crime report would haunt them. With constant anxiety about presenting at CompStat looming, the NYPD would develop a top-down management style that, to some extent, still exists.

Bratton was not without other weapons in this battle against crime. CompStat was the main weapon in the arsenal, but specific strategies were also developed that were added to the playbook. While Lee P. Brown tried to change the culture from the bottom up with the beat cop being the key, Bratton took the opposite approach. Brown (1992) developed a community policing guidebook explaining the principles of community policing. Brown was going to change the culture from individual members of CPOP to changing the whole department. It never gained complete traction as the culture at NYPD was difficult to pierce. Bratton, however, through fear, intimidation, and some level of inspiration and pride, got buy-in. The culture did change, and quite drastically. While Brown sent out his community policing guide that most did not take very seriously, Bratton released police strategies to fight crime. These gave some lasting guidance and, because of CompStat, gained traction.

Police Strategy No. 1 was *Getting Guns Off the Streets of New York* (Giuliani & Bratton, 1994a). With both Mayor Giuliani and Commissioner Bratton's names on the cover of the booklet, the game plan was set. This was something street cops could relate to. For many years they were told not to make low-level arrests. The gloves were off. The strategy was fairly specific and contained excellent guidance.

The strategy talks about the widespread use of handguns at the time. It points out the enormous increase in their use and the importance of getting illegal guns off the streets. It advised that 90 percent of the guns come from other states. The strategy first suggests refocusing investigative efforts. Detectives will now be better utilized to determine where the guns are coming from and to identify those who provide them.

More importantly, it is in this booklet where we see the expansion of the Street Crime Unit. This was a citywide plainclothes unit that aggressively fought crime. They were to target high-gun areas. Importantly, the aggressive tactics of this unit would later become a key issue in the stop-and-frisk controversy.

Training would also be increased to teach patrol officers and detectives how to properly perform their new roles. The Department was also to secure committed support from the public and other agencies. As we shall see, the widespread use of overly aggressive police tactics would fly in the face of getting public support.

Joint Firearms Task Forces would be formed to help take advantage of federal and state resources. Gun tracing to determine where the guns come from with the help of the federal government was also important. Additionally, warrants would also be more strictly enforced. More advanced technologies for their day would also be deployed. Gun exchange or buy-back programs were to be used. Overall, this was an overly aggressive focus of resources on this specific issue of illegal guns. Parts of this strategy would ultimately be very problematic. Namely, the expansion of plainclothes units became myopic in their focus. Certainly, there are very good aspects to this. However, as we will see, the lack of buy-in from the public would be exacerbated, in part, due to the overly aggressive tactics taken by NYPD.

Other crime-focused tactics were also developed during this period. *Curbing Youth Violence in the Schools and on the Streets*, *Driving Drug Dealers Out of New York*, *Getting Guns Off the Streets*, *Breaking the Cycle of Domestic Violence*, *Reclaiming the Public Spaces of New York*, *Reducing Auto-Related Crime in New York*, and *Reclaiming the Roads of New York* were all crime control-oriented strategies developed during this time. All of these were essentially outward looking. That is, preventing crime by the public.

There was only one strategy—*Rooting Out Corruption, Building Organizational Integrity in the New York Police Department*—that did not focus externally on crime but looked internally at preventing corruption and brutality. This is important, as the NYPD at this point was still concerned about the integrity of its officers. In these initial years, there was still some focus on corruption. As we shall see, as time goes on, the crime control strategies remain supreme and the integrity issues take a back seat. This is supported by research in later years showing that the NYPD initially had increased the pressures on officers to maintain integrity in the crime statistics and uphold Constitutional rights. However, as the CompStat program continued to go forward in future years, the pressure to maintain the integrity in the crime numbers and due process rights decreased (Eterno, Verma, & Silverman, 2016).

CompStat meetings rarely focus on illegal or unethical behavior by officers. Few meetings would focus, for example, on the number of civilian complaints. Few commanders were concerned about such issues. At this point, bringing down the numbers of index crimes was the major concern of commanders. The strategies were aimed at moving the NYPD into an aggressive crime control mode. The titles themselves are revealing. A short synopsis of the strategies will help the reader to understand the culture of the time.

The second strategy is about curbing youth violence (*Curbing Youth Violence in the Schools and on the Streets*, Giuliani & Bratton, 1994b). The booklet first defines the problem and, again, turns to pointing out that there is a surge in gun violence among youth. It also talks about absenteeism from schools, among other issues. One of the strategies is to make schools the focal point of youth violence reduction efforts. In the past, when not invited, the police did not intrude on schools. By creating school safety plans and safe corridors, the police would become more involved. Safe corridors are paths for youth to get to schools safely without being accosted by gangs or others making it unsafe to attend. Arrests of violent youth would also be thoroughly investigated by detectives and databases would be checked to determine what this individual is doing. Each precinct would have three instead of one youth officer so that more attention could be focused on issues and individuals. Collaborating with school authorities to develop better protocols to manage violent youth would also enhance the NYPD's efforts.

Importantly, many school leaders, just like precinct commanders, are well aware of their being judged by the level and number of incidents that occur in them. Consequently, school authorities, just like precinct commanders, loathe to have any incidents recorded. Just as commanders are judged by index crime, school authorities are also judged by violence in their areas of responsibility. Because of this, these data can also be inaccurate due to manipulation (Eterno & Silverman, 2012). For example, former Assistant Secretary of Education Diane Ravitch writes, "When numbers become the goal, then numbers displace judgment, honesty, and appropriate behavior. This misuse of data is dangerous and misleading in police work as it is in education and other areas of social policy" (Ravitch as cited in Eterno & Silverman, 2012, back cover).

Playing with the numbers is not the only issue. This strategy also creates a juvenile database which, today, is very controversial. As the Legal Defense Fund (2025, n.p.) writes, "The NYPD targets people for heightened surveillance relying, in part, on a secret Database which the NYPD created by designating thousands of New Yorkers as members of what they call 'gangs' or local street 'crews'." Again, the roots of such major concerns with police can be traced back to the crime control focus of these years. While there are positive aspects to such strategies such as developing partnerships with the school authorities, the side effects, rarely explored at the time, become more obvious as time goes on. Of course, the abuse of stop and frisk, as we will see, is also a major debilitating side effect that becomes more malignant over time.

One of the menaces of American culture is illegal drugs. Numerous strategies have been made throughout the years such as drug courts (diversion from the criminal justice system), health and education approaches (e.g., "Just Say No"), numerous rehabilitation programs of various types (e.g., boot camps), and many other strategies. Over the years, the level of illegal drug use has not declined substantially. Indeed, even with huge advances in medicine, we have seen a substantial increase in deaths due to drug overdoses in the last decades (see Figure 3.1).

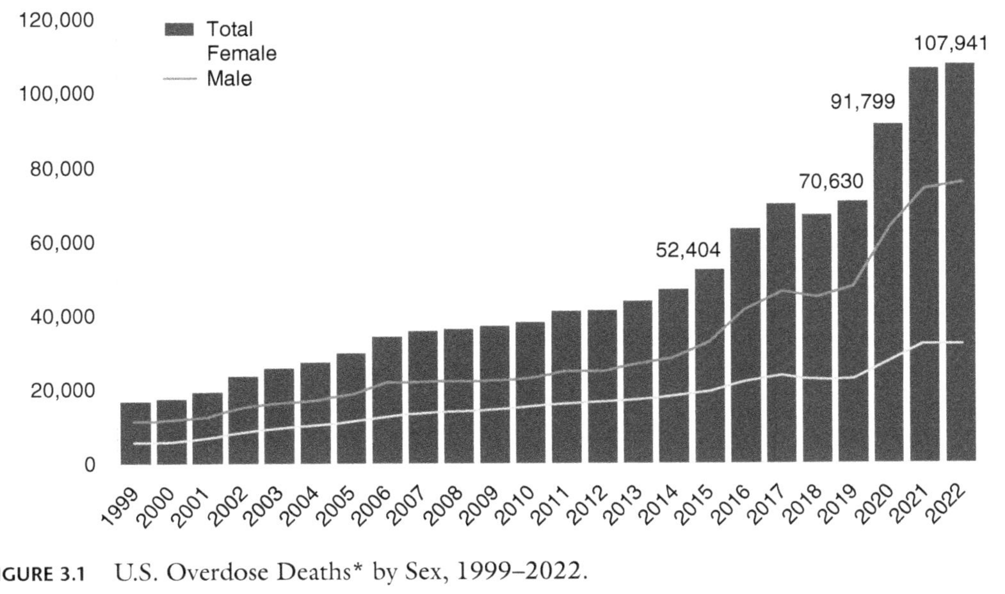

FIGURE 3.1 U.S. Overdose Deaths* by Sex, 1999–2022.

Source: Center for Disease Control and Prevention, National Center for Health Statistics, Multiple Causes of Death 1999–2022 on CDC WONDER Online Database, released 4/2024.

Note: *Includes deaths with underlying causes for unintentional drug poisoning, suicide drug poisoning, or drug poisoning of undetermined intent as coded in the *International Classification of Diseases,* 10th revision.

America is a drug culture that, unfortunately, attracts illegal narcotics trafficking from around the globe. One of the weaknesses of CompStat is that it has a very short-term focus; namely, the next CompStat meeting. This strategy, *Driving Drug Dealers Out of New York* (Giuliani & Bratton, 1994c), aims at reducing the street-level or more visible signs of illegal drugs. Some of the statistics used in this strategy are from the Arrestee Drug Abuse Monitoring Program. Unfortunately, this program no longer tracks drug use by arrestees. However, the booklet points out that, at the time, illegal drug use among arrestees increased from 42 percent in 1984 to 85 percent in 1986. Such increases cannot be disregarded. One of the key parts of the strategy is to give patrol (typical street officers rather than specialists) more responsibility for the strategy's success. This means that regular officers working in the precincts will now be engaged in this fight. This is different from in the past, when patrol was generally—though not specifically told this—not heavily engaged in this type of enforcement. This is again where we now see more and more officers engaged in enforcing even low-level activity such as marijuana violations. The precipitous rise of arrests for minor marijuana violations, especially in minority communities, was yet another debilitating side effect of the extreme focus on crime control. Levine's work in this area is particularly illuminating. In essence, his work shows how police are incentivized to make marijuana arrests, leading to a meteoric rise in arrests for very minor violations. This rise parallels the rise in stop and frisk at the time (Levine & Siegel, 2015).

Police Strategy No. 4 is *Breaking the Cycle of Domestic Violence* (Giuliani & Bratton, 1994d). This is still a major problem for the NYPD today. Murder attributed to domestic violence accounts for over 20 percent of the homicides in the city and this trend does not seem to ebb (Eterno, 2025). The strategy involves what we see as typical of NYPD of the time. Recording and tracking incidents, changing department directives, refocusing resources such as establishing a Domestic Violence Officer in each precinct, changing training such that newly collected data would be properly analyzed for trends, involving detectives and youth officers, among other items. Overall, these are excellent ideas. The booklet also involves some level of changing the police culture such that domestic violence is taken more seriously. The publication also calls for evaluation of these tactics. However, as recent data indicates, much work in this area has yet to be fully realized even 30 years later.

The fifth strategy is entitled *Reclaiming the Public Spaces of New York* (Giuliani & Bratton, 1994e). This document begins by talking about what a decent society is and the need for it. It states, "A decent society is a society of civility." In my experience, such broad statements lead to widely varying opinions. A decent society could be nearly anything depending on the person you speak to. The document then moves to discuss the return of quality of life. Again, this can be subject to interpretation. Nevertheless, the strategy is clearly focused on what many have seen as nuisances such as squeegeeing your car by a homeless person, street prostitution, loud music, the considerable number of homeless people, and so forth. This booklet invokes Wilson and Kelling's (1982) broken windows theory. The authors also cite Wesley Skogan and disorder. While these theories have some level of support, the antithesis of these theories is never mentioned. Many, including scholars, argue very differently. For example, labeling or societal reaction theory argues nearly the opposite. That is, if government gets involved, especially the police, individuals so targeted become stigmatized and, therefore, lose opportunities, will not be able to develop good peers, and ultimately will change their self-concept to one of being deviant. That is, by focusing on exceedingly minor violations, those so targeted are *more* likely to become deviants. The NYPD, in this strategy then, has adopted a point of view that may or may not be accurate. Let us assume, as NYPD does, that these are issues. Is law enforcement the most appropriate way to handle it? Note that the NYPD sees this strategy as the lynchpin to all the strategies. Unfortunately, as we shall see, the terrible side effects of this are rarely a concern during these and many subsequent years. Liberty, Constitutional rights, democracy, and in essence balancing crime-fighting with due process are simply glossed over. Later in this book, we shall see the end result of such aggressive policing including the defund the police movement, consent decrees against police, legalizing marijuana by states, unconscionable racist behavior by police, and more. While this strategy has its heart in the right place, fixing numerous societal ills, one cannot help but attribute the zero-tolerance strategy by police as one likely to lead to evoking some terribly negative reactions.

Precinct commanders are now charged with eliminating many of the lower-level issues. Again, no one disagrees with the problem, it is assigning the clean up to the police that will later haunt the nation. The strategy generally sees precinct commanders as the people who will end these societal ills.

Illegal activity such as bicyclists (specifically the booklet targets delivery people and messengers), peddlers, loud radios, drunken individuals, noise complaints, and so forth will now be subject to zero tolerance. Collaborating with communities, understanding the social contract, developing a whole-of-government approach, and so forth and not on the radar. Precinct commanders will solve these "anti-social" behaviors. The police will also solve the issue of the mentally ill on the streets. Desk appearance tickets (used for less than felony violations of the law) and summonses are expected to be key tools to combat these problems. Also, once again, the NYPD creates yet another database, the Emotionally Disturbed Persons Database, to confront these quality-of-life concerns.

It will be years later in 2014 when Mr. Eric Garner dies in police custody while being arrested for selling "loosie" cigarettes. A terrible tragedy resulting from overly aggressive zero-tolerance quality of life enforcement. It will not be until many years later that a Chief of Interagency Operations is formed such that numerous other agencies can more easily offer their expertise to help to deal with quality-of-life issues. Police legitimacy is not even a thought. One can appreciate the scope of the problems but, leaving this to commanding officers of precincts alone to solve these issues is a stretch, at best. Precinct commanders would appear to be superheroes able to leap tall buildings in a single bound. As we shall see, they are as human as the rest of us. All of us empathize with the issues but we need to develop a lessons learned mentality.

While many issues with police do begin here, we must also recognize the success of the era as well. Like a double-edged sword, the problems for the future are germinated here but we also see the huge decline in crime that cannot be denied. Quality of life also drastically improves. Yet, what is the cost? Not simply in dollars and cents but in more far-reaching and sophisticated consequences such as abuse of police power, manipulation of police reports, and, worst of all, unconstitutional and racist behavior—eminently predictable—by law enforcement.

The next booklet, *Reducing Auto-Related Crime in New York* (Giuliani & Bratton, 1995a) is much of the same. However, some changes in policy such as having victims sign sworn statements that they are not committing insurance fraud clearly had an effect. This policy change is rarely mentioned but is one of the keys to reducing the number of auto thefts in the city. In those years, even middle-class owners would do insurance fraud. It was fairly common. Such policy shifts need to be examined by those who suggest that the reduction in insurance claims is due to the NYPD's fight against auto crime. Rather, it is far more likely that the decrease, at least in part, is due to the shift in policy on insurance fraud.

The next booklet, *Rooting Out Corruption; Building Organizational Integrity in the New York Police Department* (Giuliani & Bratton, 1995b), is critically important. During these early years there was a concern about corruption. These changes are occurring right after the Mollen Commission in the early 1990s. Officer Michael Dowd in the 75 Precinct was the leader of a vast array of corrupt officers who took advantage of the "blue wall of silence." As an officer, he understood the police culture and that officers do not "rat each other out." In this booklet, the department does demand strict integrity. As we shall see, however, this booklet will soon become a relic of the past, while other strategies increase in power and influence. Illegal quotas, crime report manipulation, unconstitutional and racist stops, and so forth become the NYPD way. In these early years, however, there was a concern. Indeed, there was an increase in stressing integrity in these years that will soon fade away (Eterno et al., 2016).

The last booklet is titled *Reclaiming the Roads of New York* (Giuliani & Bratton, 1995c). The focus is on traffic. Executive officers of precincts would be charged with going to TrafficStat. TrafficStat was yet another version of CompStat but was focused on traffic accidents. Such "stat"-type meetings would soon become all the rage of the NYPD, and, in turn, other agencies, then the nation, and even the world. DomStat, for example, was used for domestic violence and so forth.

Commanding officers already had way too much to do with CompStat and other work. Thus, the important task of traffic was now relegated to the executive officer. TrafficStat could then be a training ground to help captains learn the ropes before going to CompStat. Executive officers, also known as XO's, were generally new captains. Commonly, during these early years, CompStat and the like were "baptism by fire." No one quite knew what to expect. Executive officers, in particular, were very concerned, especially since many of them were still on probation. The XO is the next person in the chain of command to be in charge of a precinct. They too were overwhelmed with work. In some cases, they would have to cover many commands in the entire borough, and sometimes cover Long Island or the upstate counties where officers are permitted to live in case of an off-duty incident (known as the "duties"). The executive officer, the second in command at the precinct, now had to not only know and help the commanding officer but also had these additional chores. In some patrol boroughs, the executive officer also had to do numerous 4 by 12 and 12 by 8 "duties." Regardless, much emphasis was placed on the power of these mid-level commanders and executives. With little or no training on all these additional responsibilities, it would simply be a matter of time before the cracks in the plan would show themselves.

Understanding These Years

Performance management via CompStat had many successful aspects to it. One example is that it prevented the silo effect. This is when units and bureaus in the agency work on their own without any significant attachment to an overall plan. CompStat brought all agency entities together. The commanding officer of the precinct was now accountable for everything that occurred in his or her precinct or area of concern. It was clearly a geographical boundary of responsibility. Another example of the positive aspects of CompStat included a clear effect on crime rates. With the entire department focused on crime control, the effect was profound. Every part of the agency was focused on this goal.

The underside of CompStat, however, was rarely discussed. Nearly everyone jumped on the bandwagon. Nevertheless, the weaknesses were evident. At times, commanders were bullied or embarrassed at meetings. Fear was the main motivator (Eterno & Silverman, 2012). In a few short years, crime report manipulation was well known among the rank and file. That is, commanders in fear of presenting would resort to changing crime reports to downgrade their crime statistics. Crime control became everything. Little or no attention to the dangerous side effects were accomplished. Nearly anything would be done, including unethical behavior, to lower the crime numbers. Specifically focused on index crimes, the department became enslaved to the CompStat god. It would not be long before problems would arise.

One of the major tactics to reduce crime was stop and frisk. Initially, this was simply a tool for investigation. It would become a key method to reduce crime. In less than ten years, the department would slip into illegal and racist behaviors in the name of crime-fighting. Like many good innovations, CompStat would soon fall prey to greed and corruption as they fought to outdo their success every year. Initially, the performance management system was an excellent innovation (Silverman, 2001). However, the seeds of illegal activities and racism would soon germinate and grow like a weed.

Summary

CompStat (compare statistics) was developed by William Bratton and his associates. This performance management system was focused almost exclusively on reducing crime reports. It was an extraordinarily successful innovation that was emulated around the world by law enforcement agencies and others. Specific strategies were also developed during this era. Most were focused on crime control as well. These strategies included extremely aggressive methods. The CompStat process, while successful at reducing the number of crime reports, set the stage for problems with respect to unconstitutional and racist behaviors by police agencies. CompStat's top-down leadership style with little focus on due process rights would come back to haunt law enforcement in the following decades; for example, leadership based on fear, a hyperfocus on crime numbers to determine success or failure, and the creation of overly aggressive units often with little supervision. CompStat ultimately turns out to be a double-edged sword. It helps to reduce crime but, at the same time, threatens the basic Constitutional rights of citizens, encourages simplistic and quick answers to complicated issues (e.g., more summonses, arrests, stops), uses fear to motivate, encourages crime report manipulation, and limits community interaction.

Discussion Questions

1. What is CompStat?
2. What is the main focus of CompStat?
3. List and explain some issues with CompStat.
4. Was CompStat initially necessary? Why or why not?
5. Discuss some of the strategies of the era. Were they helpful or hurtful? Explain.
6. Knowing that some of these innovations led to serious issues, would you do anything different? Explain.

References

Bratton, W. J. (1997). Crime is down in New York City: Blame the police. In N. Dennis (Ed.), *Zero tolerance: Policing a free society* (pp. 29–43). IEA Health and Welfare Unit.

Bratton, W. J., & Knobler, P. (1998). *Turnaround: How America's top cop reversed the crime epidemic.* Random House.

Brown, L. P. (1992). *Community policing guidebook.* New York City Police Department.

DeLorenzi, D., Shane, J. M., & Amendola, K. L. (2006, September). The CompStat process: Managing performance on the pathway to leadership. *The Police Chief, 73*(9), 34–38.

Eterno, J. A. (2025, March 12). *Community policing and women's safety and security* [Conference presentation]. Commission on the Status of Women, New York, NY, United States.

Eterno, J. A., & Silverman, E. B. (2010). The NYPD's CompStat: Compare statistics or compose statistics? *International Journal of Police Science and Management, 12*(3), 426–449. https://doi.org/10.1350/ijps.2010.12.3.195

Eterno, J. A., & Silverman, E. B. (2012). *The crime numbers game: Management by manipulation.* CRC Press. https://doi.org/10.1201/b11477

Eterno, J. A., Verma, A., & Silverman, E. B. (2016). Police manipulations of crime reporting: Insiders' revelations. *Justice Quarterly, 33*(5), 811–835. https://doi.org/10.1080/07418825.2014.980838

Geoghegan, S. (2006, April). CompStat revolutionizes contemporary policing. *Law and Order, 54*(4), 42–46.

Giuliani, R. W., & Bratton, W. J. (1994a). *Police strategy no. 1: Getting guns off the streets of New York.* U.S. Department of Justice.

Giuliani, R. W., & Bratton, W. J. (1994b). *Police strategy no. 2: Curbing youth violence in the schools and on the streets.* U.S. Department of Justice.

Giuliani, R. W., & Bratton, W. J. (1994c). *Police strategy no. 3: Driving drug dealers out of New York.* U.S. Department of Justice.

Giuliani, R. W., & Bratton, W. J. (1994d). *Police strategy no. 4: Breaking the cycle of domestic violence.* U.S. Department of Justice.

Giuliani, R. W., & Bratton, W. J. (1994e). *Police strategy no. 5: Reclaiming the public spaces of New York.* U.S. Department of Justice.

Giuliani, R. W., & Bratton, W. J. (1995a). *Police strategy no. 6: Reducing auto-related crime in New York.* U.S. Department of Justice.

Giuliani, R. W., & Bratton, W. J. (1995b). *Police strategy no. 7: Rooting out corruption; building organizational integrity in the New York Police Department.* U.S. Department of Justice.

Giuliani, R. W., & Bratton, W. J. (1995c). *Police strategy no. 8: Reclaiming the roads of New York.* U.S. Department of Justice.

Gurwitt, R. (1998, January). The comeback of the cops. *Governing*, 14–19.

Henry, V. E. (2002). *The CompStat paradigm: Management accountability in policing, business and the public sector.* Looseleaf Law Publications.

Kelling, G. L., & Sousa, W. H. (2001). *Do police matter? An analysis of the impact of New York City's police reforms* (Civic Report No. 22). Manhattan Institute.

Kocieniewski, D. (1997, October 2). Jury finds Police Department guilty of age discrimination. *The New York Times.* https://timesmachine.nytimes.com/timesmachine/1997/10/02/404667.html

Legal Defense Fund. (2025). *The NYPD gang database, explained.* https://www.naacpldf.org/case-issue/nypd-gang-database-policing-tactics/

Levine, H. G., & Siegel, L. (2015). Marijuana madness: The scandal of New York City's racist marijuana arrests. In J. A. Eterno (Ed.), *The New York City Police Department: The impact of its policies and practices* (pp. 117–161). CRC Press.

Maple, J., & Mitchell, C. (1999). *The crime fighter: Putting the bad guys out of business.* Doubleday.

Max, B. (2015, November 9). "Peace dividend" approach continues, Bratton and de Blasio say. *Gotham Gazette.* https://www.gothamgazette.com/government/5977-peace-dividend-approach-continues-bratton-and-de-blasio-say

McDonald, P. P. (2002). *Managing police operations: Implementing the New York crime control model—CompStat*. Wadsworth.

Moore, M. H. (2003). Sizing up CompStat: An important administrative innovation in policing. *Criminology & Public Policy*, *2*(3), 469–494. https://doi.org/10.1111/j.1745-9133.2003.tb00009.x

O'Connell, P. E., & Straub, F. (1999, Spring). Why the jails didn't explode. *City Journal*, *9*(2), 28–37.

Safir, H. (1988). *The CompStat process*. Police Department, City of New York.

Sanow, E. (2003, August). CompStat: The real cops on the dots. *Law and Order*, *51*, 4–8.

Schick, W. (2004, January). CompStat in the Los Angeles Police Department. *The Police Chief*, *71*(1), 17–23.

Silverman, E. B. (2001). *NYPD battles crime: Innovative strategies in policing* (Rev. ed.). Northeastern University Press.

Walsh, W. F. (2001). CompStat: An analysis of an emerging police managerial paradigm. *Policing: An International Journal of Police Strategies & Management*, *24*(3), 347–362.

Walsh, W. F., & Vito, G. F. (2004). The meaning of CompStat: Analysis and response. *Journal of Contemporary Criminal Justice*, *20*(1), 51–69.

Wilson, J. Q., & Kelling, G. L. (1982, March). Broken windows: The police and neighborhood safety. *The Atlantic Monthly*, *249*(3), 29–38.

4

HOWARD SAFIR AND BERNARD KERIK, 1996–2002

The Troubles Take Root

Courtesy, Professionalism, and Respect

The crime decline is now in motion. The new Police Commissioner, Howard Safir (April 15, 1996 to August 19, 2000) takes command. The new team is in place. Mr. Safir was moved from the Fire Department to the New York City Police Department (NYPD). Bratton, before leaving, has the entire fourteenth floor painted red, as the running joke in Headquarters is that it is to "welcome" the new commissioner. With extremely aggressive crime-fighting strategies and CompStat performance management firmly in place, Safir must try to usher in his style of leadership. His answer is *Courtesy, Professionalism, and Respect* (CPR) (Silverman, 2001).

What Is CPR?

Few, if any, changes are made to the successful and aggressive crime-fighting style developed by Bratton (1997). The NYPD doubles-down on its crime-fighting approach, CompStat. With the award-winning innovation going full speed ahead, Mr. Safir, however, develops his brand of leadership, attempting to tone down officers' overzealous zero-tolerance, crime-fighting behaviors with a new strategy called *Courtesy, Professionalism, and Respect* (CPR). Mr. Safir helps to run CompStat, so fear remains the main method of motivating commanders and others. However, CPR will now theoretically require officers of all ranks to treat those, especially outside the agency, differently. There is a real concern with treating communities with dignity. The balance between crime fighting and due process is a difficult one for police managers. This program was an attempt to grapple with that issue. For example, the NYPD writes, "If crime levels decline, but members of the community are reluctant to approach police for fear of a negative encounter, then we have not truly met our obligations to the public" (New York Police Department, 1996, p. 1). This program is an excellent insight into one of the key issues with the aggressive police crime-fighting style in place at the time. That is, if police become overly aggressive, they will likely alienate the communities they serve. This, in turn, may actually lead to an increase in crime as, for example, less information

DOI: 10.4324/9781003593256-4

will be given to the police by an untrustful public. CPR is essentially an attempt to balance the aggressive crime-control strategy with a community-oriented approach.

This was exactly what the department needed. Unfortunately, it was, in many respects, a paper tiger. Although, as we shall see, there was a measurable impact—it was not long-lasting or taken as seriously as it could have been. Why? Its major issue is that it stresses positive interactions with the public and even suggests it should be the same within the department. For example, the department writes, "For Courtesy, Professionalism, and Respect (CPR) truly to become part of our culture, it must not only be practiced when we come in contact with the public, but also in interactions among ourselves" (New York Police Department, 1996, p. 3). While this is a key point, the main issue is that high-level management is literally bullying and browbeating commanders at CompStat meetings (Eterno & Silverman, 2006, 2010, 2012). The twofold message was apparent. High-level managers would berate their commanders, yet the lower ranks were expected to be "courteous." Had upper management at least considered the effect of their mixed messages, CPR may have had a more lasting impact. Had high-level managers at the CompStat meetings been more courteous, or at least respectful, to their mid-level subordinates, this would likely have been a much more groundbreaking initiative. Instead, the program, as well intentioned as it was, simply added, albeit halfheartedly, another layer of pressure onto officers of all ranks. Not only did crime have to go down, but now officers were supposed to treat everyone with CPR. So, while high-level managers scream, yell, and, at times, berate commanders in front of their peers, everyone else must have CPR. Management by fear remained out of control. A team approach to management may have made a more meaningful change in the culture. The hypocrisy from higher-ranking officials would ultimately greatly diminish the impact of what was an excellent initiative.

Main Concepts

In this section, I will discuss some of the main concepts and ideas. One of the main concepts is "acknowledging the rights and dignity of those we come in contact with" (New York Police Department, 1996, p. 4). This is certainly an important aspect of police work, let alone CPR. It relates to stop and frisk because basic rights, such as those in the Fourth Amendment—including the right to be free from unreasonable search and seizure—are, at least to be "acknowledged." Officers were taught in the Police Academy and later during in-service training to follow laws and court cases. This appears to be, at some level, a reinforcement of those lessons. The department goes on with, "Acknowledging the diversity, traditions, and cultures of others" (New York Police Department, 1996, p. 4). Again, such cultural awareness training was commonplace in the Police Academy in the social science curriculum. The CPR initiative seems to be reinforcing the importance of Police Academy coursework.

This is critically important as the NYPD was accused in the stop-and-frisk program of violating the rights and dignity of numerous citizens, especially minority youth. Stop and frisk is supposed to protect society from illegal criminal behavior. Since forcible stops involve very close personal contact with suspects, CPR would help minimize the negative impact of such intrusions. Patrick Kelleher, the First Deputy Commissioner at the time, is quoted as saying, "There is no greater detriment to officer safety or successful completion of the Police mission than a lack of respect for the Department or the community we serve" (New York Police Department, 1996, p. 4). This is a particularly important statement as it sternly advises that officer safety could be affected by the way in which officers treat others. These high-level managers certainly are looking for officers to conduct themselves according to CPR. However, the "do as I say, not as I do" mentality of the time was a weak leadership style, at best. Without setting an example, especially, but not exclusively, at CompStat meetings, the rank-and-file would only take the program halfheartedly.

Interestingly, once again, the Department makes commanding officers accountable for their subordinates: "Commanding officers will be responsible for the quality of service provided to the public" (New York Police Department, 1996, p. 6). Once again, commanders are put on the hot seat to reduce crime and also, at the same time, to make sure that officers are doing that job with CPR. Once more, there is an attempt to change a culture. In this case, the balance between crime control and basic rights is on the shoulders of precinct-level management. They are, at least on paper, held accountable for CPR of their officers at CompStat. Again, CPR is a commendable program, but rarely are commanders held accountable for CPR as they are for crime control. Commanders were counting every index crime in their respective commands. They were very worried about crime. However, much less attention was given to these types of community interactions. They were not brought up at CompStat like index crime numbers were. Rather, they were an afterthought, if that. The Department, however, did review civilian complaints. In fact, these were part of the commander's profile and could be looked at by the high-ranking inquisitors. Nevertheless, few were afraid of those numbers compared with index crime.

Yet, at least formally, a change could be seen. Nearly all Department documents and even patrol cars would have the *Courtesy, Professionalism, and Respect* emboldened on them. Training, including those of executives, was changed to reflect the new strategy. There were measures put in place to monitor CPR. The Department would use its force monitoring system to watch suspect officers. Most of these issues, however, were falling on low-level officers. Rarely were higher ranks held to the standard. Even lower ranks' aggressive behaviors might be tolerated if they had, for example, impressive arrest records. Civilian complaints were theoretically examined closely for violations under CPR. This was nothing new, however, as the Department already had, as mentioned, a force monitoring system that most were aware of. As we shall see, CPR did have some impact, but not nearly the same effect as CompStat's national and international appeal. The lack of influence of the Civilian Complaint Review Board (CCRB) and, in turn, the CPR, may be due, at least in part, to the Police Commissioner having control of punishment with respect to CCRB complaints. One would think this would be healthy, but few commissioners have been responsive to CCRB since it became a separate agency in 1993 (CCRB, 2025). In general, only the most egregious violations are likely to receive penalties. These tend to fall on lower-ranking officers. The CCRB, then, only recommends penalties (CCRB, 2025). The CCRB during these years also had a negative reputation with respect to its investigations. For example, the United States Commission on Civil Rights (USCCR), in writing about police practices in New York City, states:

> Accordingly, the CCRB's ineffectiveness in investigating claims influenced the amount of actual discipline imposed against officers with substantiated misconduct complaints. In 1996, for example, the police department disposed of only 176 substantiated complaints. One hundred and one of those complaints were dismissed on the grounds that the evidence against the officer was insufficient to support a prima facie case even though the CCRB had previously investigated the complaint and concluded that credible evidence

> supported it. This low percentage of substantiated cases resulting in police officer discipline may have been, in part, a reaction by the NYPD to the relocation of the CCRB outside the police department .... Even aside from the CCRB's problems, therefore, the NYPD may not have taken strong measures to ensure that proper discipline was meted out to officers who were guilty of misconduct.
>
> *(USCCR, 2000, chap. 4)*

The lack of discipline based on CCRB complaints by police commissioners continues to this day. During this time period, however, CPR encouraged changes in behavior, but its impact was tepid, at best, especially compared to CompStat. Both civilian complaints and awards for liability were extremely high in spite of CPR (Eterno, 2001, 2003).

We note that there was a modicum of concern from officers of all ranks about upholding Constitutional rights. In a survey of all ranks, officers who worked during Mayor Giuliani's tenure indicated a very modest but important increase in pressure to obey Constitutional restrictions. In the era before Mayor Giuliani 44.6 percent of officers indicated that they *felt high pressure to obey* these legal restrictions. During Mayor Giuliani's years, including those of CPR's zenith, 46.9 percent of officers similarly felt *high pressure to obey* these restrictions (Eterno & Silverman, 2013). While this is a modest 2.3 percent difference, there is a demonstrable rise from previous mayors. Further, 20.7 percent felt *little to no pressure to obey* these restrictions before Mayor Giuliani's tenure while only 17.2 percent felt *little to no pressure to obey* during his tenure. Again, while there is only a modest 3.5 percent difference, there is some modest evidence (note that the remainder were in the middle, feeling moderate pressure). This is important as CPR does have some demonstrable impact, albeit not lasting nor as powerful compared with crime-control policies. In the following paragraphs, I shall show some other indicators as well.

Other evidence, too, demonstrates a modest increase in officers obeying legal restrictions during these years (Eterno, 2001, 2003; Eterno, Verma, & Silverman, 2016). Trends showing increased obedience to the law, especially stop and frisk, will reverse under Mayor Bloomberg. For now, however, the evidence indicates that officers are generally in compliance with legal restrictions such as stop and frisk, albeit with some concerns. Other than the survey, another indication of this is seen in civilian complaints for abuse of authority. In 1993 there are 1,246 complaints. In a few short years, in 1996, they increase to 2,828. In 1997 and 1998, the first full years of CPR, we see a leveling off at 2,631 and 2,646, respectively (Eterno, 2001).

Another study also indicates during this time officers tend to be following legal guidelines. A survey of 1,259 police officers from every precinct in New York City was conducted in the summer of 1997 (Eterno, 2001, 2003). Officers were placed into hypothetical legal situations called vignettes based on court cases. These included stop and search situations examining Fourth Amendment law or its equivalent in the New York State Constitution. These situations included car and person stops as well as weapon and drug searches. When the situation was illegal, only 15.6 percent of officers would likely violate legal restrictions. Additionally, it was found that those officers who tend to be more aggressive (accept zero tolerance) tend to be more illegal in their search behaviors, and less aggressive officers tended to search in 14.4 percent of the illegal situations, while aggressive officers did the illegal search in 24.9 percent of the illegal situations. This 10.5 percent difference was statistically significant. Ultimately, I suggest that if zero-tolerance policies are adopted they need to be carefully balanced with due process programs such as CPR (Eterno, 2001). Again, the police must maintain an equilibrium between aggressive crime-fighting and legal rights.

In that same survey, I also examine car stop and person stop situations (Eterno, 2003). The car stop is a hypothetical situation given to officers based on the bright-line rule (i.e., a clear, unambiguous legal standard) court case, *Delaware v. Prouse* (1979). The rule constructed by the United States Supreme Court is that officers cannot stop a car merely to check a driver's license or registration. Officers, therefore, were asked about their likelihood of stopping a car to check a license and registration. In this scenario, approximately half of the officers followed legal parameters and would not stop the car. A relatively small percentage of officers, 14.5 percent, violated legal restrictions, with the remainder in the middle. Given this type of action is basically unsupervised and hidden from public view at the time, we can be confident that most officers are, at a minimum, considering legal parameters. With respect to person stop situations, however, the results are more illegal. In an ambiguous case of New York State, *People v. Martinez* (1992), officers are not supposed to pursue suspects who turn and run without provocation. This goes against the commonsense finding of *Illinois v. Wardlow* (2000), which was a United States Supreme Court case that came to just the opposite conclusion: that if someone turns and runs from officers, it is prima facie evidence of criminal activity (reasonable suspicion). Regardless of the ambiguity of the law, officers were more likely to violate the law by running after the suspect (compared with the car stop). On a scale of 1 to 8, with 1 being definitely not searching and 8 being definitely searching, officers were more likely to follow the law in the bright-line person stop case compared with the ambiguous, person stop case (M = 3.32 versus 3.72). Both cases were essentially illegal but, again, it must be emphasized that since the case is extremely ambiguous, it cannot be said that officers are definitely violating legal restrictions since the case is so unclear. While most officers did follow the guidelines and did not "run after" the suspect, there is more of a concern with person stop situations given the higher level of violation by officers compared with the car stop. The implications of this are that bright-line rules are important and seem to be effective, albeit small (Eterno, 2007). Additionally, we can say that person stop situations seem a bit more troublesome for officers in terms of legality, even in this early stage of the stop-and-frisk controversy. On average, officers do seem to follow legal guidelines. However, there is concern particularly in ambiguous rulings for person stops (Eterno, 2003).

In sum, with CPR there was an expectation that while officers may be browbeaten at CompStat, contemporaneously lower and middle ranks should treat civilians and other Department members with CPR. Evidence, although weak, does show a modest impact on officers' behavior. Pressures to obey the law increased, civilian complaints leveled off, and officers' judgments in hypothetical legal situations were generally obedient with some concerns especially in non-bright-line person stop situations. The Department did do some integrity testing during the period as well. This even came down to how officers answered telephones. The pressures on most ranks (with the exception of the highest-ranking officials), then, continued to mount. Based on all this, I conclude that CPR had some impact. Had it been a management principle for leadership, the future of CPR may have been far more influential for Mr. Safir and NYPD.

Shocking Police Misconduct

In New York City during this time, there were incidents of alleged police abuse of authority surrounding Fourth Amendment law, including police brutality and stop and frisk. The three most important were Abner Louima, Amadou Diallo, and Patrick Dorismond (Eterno, 2003). Mr. Louima was on August 9, 1997. Mr. Diallo occurred on February 4, 1999. Mr. Dorismond was on March 16, 2000. All three controversies occurred under Mr. Safir's tenure as Police Commissioner. Each led to some level of community unrest, especially among minorities.

Abner Louima was an unarmed Haitian legal immigrant who was arrested when police were called to a Brooklyn nightclub. Mr. Louima was arrested for obstructing governmental administration, resisting arrest, and disorderly conduct. On the way back to the precinct, officers beat the handcuffed prisoner with batons and fists. Later, at the precinct, officer Justin Volpe brutalized his prisoner by placing a stick in his rectum, squeezing the prisoner's testicles, among other atrocities (*United States v. Volpe*, 1999). Officer Volpe was convicted of the sexual assault among other charges and was sentenced to 30 years in prison without the possibility of parole. He was, however, released in 2023 after serving 24 years of his sentence. The City also settled a lawsuit for $8.7 million, which was the largest settlement for police brutality at the time (Chan, 2007). This incident shocked the city and the nation, leading to huge unrest.

A second incident soon after would also send shockwaves through the NYPD. The shooting death of an unarmed immigrant from Guinea, Amadou Diallo. Mr. Diallo was shot numerous times during a forcible stop by the extremely aggressive crime-fighting citywide Street Crime Unit. The Unit had been recently tripled in size by Police Commissioner Safir. Their motto was, "We own the night." Four plainclothes officers of the unit were patrolling in the Bronx. They noticed Mr. Diallo, who apparently fitted the description of a suspected rapist. He was outside his apartment and was said to be going out for a snack (Weiss, 1999). The four officers passed the apartment, parked their unmarked car, and got out to determine what the suspect was doing. The officers were unable to use their car as cover nor was there any other readily available cover between them and Mr. Diallo. This may have contributed to the officers firing their guns without accurately assessing the situation. Mr. Diallo, an unarmed Black male, did not obey the officers' commands to stop, and fled into the poorly lit vestibule to his apartment. He then turned to face police, not obeying commands, with his wallet in his hand. At least one of the officers shouted "gun" (Weiss, 1999). The officers, tragically, mistook the wallet for a gun and fired 41 shots at Mr. Diallo, killing him. The two closest officers emptied their 9-millimeter handguns, firing 32 rounds with the remainder coming from the other two officers. This could have been a situation called rapid reflexive response. This is when one officer opens fire and, then, in turn, with little or no assessment of the situation, others open fire as well. Dr. James Fyfe, a world-renowned expert on police shootings, testified that given the actions of the suspect, among other factors, the officers acted within the scope of NYPD guidelines (Court TV, n.d.). It was suggested that officers' bullets ricocheted back at them, creating the appearance of shooting but that was not considered accurate based on the investigation (Weiss, 1999). All the officers were acquitted of criminal wrongdoing (Fritsch, 2000). The City settled for $3 million (Stanford University Libraries, n.d.).

The Diallo case is one of the most egregious in terms of catalyzing criticism of stop and frisk. Minority communities were exceedingly agitated (Harring, 2000). The aggressive unit known for its forcible stops was brought to the forefront. This case marks a turning point in race relations and issues with police behavior. Additionally, numerous issues were brought up with the incident, regardless of the verdict. For example, with no supervision present and four plainclothes officers working in one unmarked vehicle, questions soon arose. It is this case, in particular, that led to NYPD looking into its *Terry* stop behaviors.

A third incident was the apparently accidental shooting of Patrick Dorismond, an unarmed Black security guard (not working at the time of the incident). Mr. Dorismond was approached by an undercover narcotics detective, Anthony Vasquez. Mr. Vasquez asked Mr. Dorismond if he had any illegal drugs on him. Mr. Dorismond was offended by this and a struggle ensued. During the struggle, a grand jury determined the detective's gun fired one time into Mr. Dorismond's chest, killing him. As a result of the grand jury acquittal, no charges were filed against the detective. However, a civil suit was settled by the City, awarding the family of Mr. Dorismond $2.25 million. While there was no conviction, the case also represented another race-based incident in the city by police. Mr. Giuliani was quick to release Mr. Dorismond's juvenile record (which was sealed at the time) and also slow to show sympathy for the deceased. Minority communities were again appalled by yet another incident (CBS News, 2000).

NYPD Response

While the officers were ultimately acquitted, the Diallo incident marked a turning point for the NYPD. The importance of balancing aggressive crime-fighting strategies became a major concern to higher-ups. While due process issues were generally given a nod, the idea was that the crime-fighting mission was the penultimate job of police (Henry, 2002). NYPD would brag year in and year out about its crime rate decreases. Often, little to no attention was given to due process issues. With mounting pressure, especially from minority communities, the Department could no longer ignore the outcry. Initially, some minor changes were made.

Almost immediately after the Diallo shooting, the NYPD reacted with changes. They re-trained the entire Street Crime Unit in March 1999—only a few short weeks after the tragedy. Additionally, more frontline supervision was required for plainclothes units. Since no direct supervision was present when Mr. Diallo was shot, that lack of supervision was considered a likely factor contributing to the tragedy occurring (Eterno, 2003). It should be noted that many other agencies emulated the aggressive crime-fighting style of NYPD. While they tended to copy the aggressiveness, they tended not to copy or even study these critical changes based on lessons from these incidents (Eterno & Silverman, 2012).

The Diallo shooting was a key turning point for the NYPD. In the wake of the shooting, community unrest, especially from minorities, was clear. Demonstrations led by community leader, Al Sharpton, were commonplace. Indeed, immediately after the Diallo shooting there were calls for the arrest of the officers among other outcries. Although the officers were eventually arrested and tried, the Department initially waited for a Grand Juries finding before it moved. Mr. Sharpton and his followers were protesting at Police Headquarters during this time. Some of them were arrested in an attempt to bring attention to the officers who, thus far, were not taken into custody (Cooper, 1999). It was evident that this was not an issue that would simply go away.

Stop and Frisk Unit

The Diallo tragedy sparked the NYPD to examine their stop, question, and frisk reports, also known as UF-250s. The UF stands for Uniformed Forces and was the code associated with the form. It was, during this time period, a handwritten form used to document certain forcible stops by NYPD officers. The Patrol Guide (NYPD's rules and regulations) at the time only required these reports to be written when: 1) force was used; 2) a frisk or search was done; 3) the person stopped was arrested; and, 4) the person stopped refused to provide their identity.

After Diallo, the NYPD brass was particularly interested in the stops of the Street Crime Unit and other stops as well. A "stop and frisk" unit had to be formed to put all of these handwritten reports into a database. I was made the commanding officer of that original unit. It was staffed with many officers who were about to be promoted. Before promotion, they would be reassigned to this unit. We also had a cadre of various officers and staff who were either temporarily transferred to the unit or were already in the overhead command (like myself) and given this task. Given my background in research and my rank as captain, I was given overall command of the unit. This was an exceedingly difficult assignment. All facets of the Department were called in to assist. A computer program had to be created to enter the forms into the newly formed database. The unit was in Headquarters and was situated in an old communications area. This allowed access to computer terminals. Management Information Systems Development (MISD) had computer programmers develop the necessary computer program place on the mainframe computer. We then had to train numerous temporary workers who were hired to type in the information on the forms into the database. All of these workers had to be trained on rules to follow and NYPD nomenclature. For example, CPW means Criminal Possession of a Weapon. CPCS means Criminal Possession of a Controlled Substance. Numerous other abbreviations and rules had to be created. Most important was that the collection of the data needed to be done in a consistent manner. The unit initially ran 24 hours a day, 7 days a week. It was an enormous undertaking. Another captain was brought in to oversee night shifts. I was on call 24/7 as well.

During this time, I also worked closely with the higher echelon such as the Deputy Commissioner of Legal Matters, Deputy Commissioner of Strategic Initiatives, and Assistant Commissioners in several areas. There were regular meetings and progress reports. Eventually, years later, the stop-and-frisk report prepared by officers in the field was made electronic. At this time, however, the tedious job of putting the reports onto computer was endless. We concentrated on the most recent years first. Eventually we had a few years of reports, and data were made available to both NYPD and some outside groups that were scrutinizing the stop-and-frisk practices of the NYPD.

To that end, two of these groups become critical. First was the New York State Attorney General, Eliot Spitzer. Second were the plaintiffs in a civil suit against the Department. The original case was *Daniels v. City of New York* (2001). I was deposed along with others at the NYPD in that case in 2002. My testimony was in November of 2002.

Ultimately, the Department truly did Herculean work to get this data. The unit even did work during 9/11, collecting DNA data and putting that information into a database as well. Regardless of that work, the data on stop and frisk were available in 1999 for Eliot Spitzer to conduct a full analysis of the UF-250s. The New York State Office of the Attorney General's report (1999), written with the assistance of Dr. Jeffrey Fagan, a professor at Columbia University, was exceedingly critical of the NYPD.

Given the outcry from minority communities, Eliot Spitzer, then-New York State Attorney General, closely examined and analyzed the stop-and-frisk practices in New York City.

New York State Attorney General's Report on Stop and Frisk

On December 1, 1999, the Attorney General's Report on racial profiling by NYPD was released (New York State Office of the Attorney General, 1999). The quantitative analysis, a key part of the report, was based on the stop-and-frisk reports provided by the Department and created by the aforementioned unit. The report blasted the practices of the NYPD. It does contain, however, a wealth of information in its nearly 200 pages. It does not, however, contain most of the NYPD viewpoint since they were not consulted before the report went public. This is critically important, and generally overlooked when cited. Importantly, during this time period, the NYPD, in general, defends itself well, and numerous attacks fail to completely change NYPD forcible stop practices. It is not until about a decade later that these initial issues become exacerbated by an NYPD either unwilling or unable to grapple with many of these arguments going forward. Again, the NYPD does effectively manage these attacks, but a decade later they totally abuse the settlements and powers given to them by increasing their stops by over 600 percent. At that point, it is obvious to all that the Department simply abused its authority and the goodwill of so many involved. So, the seeds are planted here and the NYPD, unfortunately for them, fails to heed the messages.

The report, including its widespread critique of the NYPD, is clear. Its strong wording shows major concerns with the NYPD's practices. As we shall see, it makes many compelling arguments attacking them. Ultimately, however, the NYPD initially overcomes these arguments. The investigation begins in March 1999. Again, note the timing: right after the Diallo shooting.

One of the key findings in the report that comports well with other research of the time is that approximately 15 percent of stops, *regardless of race*, are not supported by legal criteria. Additionally, over half of stops are within legal parameters *regardless of race*. A survey of officers discussed earlier, which I conducted in 1997, also shows about 15 percent were not following legal parameters and over half were following the law (Eterno, 2003). Both results are remarkably similar. The New York State Office of the Attorney General (1999, pp. 14–15) states:

> Citywide, 61.1% of all sampled UF-250 forms contained factual bases provided by officers that, as stated, were sufficient to justify a "stop" based on "reasonable suspicion." … Citywide, 15.4% … were not sufficient to justify a "stop." … Citywide, 23.2% of forms completed by members of the SCU did not provide a factual basis for the "stops" …. Notably, based on the sample, racial minorities were no more likely than whites to be subject to "stops" where the factual basis stated did not meet the legal standard of "reasonable suspicion."

This result is especially important for at least two reasons. First, 23 percent of the forms completed by the Citywide Street Crime Unit (SCU) are illegal. The survey discussed above shows that approximately 40 percent of forcible stops by anticrime are illegal (Eterno, 2003). Here, the Attorney General is actually showing a more promising result. That is, exceedingly aggressive SCU officers are not nearly as illegal as one might expect. This may be due to the widespread training of SCU officers. Anticrime are precinct officers who are selected by commanding officers of precincts. With CompStat looming over commanders' heads, precinct officers may be more susceptible to conducting illegal stops. While the SCU will later be a concern, and even disbanded later in 2002 (Rashbaum & Baker, 2002), much of that work was then transferred over to precinct anticrime officers. It would appear, then, that this was not a solution and it arguably, based on this evidence, exacerbated a long-standing problem at NYPD. Second, in terms of legal criteria, officers showed no difference with respect to race.

That is, they equally applied legal guidelines regardless of race. While much is made of officers stopping too many minorities based on population counts, little attention is given to the above result. What this may mean is that officers generally follow legal criteria. Importantly, however, as we shall see in future chapters, a broader policy by higher-ups such as the police commissioner and/or the mayor is a likely candidate for issues related to racism and unconstitutional behavior by officers.

Overall, however, the New York State Office of the Attorney General's Report (1999) is extremely critical of NYPD practices with respect to stop and frisk. The report is very thorough, and its legal analysis does include extensive discussion of the *De Bour* case. As discussed, this is the New York State Court of Appeals case that holds New York State officers to some different criteria compared with *Terry v. Ohio* (1968). As already talked about, the *De Bour* case creates a four-tiered approach to police intrusions. To quickly review, at the first level, officers must have an objective credible reason, not necessarily criminal behavior, to request basic information. This might include reason for conduct, identity, why a person is at a location, and similar information. The second level is the common law right of inquiry. The officer, in this case, may go beyond simple basic information such as identity and probe for other information. At both of these levels, the person is free to go and may not be forcibly detained. The next level is forcible stopping; this is based on reasonable suspicion, which is similar to *Terry*. However, in New York it is slightly more than *Terry*, where the officer has a slightly greater burden to show evidence. The evidence must be particular to an individual. The fourth level is based on probable cause and allows the officer to arrest.

The New York State Office of the Attorney General's Report (1999) also discusses the NYPD approach to stop and frisk as a crime-fighting tool. Broken windows theory (Wilson & Kelling, 1982; Kelling & Coles, 1996) is discussed, as well as the importance of enforcing minor violations. The pressures of CompStat are also covered, indicating an understanding of Department culture. An understanding of NYPD's proactive policing strategy is developed. Further, the report also outlines NYPD training on the law, which was fairly extensive at the time.

The report focuses on select scientific research which has shown some issues at NYPD, such as Skolnick's classic work, *Justice without Trial* (1975). The report also covers officers' attitudes toward stop and frisk: "From their point of view, 'stop & frisk' is where 'cops put' their lives on the line to deter, investigate, and solve crime." Every such encounter raises the question "whether the cop is going home at the end of his tour" (New York State Office of the Attorney General, 1999, p. 73). Concluded one officer: "This is about going home" (p. 69). Officers are taught in nearly all circumstances the possibility of danger. This includes car stops, domestics, and other situations. While the report suggests that stop and frisk is singled out as "dangerous," this is not the case. Nearly all personal encounters are taught this way to officers. In other words, stop and frisk is not especially different in this way from other topics. The report never points this out, strongly suggesting officers' attitudes toward stop and frisk are, in particular, overly stressing the possibility of danger.

Furthermore, it is equally clear that officers at NYPD are highly trained and understand legal criteria: "To be sure, every officer interviewed by the OAG [New York State Office of the Attorney General] could identify the basic legal standards: 'reasonable suspicion' v. 'mere suspicion,' and 'common law inquiry' v. *Terry* 'stop'." (p. 69). This is not a trivial point. The training on stop and frisk at the time is clearly, at a minimum, informative and, as demonstrated, showing that officers are retaining the information taught. This, too, compares well with the findings of another study done at the time (Eterno, 1999, 2003).

The report also contains a detailed statistical analysis. Without going into specifics, the essential findings are that NYPD is engaging in illegal and racist behaviors:

> This [sic] data—which covers the period January 1, 1998 through March 31, 1999—has been compared with census data, crime statistics and other demographic information to yield, for the first time, a statistically valid, quantitative view of the practice of "stop & frisk," including: (1) the rates at which "stops" occur to people in different racial groups and in different locations throughout the City; (2) the extent to which such "stop" rates are predicted by crime data; (3) the facts articulated by police officers as the basis for making "stops"; and (4) the extent to which those facts, as stated, articulate "reasonable suspicion" of potential criminal activity as required by Terry v. Ohio and its progeny. This data provides a unique view of "stop & frisk" tactics. After years of relying upon individual accounts provided either by officers or by civilians who are "stopped," the OAG's analysis demonstrates, in objective, statistical form, the actual patterns and trends that occur daily on New York City's streets. Impressions and assumptions can now be evaluated in light of hard data and statistically impartial facts. Among the key findings of this research are the following: There is a strong statistical correlation between race and likelihood of being "stopped." ... While crime rates partially explain the high correlation between race and likelihood of being "stopped," they do not fully explain this correlation. In other words, even when crime data are considered, minorities are still "stopped" at a higher rate than would be predicted by both demographics and crime rates. ... In roughly one out of every seven "stops" conducted by the NYPD, the facts that the police officer articulates for making the "stop," as stated in the UF-250 form, fail to meet the legal threshold of "reasonable suspicion."
>
> *(New York State Office of the Attorney General, 1999, p. 88)*

Were the stops unconstitutional? As discussed earlier, about 15 percent of stops were found unconstitutional: "For the citywide sample, 15.4% of all rationales provided by officers in the UF-250 forms, without more, failed to articulate facts sufficient to establish the requisite 'reasonable suspicion'" (p. 172). While this does not seem unusual, it should be noted that the OAG was the only one to determine if the stop met the legal requirement. There was no input from the NYPD or even an outside authority. Nevertheless, the level is not unexpected or necessarily outrageous given other research of the time (see Eterno, 1999, 2003). Perhaps most concerning was the suggestion of racism by police. For example, "as noted in Section I.A., the SCU was far more likely to 'stop' Blacks than were precinct level commands" (New York State Office of the Attorney General, 1999, p. 174). Ultimately, the Attorney General has been in contact with the NYPD. The data, supplied by NYPD, is just one example. The Attorney General did not, however, put NYPD's response into their report. However, media reports, as well as another investigation, did include the NYPD response. The United States Commission on Civil Rights' report documents NYPD responses. After discussing those, the *Daniels* case will be explored.

United States Commission on Civil Rights

At this time, NYPD's stop-and-frisk practices were under enormous scrutiny. In May 1999, another investigation was conducted into police practices and civil rights in New York City.

While the Spitzer report failed to incorporate or even ask NYPD for its response, the Civil Rights Commission listened and incorporated the NYPD viewpoints. A *New York Post* article, while critical of NYPD, summarized this situation as follows:

> Police Commissioner Howard Safir, in a press release yesterday, blasted Spitzer for issuing a "critically flawed" report without showing it to the NYPD first so it could correct some misconceptions. Safir's biggest contention was that Spitzer failed to acknowledge "the race of the individuals stopped strongly correlates with the descriptions of persons committing violent crime as identified by their victims."
>
> *(Newfield, 1999, n.p.)*

The New York State Office of the Attorney General failed to even ask the NYPD for its responses before publishing their extremely critical report (1999). However, the United States Commission on Civil Rights (USCCR), in its report (2000), not only asked but incorporated, mostly in a series of endnotes, the NYPD position. The most important of those responses are explained in the following paragraphs.

One of the first NYPD responses is, "several criminal justice experts consider the Department an example of proper policing." While the experts are not named in the document, there are well-known works very favorable to NYPD policing (USCCR, 2000, fn. 1). We can surmise, however, based on publications shortly after this report. One example is Zimring (2007), who certainly argues that the NYPD was almost completely responsible for the crime drop. Henry (2002), too, is very favorable to the NYPD.

In another citation, the NYPD suggests that the law of stop and frisk is ambiguous: "Some authorities, such as New York Governor George Pataki and former New York State Supreme Court Judge Harold Rothwax have considered stop and frisk law ambiguous" (USCCR, 2000, fn. 46). Another issue is that the stop-and-frisk reports often do not need to be recorded by officers (fn. 70). The NYPD also states that, "Data extracted from NYPD database may not be proper for analysis" (fn. 75). The NYPD also made the assertion that there are no quotas on stop-and-frisk reports (fn. 78). While this may or may not have been accurate at the time, in the following decade the evidence of quotas is overwhelming and they were likely responsible, at least in part, for the tremendous increase in forcible stops, as we shall see later in this book.

The NYPD also advised that the USCCR did not properly understand or analyze the data (fn. 93). This is a typical response when a study does not show anyone in a good light. Furthermore, the USCCR study is misleading in that they do not consider crime data (fn. 94). More specifically, the NYPD response (USCCR, fn. 119) is:

> [T]he Police Commissioner has acknowledged that blacks and Hispanics are stopped in numbers greater than their proportion to the population. A more plausible interpretation is that officers are stopping individuals based on descriptions given by current victims as well as descriptions collected from continuing crime patterns (e.g., rape pattern, robbery pattern) in the area being policed. Those individuals who fit these pattern descriptions (from either immediate incidents or continuing patterns) along with those who officers actually observe committing crimes or violations are those most likely to be stopped by police. ... complaint data is an extraordinarily strong indicator of the demographics of the individuals' committing actions that would lead an officer to develop the reasonable suspicion necessary to conduct a street stop.

The NYPD response was written directly into the USCCR. Since the New York State Office of the Attorney General's report (1999) never solicited input from the NYPD, it never contained the response. However, the response to the Attorney General's report is seen in the USCCR report and in news media. Overall, the NYPD challenges the methods, analysis, and findings. The arguments are sensible and, combined with other factors, will lead to an initial settlement, as we shall soon see.

September 11, 2001

Bernard Kerik becomes Police Commissioner on August 21, 2000. Again, more of CompStat and more top-down management. Loyalty to Mayor Giuliani was essential. Terrorism, prior to 9/11, was not a priority. For example, only a few months before the millennium celebration, as commander of another unit called Mapping Support, I was asked for maps of the Times Square area by the New York City Joint Terrorism Task Force. I prepared maps for them. However, at the time, I was questioned about giving those maps to the Task Force. The worry of my superiors was that those maps looked too good and may have shown up on the news. If they did, I was scolded, "You will make the mayor look bad because his maps will not look as good." While I talked about the safety of the public and the fact that this was a "joint" task force including our own detectives, my pleas were ignored. It was all about making the mayor look good. Despite the 1993 attack at the World Trade Center and other alarming events such as the Oklahoma City bombing of the federal building, the general sense of the time was one of political loyalty to the mayor and other powerful figures. With Commissioner Kerik, the importance of loyalty was dramatically increased.

September 11, 2001 changed the entire dynamic. The landscape drastically changed, as did the NYPD. Certainly, Police Commissioner Kerik and the mayor led the city through those exceedingly challenging times and must be given some credit for that. Importantly, however, the respect for first responders grew dramatically. In terms of stop and frisk, the danger of terrorism moved the pendulum toward law enforcement. Laws were passed, such as the USA PATRIOT Act (2001), which gave law enforcement additional power. The fear of the attack would change the balance of power toward the executive branch and police. In times of crisis, this is not unusual. For example, habeas corpus has only been suspended three times in the history of the United States. The first time was in the civil war. The second was after the bombing of Pearl Harbor and the internment of the Japanese under Executive Order 9066. The third, and to the point here, was during the period after 9/11. This should show readers the importance of the terrorist attack.

During this time, then, the civil court case on stop and frisk was still in its initial stages where each side was making its points and going before Judge Scheindlin, who had the case in the United States District Court for the Southern District of New York. The New York Civil Liberties Union and the Center for Constitutional Rights (CCR) on balance decided it was time to settle. The City agreed.

Daniels v. City of New York

On March 8, 1999, a civil suit against the NYPD was brought to Federal District Court of the Southern District of New York (*Daniels v. City of New York*, 2001). Judge Shira Scheindlin was assigned the case. The essence of the case is that, in the wake of the Diallo shooting, plaintiffs sued the NYPD. More specifically, they argued that the NYPD Street Crime Unit was targeting minorities and conducting illegal racial profiling. The Center for Constitutional Rights and the New York Civil Liberties Union were the legal team leading the lawsuit. Numerous motions and other legal moves were made, making the case complicated (*Daniels v. City of New York*, 2001). The City's lawyers, called Corporation Counsel, initially tried to prevent stop-and-frisk reports from being released, at least early on. Ultimately, the plaintiffs did get the database, and numerous analyses were conducted with that data, including the aforementioned New York State Office of the Attorney General's report (1999).

Once the data were released, as we have seen, studies outside the NYPD at this point tend to show that the Department is engaged in widespread racial profiling. However, the NYPD, in its defense, strongly suggests otherwise. In particular, its argument is that the forcible stops are tailored to the descriptions of perpetrators as given to them by complainants. They indicate that stops can only be based on the descriptions they get and not on population figures. Thus, the basic argument of the police is that they develop reasonable suspicion (the legal standard to conduct a proper forcible stop) based on the information they are given. That is, the population numbers have little to do with developing reasonable suspicion but, importantly, complainants' descriptions of perpetrators are what police must work with. Additionally, the Department argues that the law is ambiguous in this area among some other arguments, all of which are publicly available (e.g., USCCR, 1999).

According to court records, numerous motions are made in the case (*Daniels v. City of New York*, 2001). Ultimately, the Judge ordered the release of the data and very public arguments are made (*Daniels v. City of New York*, 2001). Essentially, the argument of the plaintiffs is that they are being harassed and specifically targeted by police. The New York State Office of the Attorney General's report (1999), in particular, suggests the police are stopping minorities way out of proportion to their numbers in the population. Additionally, very few guns are removed from these stops and, in fact, stops of Whites are more likely to get a gun (Eterno & Silverman, 2012). As indicated, the City argues that the police are well trained, stop suspects properly, and do not racially profile. One key argument is pointing to the criminal complaints, including the descriptions of perpetrators, and showing how that data neatly lines up with forcible stops. Ultimately, after years of wrangling in the courts, both sides agree to a settlement early in Michael Bloomberg's tenure as mayor. On December 12, 2003, a settlement was made. However, this settlement will later be contested and explode in the *Floyd v. City of New York* (2013) case. This shall be covered in the next chapter.

Before the end of the Giuliani administration, the NYPD was responding to the many charges of racial profiling. They re-trained all of their officers on stop and frisk. They disbanded the citywide Street Crime Unit (Center for Constitutional Rights, 2025). Additionally, they penned racial profiling policies forbidding the practice. They did respond to their critics and to lawsuits. While the settlement in *Daniels* was not to come until the next administration, much of the groundwork for that settlement was already in place. It is quite likely that the intervention of 9/11 made all parties more likely to give a little to one another. The events of 9/11 were devastating to the city—especially to first responders. Funerals in and around the city related to 9/11 deaths were everywhere. There can be no doubt that the pendulum had swung in favor of law enforcement and giving them the benefit of the doubt. Soon, a settlement will come but, unfortunately, as we will see, the next administration, instead of reaping the benefits, would abuse its authority so much that another lawsuit would soon be in the works.

Summary

Howard Safir becomes Police Commissioner in early 1996. He develops a new program called *Courtesy, Professionalism, and Respect* (CPR). This new initiative is an attempt to help with community relations to balance the aggressive crime-fighting strategy that is fast becoming the rage of the nation called CompStat. While CPR has many promising ideas, it fails to get full traction as crime control overwhelms its impact. As aggressive crime-fighting continues, there is some community unrest, especially among minorities. At the time, stop and frisk is one of the aggressive tactics used by NYPD that is raising questions. When an unarmed Black male, Amadou Diallo, is fatally shot 41 times by an aggressive NYPD unit called the Street Crime Unit, relations reach boiling point. The NYPD is sued and both sides make their arguments to the public and the court. The federal case, *Daniels v. City of New York* (2001), becomes a focal point for both sides to square off.

Discussion Questions

1. What is the *Courtesy, Professionalism, and Respect* program?
2. Why do you think this program may be necessary?
3. Who is Amadou Diallo? Why is he so important?
4. Why is the NYPD sued in *Daniels?*
5. What are the plaintiffs' arguments? NYPD's arguments?
6. Do you think the plaintiffs or the NYPD have a better case? Why?

References

Bratton, W. J. (1997). Crime is down in New York City: Blame the police. In W. J. Bratton, N. Dennis, R. Mallon, J. Orr, & C. Pollard (Eds.), *Zero tolerance: Policing a free society* (pp. 29–43). IEA Health and Welfare Unit.

CBS News. (2000, March 25). *No trial for Dorismond shooter.* https://www.cbsnews.com/news/no-trial-for-dorismond-shooter/

Center for Constitutional Rights. (2025). *Daniels v. City of New York.* https://ccrjustice.org/home/what-we-do/our-cases/daniels-et-al-v-city-new-york

Chan, S. (2007, August 9). The Abner Louima case, 10 years later. *The New York Times.* https://archive.nytimes.com/cityroom.blogs.nytimes.com/2007/08/09/the-abner-louima-case-10-years-later/

Civilian Complaint Review Board (CCRB). (2025). *Complaint process.* City of New York. https://www.nyc.gov/site/ccrb/complaints/complaint-process/complaint-process.page

Cooper, M. (1999, March 10). 12 arrested during sit-in to protest Diallo killing. *The New York Times.* https://www.nytimes.com/1999/03/10/nyregion/12-arrested-during-sit-in-to-protest-diallo-killing.html

Court TV. (n.d.). *NY v. Boss et al: Dr. James Fyfe readback.* https://www.courttv.com/title/48-ny-v-boss-et-al-dr-james-fyfe-readback/

Daniels v. City of New York, 138 F. Supp. 2d 562 (S.D.N.Y. 2001). https://law.justia.com/cases/federal/district-courts/FSupp2/138/562/2462331/

Delaware v. Prouse, 440 U.S. 648 (1979)

Eterno, J. A. (1999). *Deciphering legal decisions on the street: A case study of the New York City Police Department* [Doctoral dissertation, University at Albany, State University of New York].

Eterno, J. A. (2001). Zero tolerance policing in democracies: The dilemma of controlling crime without increasing police abuse of authority. *Police Practice and Research: An International Journal, 2*(3), 189–217.

Eterno, J. A. (2003). *Policing within the law: A case study of the New York City Police Department.* Praeger.

Eterno, J. A. (2007). Understanding the law on the front lines: The need for bright-line rules. *Criminal Law Bulletin*, *43*(5), 706–725.
Eterno, J. A., & Silverman, E. B. (2006). The New York City Police Department's CompStat: Dream or nightmare? *International Journal of Police Science and Management*, *8*(3), 218–231. https://doi.org/10.1350/ijps.2006.8.3.218
Eterno, J. A., & Silverman, E. B. (2010). Understanding police management: A typology of the underside of CompStat. *Professional Issues in Criminal Justice*, *5*(2&3), 11–28.
Eterno, J. A., & Silverman, E. B. (2012). *The crime numbers game: Management by manipulation*. CRC Press.
Eterno, J. A., & Silverman, E. B. (2013). *Crosstabulations for Eli Silverman testimony in Floyd v. City of New York* [Unpublished raw data].
Eterno, J. A., Verma, A., & Silverman, E. B. (2016). Police manipulation of crime reports. *Justice Quarterly*, *33*(5), 811–835. https://doi.org/10.1080/07418825.2014.980838
Floyd v. City of New York, 959 F.Supp.2d 668 (2013)
Fritsch, J. (2000, February 26). The Diallo verdict: The overview; 4 officers in the Diallo shooting are acquitted of all charges. *The New York Times*. https://www.nytimes.com/2000/02/26/nyregion/diallo-verdict-overview-4-officers-diallo-shooting-are-acquitted-all-charges.html
Harring, S. L. (2000). Another "tragic accident" in New York's war on street crime? *Social Justice*, *27*(1), 9–18. https://www.jstor.org/stable/29767188
Henry, V. E. (2002). *The CompStat paradigm*. Looseleaf Law.
Illinois v. Wardlow, 528 U.S. 119 (2000)
Kelling, G. L., & Coles, C. M. (1996). *Fixing broken windows: Restoring order and reducing crime in our communities*. Martin Kessler Books, Simon & Schuster.
New York City Police Department. (1996). *Courtesy, professionalism and respect handbook*. NYPD.
New York State Office of the Attorney General. (1999). *The New York City Police Department's "stop & frisk" practices: A report to the people of the state of New York from the Office of the Attorney General*. https://ur.ag.ny.gov/sites/default/files/reports/stp_frsk.pdf
Newfield, J. (1999, December 1). Race report is indictment of police policy: Spitzer stats bare bias in street frisks. *New York Post*. https://nypost.com/1999/12/01/race-report-is-indictment-of-police-policy-spitzer-stats-bare-bias-in-street-frisks/
People v. Martinez, 80 N. Y. 2d 444 (1992)
Rashbaum, W. K., & Baker, A. (2002, April 10). Police commissioner closing controversial street crime unit. *The New York Times*. https://www.nytimes.com/2002/04/10/nyregion/police-commissioner-closing-controversial-street-crime-unit.html
Silverman, E. B. (2001). *NYPD battles crime: Innovative strategies in policing* (Rev. ed.). Northeastern University Press.
Skolnick, J. (1975). *Justice without trial: Law enforcement in democratic society* (2nd ed.). Wiley.
Stanford University Libraries. (n.d.). *Amadou Diallo*. Say Their Names. https://exhibits.stanford.edu/saytheirnames/feature/amadou-diallo
Terry v. Ohio, 392 U.S. 1 (1968)
U.S. Commission on Civil Rights. (USCCR). (2000). *Police practices and civil rights in New York City*. U.S. Government Printing Office. https://www.usccr.gov/files/pubs/nypolice/main.htm
United States v. Volpe, 78 F. Supp. 2d 76 (E.D.N.Y. 1999)
Uniting and Strengthening America by Providing Appropriate Tools Required to Intercept and Obstruct Terrorism (USA PATRIOT ACT) Act of 2001, Pub. L. No. 107–56, 115 Stat. 272 (2001)
Weiss, M. (1999, February 12). Here is what really happened on fateful night. *New York Post*. https://nypost.com/1999/02/12/heres-what-really-happened-on-fateful-night/
Wilson, J. Q., & Kelling, G. L. (1982, March). Broken windows: The police and neighborhood safety. *The Atlantic Monthly*, *249*(3), 29–38.
Zimring, F. E. (2007). *The city that became safe: New York's lessons for urban crime and its control*. Oxford University Press.

5

THE SAFEST BIG CITY IN AMERICA? BUT CRIMINAL SUSPECTS ARE EVERYWHERE

Introduction

With the election of billionaire Michael Bloomberg as mayor on November 6, 2001, a different police commissioner would soon be appointed. Raymond W. Kelly. He was a previous police commissioner under Mayor David Dinkins with strong ties to community-oriented policing. He took office on January 1, 2002. Mr. Kelly would remain in this role until December 31, 2013 (see Table 5.1). He is now the longest serving police commissioner in the city's history. However, it would be a difficult and controversial tenure.

Recalling Mr. Kelly's previous stint as commissioner under Mayor Dinkins, one would assume that community policing would immediately be revived. Perhaps a kinder and gentler police department. With crime already down a stunning 60 percent, one would have thought police leadership would change their aggressive tactics. Furthermore, 9/11 was in the recent past, and New York City, which endured most of the attack, had a general consensus of respect for police and other first responders. The New York City Police Department (NYPD), however, would not only take on the role of guardian of crime but also that of protector from all forms of terrorism. For example, officers would soon be sent overseas with little to no training in diplomacy. New bureaus and units were formed in haste, with thousands of officers transferred to them. These officers were generally in new and unfamiliar roles, fighting terrorism and gathering and interpreting intelligence. With his experience, Mr. Kelly seemed a logical choice.

Mr. Kelly was, and is, considered one of the most respected names in law enforcement. His credentials are impeccable. He served his country as an officer in the Marines in both active and reserve capacities. As a law enforcement officer, he started his career in the NYPD in the 1960s. He rose through the ranks to Police Commissioner. When Mr. Giuliani took office as mayor, he left that position but had numerous respected, high-level positions in the interim. From 1996 to 1998, he was Under Secretary for Enforcement in the United States Department of the Treasury. From 1998 to 2000, he was Commissioner of the United States Customs Service. During this entire time, 1996 to 2000, he was on the Interpol Executive Committee. In the private industry, he was Senior Managing Director for Corporate Security

DOI: 10.4324/9781003593256-5

TABLE 5.1 List of Police Commissioners and Monitor Reports

Commissioner	*Dates in Office*	*Mayor*	*Monitor's Reports*
William J. Bratton	Jan 1, 2014–Sep 16, 2016	Bill de Blasio	#1—July 9, 2015 #2—February 16, 2016 #3—August 9, 2016
James P. O'Neill	Sep 16, 2016–Nov 30, 2019	Bill de Blasio	#4—November 18, 2016 #5—May 30, 2017 #6—June 29, 2017
		Bill de Blasio	#7—December 13, 2017 #8—July 27, 2018 #9—January 11, 2019
Dermot F. Shea	Dec 1, 2019–Dec 31, 2021	Bill de Blasio	#10—January 7, 2020 #11—October 28, 2020 #12—November 30, 2020
		Bill de Blasio	#13—September 1, 2021 #14—October 12, 2021 #15—December 14, 2021
Keechant L. Sewell	Jan 1, 2022–Jun 30, 2023	Eric L. Adams	#16—May 6, 2022 #17—October 17, 2022 #18—March 3, 2023 #19—June 5, 2023
Edward A. Caban	Jul 1, 2023–Jul 17, 2023	Eric L. Adams	No Reports
Edward A. Caban	Jul 17, 2023–Sep 13, 2024	Eric L. Adams	#20—April 11, 2024 #21—September 4, 2024
Thomas G. Donlon	Sep 13, 2024–Nov 25, 2024	Eric L. Adams	#22—October 7, 2024
Jessica S. Tisch	Nov 25, 2024–Present	Eric L. Adams	#23—February 3, 2025 #24—May 21, 2025 #25—June 3, 2025 #26—October 14, 2025 #27—October 22, 2025
Jessica S. Tisch	Jan 1, 2025–Present	Zohran K. Mamdani	#28—January 20, 2026 #29—February 26, 2026

Source: City of New York. (n.d.); Department of Citywide Administrative Services. (n.d.).

for Bear Stearns from 2000 to 2001. He also served as the Chair of the Athletic Commission from 2001 to 2002, where he resigned to become Police Commissioner again (New York State, Office of the Governor, 2017). One must give respect and courtesy to one who has served and achieved so much. While acknowledging his vast accomplishments, it must also be pointed out that, under his watch, stop and frisk went out of control. With consistent rhetoric, totally unsupported by facts, about getting guns off the streets and stopping crime, the city's population, especially minorities and youth, were subject to what we now know as racist and unconstitutional stops by police. Research on lower-level marijuana violations showed remarkably similar disparate practices (Levine & Siegel, 2015). In only a few short years, these stops numbered in the millions.

The NYPD certainly had its hands full in the first years of Mr. Kelly. With the failure of federal law enforcement to protect the City of New York, it would be left to the local police to make sure it never happened in the future. Again, at this time, there was plenty of goodwill toward law enforcement. Many would give them a "pass" or look the other way. Toward that end, what can be considered a favorable settlement for the NYPD was soon to be had. Despite the highly negative official government reports on stop and frisk from the New York State Office of the Attorney General and the United States Commission on Civil Rights, a settlement in the *Daniels* case was forthcoming. With the NYPD taking an enormous role in counterterrorism, and residents stung from the attack, everyone seemed poised for talks. The NYPD made some fairly decent arguments in their favor, and all sides were ready for calm. Mr. Kelly would start out with an amicable settlement and goodwill from all. Unfortunately, this would not last long.

Settlement in *Daniels v. City of New York*

The parties in the class action lawsuit *Daniels v. City of New York* (2001) officially had their settlement signed on December 12, 2003 (CCR, 2025a). This was signed into law by Federal District Court Judge Shira Scheindlin. This same judge would later preside over the controversial *Floyd v. City of New York* (2013) case, which reopened these issues only a few short years later in 2007. This case shall be covered extensively later in this chapter. The essentials of the *Daniels* settlement were, however, reached several months before the actual signing (New York City Law Department, Office of the Corporation Counsel, 2003). The City, in its press release, felt the terms were very favorable. Indeed, the headline of the release states, "Settlement formalizes existing policy of not stopping suspects based on racial bias" (New York City Law Department, Office of the Corporation Counsel, 2003). The details of the settlement were also quite favorable—assuming the police adhered to the agreement.

The Center for Constitutional Rights (CCR) did not see the settlement in quite the same way. They point out that the City, during the time of the lawsuit, disbanded the Street Crime Unit, which was one of the initial issues. The settlement also required the City (i.e., NYPD) to maintain an anti-racial profiling policy, monitor officers and supervisors with respect to stop-and-frisk practices, and engage in public education efforts. The results of audits of officers and supervisors must be sent to CCR on a quarterly basis (CCR, 2025a).

In the City's press release, however, were harbingers of future issues. For example, Corporation Counsel Michael A. Cardozo is quoted in the release: "This is a fair and equitable settlement that we think will let the Police Department focus on ongoing crime-fighting efforts, while at the same time being sure that racial profiling is not used by police officers" (New York City Law Department, Office of the Corporation Counsel, 2003, para. 3). It is exactly the overwhelming focus on crime control that will unravel the agreement in just a few short years. CCR will soon be back before Judge Scheindlin on these issues once again. As CCR (2025a) states, "After significant non-compliance with the consent decree and after new information released publicly by the City showed a remarkable increase in stop and frisks over the past several years, CCR decided to file a new class-action lawsuit *Floyd et al. v. The City of New York et al.*" As we shall see, the NYPD sharply raised its use of stop and frisk, claiming it was necessary to keep crime down. Despite numerous protests and evidence to the contrary, the number of forcible stops conducted by police increased exponentially with little to show for it. The brunt of the impact of these stops was felt by minority youth. The NYPD stubbornly insisted that without this insane number of forcible stops, the City would return to the "bad old days" of crime and disorder. There was absolutely no evidence for this, and the NYPD simply ignored the facts driven by the data. This would be a costly error to the NYPD and, indeed, to policing in the United States.

Aggressive Tactics, Minimal Rights

The police were in the good graces of nearly all after 9/11. It would appear that the public was likely to support the police in the future. What happened to change all of this? In New York City, the shift began in 2002. There was a myopic focus on crime control. In 2002, the first year of Commissioner Kelly and Mayor Bloomberg, there were 97,296 recorded stops (New York Civil Liberties Union, 2025). This seemed reasonable as crime was down about 60 percent from its height. No one was shocked or overly concerned. Training was done on the entire NYPD during *Daniels*, ensuring that all reasonable suspicion stops must be recorded. This is a key point since, previously, as seen in the New York State Office of the Attorney General's report (1999), the NYPD only recorded certain stops that fitted into four categories (see page 26). This limited recording policy ended on January 1, 2001 (Eterno & Silverman, 2013a). From that point forward, all reasonable suspicion stops had to be recorded throughout the NYPD. Training was accomplished by the Office of Management Analysis and Planning in conjunction with the Legal Bureau. So, moving forward, in 2002, the number of stops can be properly compared with future years' numbers without concern that increases are due to this policy change.

Through 2011, the sheer number of stops rose dramatically and steadily. In 2003, 160,851 stops were recorded. In 2004, 313,523 stops were recorded. In 2005, 398,191 stops were recorded. In 2006, 506,401 stops were recorded. In 2007, there is a leveling off to 472,096. I note here that on January 1, 2008, the CCR filed a lawsuit against the City in *Floyd v. City of New York* (2013). It is likely that the plaintiffs were having conversations with the City before filing. We cannot definitely say that the leveling off this year is due to those conversations, but it seems a likely possibility. Nevertheless, the numbers rise again thereafter: 2008 sees 540,302; 2009 has 581,168; 2010 has 601,285; and in 2011, a peak of 685,724. The last year of the Bloomberg/Kelly administration saw the beginnings of the precipitous decline, with 532,911 (New York Civil Liberties Union, 2025). This turnaround is likely due to negative publicity, community outrage (especially from minorities), and the *Floyd* case. What is the cause of such a sharp increase? Did individual officers suddenly feel the need to forcibly stop people? What caused this apparent insanity in the ranks? With crime already down to record lows, no one was thinking there was a need for such activity except for an upper-management culture hell-bent on making sure the crime numbers continue to decrease (Eterno & Silverman, 2012).

News Reports

During Mayor Bloomberg's tenure, the media coverage with respect to the NYPD and especially stop and frisk was both controversial and on polar extremes. Some coverage was very favorable to the crime-fighting image painted by the Mayor and the police. Others, however, were exceedingly critical. The divisiveness was extraordinary, and some of this continues to this day. The positive coverage came mostly from the more conservative outlets such as the Manhattan Institute (a conservative think tank), the *New York Post*, and the *New York Daily News*. Before discussing this coverage, however, it is particularly important to note that eventually the editorial board of the *Daily News* realized, albeit quite late, that it was wrong with respect to its defense of stop and frisk. It belatedly admitted (after it became painfully obvious that the facts did not support their views) that their position supporting the overwhelming increase of stop and frisk "was wrong" (Charney, 2016). In general, the positive coverage supporting stop and frisk under Mayor Bloomberg essentially ignored the statistics, scientific research, and public opinion, especially the voices of minorities and community groups.

At the time, the Manhattan Institute, the *New York Post*, and the *New York Daily News* became the mouthpiece of City Hall and the NYPD. They supported a policy of aggressive and substantial increases in the practice of stop and frisk. Mac Donald (2010), for example, parrots the NYPD's position, "The attack on the Police Department's stop-and-frisk data is based on the false premise that police activity should mirror census data, not crime. If the critics get their way, it would strip police protection from the New Yorkers who need it most." This argument is simply not accurate. It essentially supports government overreach and abuse of authority. The main idea of the opinion piece is that if police do not conduct hundreds of thousands of forcible stops, especially of minorities, crime will go up. The argument then goes on to suggest that minorities, therefore, will suffer. The author argues that critics are essentially stating that stops should be compared to the population and not suspects. Nothing could be further from the truth. While one academic suggested this, it was never the key argument of critics. Rather, the author fails to contend with the main arguments against wild increases. For example, crime went down 60 percent *before* the ramping up and abuse of the stop strategy. This means that with around 100,000 stops per year, the NYPD was able to combat crime quite effectively. Furthermore, when the foolish increases in forcible stops were eventually reversed, we still see enormous decreases in crime. That is, crime continued to ***decrease, including homicides***, despite the reduction in stops. The argument in support of hundreds of thousands of stops every year simply makes no sense whatsoever. Additionally, stops should never be based on racial makeup or census population (the first suggested by the author of the op ed and the second suggested by "critics"). Rather, as indicated by the judge in the case, neither is accurate. Stops, rather, must be based on Constitutional or legal rules; namely, reasonable suspicion. To put it succinctly, neither population nor crime figures will alone support the Constitutionally required legal criterion. If the police cannot find a way to work within the Constitutionally required criterion, then they must not use the tactic. In other words, if police do not have reasonable suspicion, they must find another way to do their jobs. The author is arguing that it is essential to reduce crime. To some extent, yes, but this must be done legally and not be abused. Furthermore, the argument does not, and never was, supported by the facts (even those known at the time). Phenomenal increases in forcible stops do not, and never did, equate with huge decreases in guns, crime, or murders. The stop policy is a failure on its most basic level—crime reduction. This has been demonstrated over and over again. As seen, crime was drastically reduced without the hundreds of thousands of stops, and continued to go down without the abuse of stop and frisk. Further, while the stop procedure is clearly an important one, police must follow the law. Just as we do not want police to shoot their guns arbitrarily, we also do not want arbitrary stops. The stop practices of the Bloomberg/Kelly era were, without a doubt, an abuse of authority. It was not the individual officer who should be blamed, but the top-down performance management system that made stops part of a "numbers game" (Eterno & Silverman, 2012). Hundreds of thousands of stops of mostly minority youth did not work to reduce crime, take guns off the streets, or protect anyone. Indeed, this was alienating minority youth, making their attitudes toward police unnecessarily worse, and unconstitutional behavior. While working within legal limitations is harder for the police in democratic societies, the system is designed that way. Our founding fathers feared overreach by government, and this practice is an example of exactly that. It was based on quotas, stereotyping, and upper management that failed to acknowledge the facts, leading to vast repercussions. To be clear, no one wants to see high crime, but, as is the case here, government overreach can be just as damaging. One would think that conservatives in particular would see overregulation and government abuse as problematic. Rather, the parroting of police officials without evidence to support the practice was commonplace. Eventually, the *New York Daily News* saw that their position was untenable (that crime numbers and stops are strongly related), but others still cling to this fantasy without reviewing facts. Thus, the relationship between crime and forcible stops is a complicated one. Abuse of stop and frisk was not only unnecessary but harmful. All one had to do was stick to the law and analyze the numbers. The only reasonable conclusion is that the NYPD's practice of stop and frisk during these years was abuse.

The *New York Post* was equally vocal and just as stubborn—failing to acknowledge even the most basic statistics. On September 19, 2013, the *Post* was already ringing alarm bells that somehow the city would soon be plunged into anarchy due to the stop-and-frisk ruling in *Floyd*. It was too quick with its article, "Gun Crime Up After Stop-and-Frisk Ruling" (Schram & Conley, 2013). The article proclaimed that gun crime is up already, and the police are no longer proactive. Today, of course, we know all of this is simply rhetoric. The failure to take an analytic approach and simply mimic authorities was fatal. Crime, of course, continued to decrease and, in fact, continued to inch down for many years to follow. While I do not claim that the city is a panacea for life, the lack of stop and frisk did not turn the city into a den of iniquity. Rather, crime continued to decline. While I am not opposed to some level of stop and frisk that is based on legal criteria, the fact is, the city never experienced the atrocities foretold by such blatantly one-sided "news" coverage. The suggested increase in crime never occurred. Further, such stories seem to attempt to construct a panic based on a false premise. The predicted Wild West scenario was just another exaggeration. The facts simply demonstrate that such defenders of the wild increases in stop and frisk (i.e., the defenders of the status quo) were patently and predictably wrong. While police need to have the tools to fight crime, incredulous and unlimited stop and frisk is not necessary or even desirable. It is simply damaging. Any unbiased study of the New York City experience will bear this out.

On the other side were various groups sounding the alarm about the unbridled stop-and-frisk practice by the NYPD. Among others, Dr. Eli Silverman and I were outspoken critics of the NYPD's unproductive, racist, unsupported, and, as indicated in *Floyd*, unconstitutional program. Dr. Silverman and I penned many editorials, books, scientific peer-reviewed articles, and other materials. I will briefly mention only a couple of them. First, there is one entitled, "Mike Bloomberg's Fact-Free Defense of Stop-and-Frisk" (Eterno & Silverman, 2013b). In this op ed, Dr. Silverman and I go step by step, explaining the flaws in the NYPD's arguments supporting stop and frisk. For example, we discuss how so few guns are taken off the streets by the tactic (0.2 percent of stops result in guns) and how other tactics are far more effective, how crime was not significantly impacted by the numerous stops (crime was already down 60 percent before they even took office), that crime would not increase if stops were reduced (we use murder statistics showing little impact by the increase in stops and also show how the murders went down even when stop and frisk ***decreased***), and how minorities are alienated by the practice. Also, based on our surveys, we point out that the pressures on officers to write stop-and-frisk reports during Mr. Kelly's tenure drastically increased. Simultaneously, the pressure to obey legal rules significantly ***decreased*** (see Tables 5.2 and 5.3).

TABLE 5.2 2012 Survey Findings: Year by Stop Pressure

*Crosstab—Year Categorized * Stop Pressure Categorized*

			Year Categorized			
			before 1995	*1995 until 2001*	*2002 until 2012*	*Total*
Stop Pressure Categorized	low	Count	297	127	205	629
		% within year categorized	57.8%	36.7%	24.4%	37.0%
	medium	Count	170	153	341	664
		% within year categorized	33.1%	44.2%	40.5%	39.0%
	high	Count	47	66	295	408
		% within year categorized	9.1%	19.1%	35.1%	24.0%
Total		Count	514	346	841	1701
		% within year categorized	100.0%	100.0%	100.0%	100.0%

Note: Gamma =.461 p <.000

TABLE 5.3 2012 Survey Findings: Year by Pressure to Obey Rights

*Crosstab—Year Categorized * Pressure to Obey Constitutional Rights Categorized*

			Year Categorized			
			before 1995	*1995 until 2001*	*2002 until 2012*	*Total*
Obey Constitutional Rights Pressure Categorized	low	Count	109	63	187	359
		% within year categorized	20.7%	17.2%	22.1%	20.6%
	medium	Count	183	132	357	672
		% within year categorized	34.7%	36.0%	42.2%	38.6%
	high	Count	235	172	302	709
		% within year categorized	44.6%	46.9%	35.7%	40.7%
Total		Count	527	367	846	1740
		% within year categorized	100.0%	100.0%	100.0%	100.0%

Note: Gamma = −.106 p <.002

Another editorial that I penned, published in *The New York Times*, explained that the vast pressures on officers to increase their numbers of stops, summonses, and arrests were due to CompStat (Eterno, 2012b). There are numerous other editorials, books, peer-reviewed articles, and materials on the topic. Also, Dr. Silverman testified in the *Floyd* case for the plaintiffs (Eterno & Silverman, 2013a). The research was clear, but few would listen. I did speak at community meetings, with members of the State Senate and Assembly (Eterno, 2012a), on CUNY television, and in other venues about the injustice and flawed logic supporting it.

While the Center for Constitutional Rights and the New York Civil Liberties Union were vocally against the practice and spearheaded the *Floyd* lawsuit, one reporter's coverage stands out above all the others by far, and that is Graham Rayman, who, at the time, was with the

Village Voice. His work helping to expose the NYPD's practices won top honors in investigative reporting in the AltWeekly Awards. A major part of his work is entitled *The NYPD Tapes* (2013), which is written in five parts: Part 1: The NYPD Tapes: Inside Bed-Stuy's 81st Precinct; Part 2: Bed-Stuy Street Cops Ordered: Turn This Place Into a Ghost Town; Part 3: A Detective Comes Forward About Downgraded Sexual Assaults; Part 4: The Whistle-blower, Adrian Schoolcraft; Part 5: The Corroboration (Gillmore, 2011).

A Failed Policy

The rise in stops and the lack of response to public outcry can be explained. Information is available from the *Floyd* case (and pre-trial motions), books, peer-reviewed materials, and other sources. Taken together, we see a picture of the NYPD emerging during this time as being enamored with their performance management system called CompStat. It is this top-down management system that drives the numbers.

CompStat (compare statistics) is the performance management system that puts fear into every commander. The NYPD and the mayor were consistently bragging about record-low crime. Year in and year out, the clamor was that crime is going down. No one wanted to be at the top when crime ticked up. However, assuming the crime numbers are accurately being recorded (note that they were being manipulated—see especially Eterno, Verma, & Silverman, 2016), it had to happen eventually. It became paranoia. It was a numbers game. Everything, I mean everything, was done to be sure numbers were going in the "right" direction. Everything was on the table: crime report manipulation; quotas for stops, arrests, and summonses; harassment of anyone suspected of causing problems; enforcement of very minor violations such as marijuana; and more (Eterno & Silverman, 2012). The focus of this book is stop and frisk, but it needs to be understood that the upper echelon were responsible. This was not, nor was it ever, a few bad apples or a few officers going rogue. The sheer scale of the increases in stops makes that obvious.

A careful analysis of various sources shows the mechanisms at work that ultimately led to the illegal, racist, and unconstitutional behaviors by the rank-and-file. One must understand that this is a top-down system from headquarters that led to illegal stops. This is the most critical piece. Without this knowledge, one is missing the essence of the entire process. Quotas—the NYPD calls them "performance goals" (they are synonyms for our purposes—although the NYPD would dispute this)—for example, are one of the key mechanisms by which the Department enforced the number of stops.

Another major flaw in the NYPD's logic has to do with crime. They continually would bark out their success that New York City was the safest big city in America. Crime went down, year in and year out. There was rarely, if ever, a notable increase in index crime since CompStat began. The constant bragging may have become an imperative (Eterno & Silverman, 2012). That is, crime had to go down, regardless of facts. It was clear that crime was down and going down. How much, however, is another question. It was inevitable that with numerous pressures on commanders from the upper echelon, the commanders would do whatever it took to look good. This could mean crime report manipulation, massive stops, and numerous other devices to save face (Eterno & Silverman, 2012). Ultimately, crime reports predictably went down year after year. However, at the same time, criminal suspects walking the streets became ubiquitous. Logically, the two cannot stand together—less and less crime, but, simultaneously, more and more criminal suspects. If the NYPD had so many suspects with the requisite

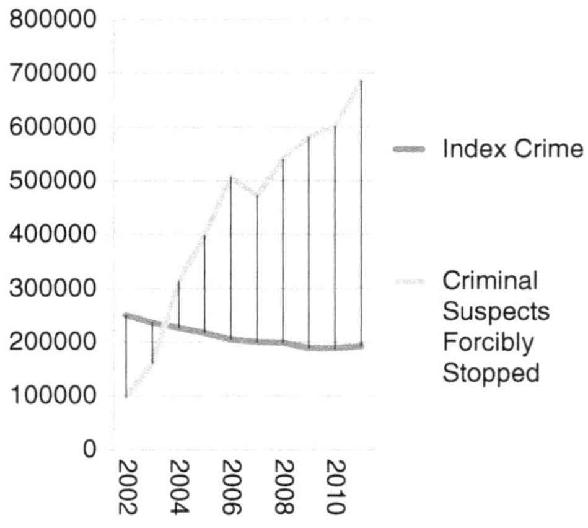

FIGURE 5.1 Reported Crime with Criminal Suspects.

legal standard of reasonable suspicion, it would appear that crime was about to happen, or was happening, nearly everywhere. The two trends cannot stand together. That is, if crime is down, there must be fewer criminal suspects to forcibly stop. It was a conundrum that the NYPD simply had no defense against. The trends, assuming NYPD is doing stops based on reasonable suspicion, should, to some extent, correlate. As one can see, the trends were in the opposite direction. There was no escape from this. Either the stops were unconstitutional or crime was trending up. With so many criminal suspects on the streets, it was a wonder that anyone survived (see Figure 5.1). The explanation for this, of course, is the pressures of CompStat. Commanders gave upper management what they wanted: namely, lower crime statistics and more stop and frisks. Logic, law, and liberty be damned.

Floyd v. City of New York: Its Depth and Difficulties

The breadth of information that Judge Scheindlin had to understand is staggering. Her opinions show a deep consideration of all the evidence presented to her. Not without controversy, nevertheless, her opinions are reasoned and logical. Key points will be reviewed, and some commentary added where necessary. I encourage readers to review the evidence and think about how they might decide on some of these weighty questions. A review of a pre-trial motion and the case itself is absolutely needed to understand the difficulties this case presented. It is one of the most impactful cases on stop and frisk that still influences New York City to this day.

Judge Scheindlin's opinion in a pre-trial motion regarding class certification in *Floyd* is particularly instructive. At this point in the history of the case, the lawsuit has already been going on for years. Based on her reasoning of the issues, we can see the evidence of the NYPD's system through her rulings. The NYPD is, simply stated, driving the stops from headquarters. The evidence is, simply put, overwhelming. In fact, as we shall see, the NYPD not only does not deny this, but their own witnesses also testify to it. At the outset, then, to be clear: this is a top-down system of management leading to unconstitutional stops. This management system, as we will see, is exported to numerous other law enforcement agencies. Similar tactics are then used elsewhere throughout the country and even in the democratic world. Some of the keys to her ruling are quite revealing and informative. Let us begin with the pre-trial motion in 2012.

In *Floyd v. City of New York* (2012), one of the key aspects of the ruling is that the NYPD has a stop-and-frisk program. That is, officers' stops are not occurring by happenstance. Judge Scheindlin writes:

> It is indisputable that the NYPD has an enormous stop and frisk program .... Decisions about the policy are made at the highest levels of the department. At the regular CompStat meetings involving the NYPD's top officials, "[s]top, question and frisk activity is commonly discussed" in detail and "[t]he process allows top executives to monitor precincts and operational units, evaluate the skills and effectiveness of managers and properly allocate resources."
>
> *(Floyd v. City of New York, 2012, § III.A)*

The judge clearly indicates in her opinion that there is a "centralized use of performance standards and quotas" (*Floyd v. City of New York*, 2012, § III.B). The evidence for this is, once again, unambiguous. The scope itself is one important aspect showing this. She points out a specific order signed by the Commissioner, stating,

> In a recent Operations Order, Commissioner Kelly directed all commands that 'Department managers *can* and *must* set performance goals,' relating to 'the issuance of summonses, the stopping and questioning of suspicious individuals, and the arrests of criminals.
>
> *(Floyd v. City of New York, 2012, § III.B)*

The opinion goes on, "Deputy Commissioner Paul Browne (the Deputy Commissioner of Public Information) has made clear that the Department continues to embrace stops as a central part of its crime-fighting strategy" (*Floyd v. City of New York*, 2012, § III.B). The opinion even goes so far as to discuss specific CompStat meetings. For example:

> At a CompStat meeting on July 17, 2008, NYPD Chief of Department Joseph Esposito (who is the highest-ranking uniformed member of the force) told the executive officer of the 28th Precinct: "Your enf[orcement] numbers are way down .... As an [executive officer] you have to look at that .... If you look at raw number of 250s [stop and frisk reports] you are down 50 percent."
>
> *(Floyd v. City of New York, 2012, § III.B)*

The case goes on to discuss whistleblower Police Officer Adhya Polanco, who points out that his commanding officer demanded quotas on arrests, summonses, and stop and frisks. This was not merely at his sworn deposition; it should be noted that there are audiotapes to support this testimony. Another whistleblower, Adrian Schoolcraft, who also has audiotapes, exposes the practice as well.

Judge Scheindlin also points to statistical evidence. In this pre-trial motion, she specifically discusses the work of Dr. Jeffrey Fagan of Columbia University. She finds his work compelling and writes:

> [A]ccording to their own records and judgment, officers' suspicion was wrong nearly nine times out of ten .... Guns were seized in 0.15 percent of all stops .... NYPD stops-and-frisks

> are significantly more frequent for Black and Hispanic residents than they are for White residents, even after adjusting for local crime rates, racial composition of the local population, police patrol strength, and other social and economic factors predictive of police enforcement activity .... Black and Hispanic individuals are treated more harshly during stop-and-frisk encounters with NYPD officers than Whites who are stopped on suspicion of the same or similar crime.
>
> *(Floyd v. City of New York, 2012, § III.C)*

Other evidence is seen from the full 198-page *Floyd* trial opinion. This opinion is just as striking. Similar evidence as above is presented and then some. The word "quota" appears 35 times in the opinion. Over 20 pages are dedicated to explaining pressures to conduct stops. CompStat is mentioned 54 times. In her introduction, Judge Scheindlin clearly understands the importance of the case. The fundamental balancing of crime control and due process is at issue. Democratic principles with respect to policing—its limits and its powers—are in play. For example, Judge Sheindlin writes, "This case is about the tension between liberty and public safety in the use of a proactive policing tool called 'stop and frisk'" (*Floyd v. City of New York*, 2013, p. 1). This insight, sometimes not well understood by those who proclaim that crime control, is the essence of police work in democracies. Often, such viewpoints fail to consider the protecting of basic rights, a necessary aspect that must be properly balanced in a democratic society, especially for those in the law enforcement community. It is a difficult concept, as such a balance makes the task of policing problematic. In a police state, officers do not worry about fair or equal treatment. They essentially do as they please. Not so in democracy. Crime-fighting is not, nor has it ever been, supreme. Rather, it is the balance that is so critical. Importantly, this balance may change over time. Police, in particular, must be keenly aware of the times. That is, they must understand the social contract and maintain legitimacy. Abuse of power can and will lead to issues for police, such as the defund movement and Black Lives Matter. Additionally, and just as important, police must recognize when the public needs more crime control, but still maintain integrity and democratic principles. For example, in times of peril, the powers of the executive branch, and, therefore, the police, expand (note that there were three instances in which the writ of habeas corpus [essentially, the ability to challenge the legality of detention] was suspended: the Civil War, World War II, and 9/11). The *Floyd* case, therefore, is a snapshot of expectations. Police power will, however, bend and flow with the times. Leadership, then, is not a simple, unthinking "crime control" response. Rather, it is far more complicated and requires an understanding of history, social issues, and, generally, cultural ebbs and flows. The *Floyd* case is instructive, not merely for its precedent, but as a critically important lesson to future generations. In 2013, this judge makes that balance, and the NYPD comes up severely lacking. The opinion is long and harsh in its tone. However, on another day and time, the case could have gone in another direction. As we shall see, the election of Mayor de Blasio prevented the case from being appealed. This shows where the city was during this time. Regardless, it is an instructive opinion.

Judge Scheindlin felt strongly that the Department basically continued its policy of unconstitutional stops even though they had been aware of the problem as early as 1999. She pointed out that the New York State Office of the Attorney General's report (1999) specifically talks about these issues and gives decisive evidence of racism and unconstitutional problems. The judge also pointed out numerous other signs and, at the outset of the opinion, is confident in a strongly worded admonition of the NYPD (*Floyd v. City of New York*, 2013, p. 11):

> With respect to both the Fourth and Fourteenth Amendment claims, one way to prove that the city has a custom of conducting unconstitutional stops and frisks is to show that it acted with deliberate indifference to constitutional deprivations caused by its employees—here, the NYPD. The evidence at trial revealed significant evidence that the NYPD acted with deliberate indifference.

The judge also points out that the use of quotas is rampant, and is extremely critical of the practice:

> Evidence at trial revealed that officers have been pressured to make a certain number of stops and risk negative consequences if they fail to achieve the goal. Without a system to ensure that stops are justified, such pressure is a predictable formula for producing unconstitutional stops.
>
> *(Floyd v. City of New York, 2013, p. 10)*

These pressures are a consistent part of her opinion. It gets more intriguing as Judge Scheindlin opines that not only were there pressures, but those pressures were focused on minorities:

> In addition, the evidence at trial revealed that the NYPD has an unwritten policy of targeting "the right people" for stops. In practice, the policy encourages the targeting of young Black and Hispanic men based on their prevalence in local crime complaints. This is a form of racial profiling.
>
> *(Floyd v. City of New York, 2013, p. 10)*

Thus, it is the pressures from CompStat that lead to unconstitutional behavior. Again, it is not individual officers; rather, a management system that is responsible for causing the unconstitutional behaviors by officers.

In addition, it is not simply a matter of quotas and pressures, but, just as important, supervision was not performing its job to ensure that police are working within legal parameters very well. In her opinion, she writes, "Much evidence was introduced regarding inadequate monitoring and supervision of unconstitutional stops" (*Floyd v. City of New York*, 2013, p. 11). We see this later in the testimony of Dr. Eli Silverman, an expert witness on policing, who cites survey research conducted on NYPD (Eterno & Silverman, 2012, 2013a, 2016). One key point presented by Dr. Silverman is that there is less pressure to obey legal restrictions during the Kelly/Bloomberg era:

> a significant post-2002 decrease in those reporting high pressure to do so. 45% of pre-CompStat retirees and 47% of early CompStat era retirees reported high pressure to obey legal and constitutional rules, while only 36% of post-Bloomberg retirees reported high pressure. Dr. Silverman testified that this represented a modest but statistically significant decline.
>
> *(Floyd v. City of New York, 2013, p. 70)*

Judge Scheindlin also discusses how minorities are singled out by the NYPD. She writes, "Both statistical and anecdotal evidence showed that minorities are indeed treated differently than whites" (*Floyd v. City of New York*, 2013, p. 13). Indeed, she finds that the City's own expert witness was making the case for the plaintiff. Dr. Dennis Smith, an associate professor of Public Affairs at New York University, testified for the city. Judge Scheindlin writes of this testimony:

> Dr. Smith's position, while surprising, is not illogical once his premises are accepted. Dr. Smith apparently does not find it plausible that officers' decisions regarding whether to stop a person may be swayed by conscious or unconscious racial bias. If a researcher begins with this premise, he will attempt to find a credible, race-neutral explanation for the NYPD's stopping of blacks and Hispanics out of proportion to their share of the population .... Rather than being a defense *against* the charge of racial profiling, however, this reasoning is a defense of racial profiling. To say that Black people in general are somehow more suspicious-looking, or criminal in appearance, than white people is not a race-neutral explanation for racial disparities in NYPD stops: it is itself a *racially biased explanation*. This explanation is especially troubling because it echoes the stereotype that Black men are more likely to engage in criminal conduct than others.
>
> (*Floyd v. City of New York, 2013, pp. 55–56*)

With respect to this part of the opinion, the NYPD has been known to develop policy and then try to find evidence for the policy. Data-driven strategies are common for police. They are well-known strategies. CompStat can be thought of as a data-driven strategy; for example, placing police officers at hot spots where crime is known to be occurring. Attacking known drug dens with officers from narcotics, as well as using local precinct police, is another example. So, first you have data that points out the issue, and then you develop a strategy to deal with the issue. However, what Judge Scheindlin is discussing is something known as "policy-based evidence making." This is a pejorative term. That is, a policy comes first, and the same body that makes the policy (in this case NYPD) tries to find evidence to support it. It is backward, illogical, flawed, and may even be damaging. It is common practice at the NYPD, and it is not good, acceptable, or healthy for the organization or the public (Eterno, 2015, pp. 1–2).

Judge Scheindlin reprimands the NYPD for its failure to develop individualized reasonable suspicion. Numerous stops do not have the requisite level of proof for a constitutionally permitted *Terry* stop. She writes, "In general, reasonable suspicion requires an individualized suspicion of wrongdoing. While the Supreme Court has recognized certain narrow exceptions to this requirement, there is no exception for stops of pedestrians for the general purpose of controlling crime" (*Floyd v. City of New York*, 2013, p. 23). This is a critical point. It is essentially saying that the reasoning of the NYPD is flawed. That is, the NYPD is claiming that nearly 700,000 stops in one year can be excused by its crime-fighting mission. However, as seen here, crime control is not sufficient to defend this widespread and racist practice. That is, even if this stopped crime, and it is very questionable that it is doing that or getting guns off the streets, at least with any critical impact, the practice offends the Constitution. Put succinctly, even if forcible stops as done by the NYPD in this case do work (i.e., quotas, pressures, stopping minorities out of proportion, and so forth), the police cannot do this and must find a method to fight crime that does not violate Constitutional rights.

She also severely criticizes NYPD's expert Dr. Smith's basic presumption that all stops by the NYPD are based on reasonable suspicion. Additionally, the lack of getting many arrests or summons (a low hit-rate) makes the practice ineffective, if not completely untenable: "But even if all stops by the NYPD were based on reasonable suspicion—which is highly unlikely for reasons already stated—the low hit rate would undermine the assumption" (*Floyd v. City of New York*, 2013, p. 23).

In another part of the opinion, Judge Sheindlin writes, "nearly 90% of the people stopped are released without the officer finding any basis for a summons or arrest" (*Floyd v. City of New York*, 2013, p. 51). And again, a few pages later:

> The City failed to establish that a significant number of the approximately 3.9 million stops that resulted in no further enforcement action were stops of people who were about to commit, but were prevented from committing, a crime. Dr. Smith's theory that a significant number of these stops resulted in the prevention of the suspected crime is pure speculation and not reliable.
>
> *(Floyd v. City of New York, 2013, p. 54)*

The NYPD's expert attempts to explain the stopping of more minorities by showing a relationship going precinct by precinct of stops closely associated to suspects' descriptions. That is, the stops by the NYPD line up neatly with what victims describe as perpetrators. This generalized explanation, which is not ***individualized***, according to the judge, actually promotes the plaintiff's position. The NYPD never offers a race-neutral explanation for its stops. She writes:

> In short, the correlation highlighted by the City and its experts in their attempt to refute the allegation of racial profiling, in fact, provides evidence of racial profiling. Rather than revealing a valid race-neutral variable that explains the NYPD's disproportionate stopping of blacks and Hispanics, the correlation highlighted by the City's experts suggests how the racial disparities identified by Dr. Fagan might have come about—namely, through a widespread practice of racial profiling based on local criminal suspect data.
>
> *(Floyd v. City of New York, 2013, p. 58)*

The judge goes on to explain that there was a code offered by the higher-ups to focus on minorities. It is established through pressure on officers, particularly through CompStat:

> In addition, I find that the NYPD instituted a policy of indirect racial profiling by directing its commanders and officers to focus their stop activity on "the right people"—the demographic groups that appear most often in a precinct's crime complaints. This policy led inevitably to impermissibly targeting blacks and Hispanics for stops and frisks at a higher rate than similarly situated whites.
>
> *(Floyd v. City of New York, 2013, p. 61)*

She continues:

> The evidence discussed in the previous section shows that senior NYPD officials at CompStat meetings routinely place pressure on commanders to increase their

> enforcement activity, including their stop numbers. The survey evidence in this section shows that subordinate managers in the NYPD have communicated this pressure to the rank and file.
>
> I find that the City's criticisms do not undermine the surveys' central finding for the purposes of this case: NYPD personnel experienced or were aware of pressure to increase the number of stops after the introduction of CompStat, and especially after the arrival of Mayor Bloomberg and Commissioner Kelly. In addition, this rising pressure for stop numbers was not accompanied by equivalent pressure to obey constitutional restrictions.
>
> *(Floyd v. City of New York, 2013, p. 61)*

One member of the higher echelon suggested that the issues with stop and frisk were due to a misconception by commanding officers of precincts. Namely, commanding officers felt that the formula to deal with the pressures of CompStat meetings was to increase forcible stops regardless of quality. Even if this is accurate, this agrees with a major theme of this book, that pressures from CompStat were responsible for the huge increase in forcible stops during Mr. Kelly's tenure (confidential communication, March 2026). Second, the higher echelon is responsible for all actions of its cadre. The upper echelon knew, or should have known, the extent of the issues with stop, question, and frisk, and addressed them.

Judge Sheindlin also directly implicates the high-ups. She specifically mentions Mayor Bloomberg and Commissioner Kelly. She implicates their policing methods and does not question their motives.

> Mayor Bloomberg stated in April that the NYPD's use of stop and frisk is necessary "to deter people from carrying guns. … [I]f you end stops looking for guns, … there will be more guns in the hands of young people, and more people will be getting killed." At the same time, the city emphasized in its opening arguments that "blacks and Hispanics account for a disproportionate share of … crime perpetrators," and that "90 percent of all violent crime suspects are Black and Hispanic." When these premises are combined—that the purpose of stop and frisk is to deter people from carrying guns and that blacks and Hispanics are a disproportionate source of violent crime—it is only a short leap to the conclusion that blacks and Hispanics should be targeted for stops to deter gun violence, regardless of whether they appear objectively suspicious. Commissioner Kelly simply made explicit what is readily inferable from the City's public positions.
>
> Commissioner Kelly responded that he focused on young blacks and Hispanics "because he wanted to instill fear in them, every time they leave their home, they could be stopped by the police." Senator Adams testified that he was "amazed" that Commissioner Kelly was "comfortable enough to say that in the setting."
>
> *(Floyd v. City of New York, 2013, pp. 297–300)*

Judge Scheindlin points out that the training is good. It has little to do with training. Rather, it is the heavy-handed policy that is the key to understanding what happened. "The gravest problems in the NYPD's stop and frisk practices stem not from inadequate training but from a divergence between the NYPD's written training materials and the 'operational policy' carried out in the streets" (Floyd v. City of New York, 2013, pp. 297–300).

The City tries to defend itself against the charges by showing a study done by the RAND Corporation. However, Judge Scheindlin attacks that study in the same way she has attacked other studies. The City also attempts to use suspect descriptions as an explanation. The case already notes that this explanation only undermines the City's position. It is not a race-neutral explanation. Additionally, this is, in this author's view, another example of policy-based evidence making. The City paid RAND for its study, and the NYPD had an enormous input in the final product (see Eterno & Silverman, 2012). Nevertheless, the judge outright dismisses this evidence, stating,

> The City attempts to rebut evidence of notice by pointing to a 2007 report by the RAND Corporation that found little evidence of pervasive racial profiling in the NYPD's pedestrian stop and frisk activity. But the RAND study used violent crime suspect data as its benchmark, which is problematic for reasons discussed.
>
> *(Floyd v. City of New York, 2013, pp. 115–116)*

The case ultimately can be described as police abuse of authority. The control of crime cannot be an excuse to violate rights. Law enforcement must work within a legal framework. In this case, the NYPD is checked and balanced appropriately.

> There is no dispute that the primary concern of a police department can and should be combating crime. At the same time, section 1983 limits the lack of concern that any municipal agency may show toward constitutional violations by its employees. The NYPD's senior officials have violated section 1983 through their deliberate indifference to unconstitutional stops, frisks, and searches. They have received both actual and constructive notice since at least 1999 of widespread Fourth Amendment violations occurring as a result of the NYPD's stop-and-frisk practices. Despite this notice, they deliberately maintained and even escalated policies and practices that predictably resulted in even more widespread Fourth Amendment violations. Moreover, while the NYPD is an acknowledged leader in the use of data collection and analysis to improve the effectiveness of policing, it has hindered the collection of accurate data concerning the constitutionality of its stops and made no effective use of the limited data that is available. The NYPD has repeatedly turned a blind eye to clear evidence of unconstitutional stops and frisks.
>
> *(Floyd v. City of New York, 2013, p. 179)*

The judge goes on, "The NYPD's policy of targeting 'the right people' for stops, by contrast, is not directed toward the identification of a specific perpetrator. Rather, it is a policy of targeting expressly identified racial groups for stops in general" (*Floyd v. City of New York*, 2013, p. 187).

Remedy

In a separate opinion, Judge Shira Scheindlin issued the remedy to the previous issues. Importantly, the NYPD did not have to end its practice of stop and frisk. Rather, there was an attempt to fix the unconstitutional practices of the NYPD. As part of the remedy, a monitor was appointed, Peter Zimroth. He was to ensure that the Court's orders would be implemented, and unconstitutional practices would end. He died in November 2021 (Roberts, 2021). He was subsequently replaced by Mylan Denerstein (NYPD Monitor, n.d.), as will be discussed in the next chapter. The monitor publishes regular reports. Ultimately, the idea is that an independent monitor can oversee what the NYPD is doing and attempt to properly apply and follow the law. The idea is that policies, training, supervision, monitoring, and discipline with respect to stop-and-frisk practices will come under the monitor's purview. The monitor is limited to stop-and-frisk practices, and once that is remedied to the satisfaction of the Court, the monitor will no longer be necessary.

A second remedy is to develop immediate reforms to stop-and-frisk practices. The Court outlined numerous issues in the opinion. These would be sent to the court as soon as practicable. These would include forms, policies, supervision, discipline, and the like. Again, the Court must approve the changes. As part of the remediation process, the Court ordered that communities must be involved. Some specific organizations are mentioned in the decision. Interestingly, what would be considered today as commonplace was the use and development of body-worn cameras by police.

The *Floyd* case is a powerful rebuke to the NYPD's centralized management system and its leadership. Scholarly research on the NYPD during this time made it clear that CompStat was going too far (Eterno, 2015a, 2015b; Eterno & Silverman, 2012, 2010a, 2010b, 2005). In one of the most direct challenges to Mr. Bloomberg and Mr. Kelly's defense of stop and frisk, Dr. Silverman and I publicly explain the emptiness of the NYPD's position (Eterno & Silverman, 2013a). With few guns being taken off the streets, and crime minimally affected by numerous stops of mostly minority youth, the practice was untenable. The remedy of *Floyd* is a separate opinion. Compared with the *Daniels* settlement, it is devastating and long-lasting (CCR, 2025b). Future chapters will address many of the issues resulting from the NYPD's aggressive and unconstitutional practices.

Removal of Judge Shira Scheindlin

The City engaged in a publicity campaign that ultimately led to Judge Scheindlin's removal from the case by an appeals panel. Such publicity campaigns are not unusual. My research with Dr. Eli Silverman was subject to such a campaign. We write about it in our book (see Eterno & Silverman, 2012). They attacked us with editorials, including one by Mr. Kelly. We were able to fend off the attacks, but the City has very deep pockets and access to media outlets. In the end, we were very confident in our research, and ultimately, much of what we stated was confirmed in the *Floyd* case. Judge Scheindlin was subjected to a similar campaign. I have gone on the record defending her from these assaults.

> Media attacks on critics of the NYPD are not new for the NYPD. I and my colleague, Dr. Eli Silverman, have been victims of similar attempts at character assassination after our research on crime report manipulation by the NYPD went public in 2010. Several editorials and Op-Eds attacked us, including one written by Kelly in the *Daily News*. Other NYPD whistleblowers—such as Adrian Schoolcraft, Robert Borrelli, and Adil Polanco—have also been punished for revealing the truth. This attempt to control debate won't succeed. Ultimately, the evidence on stop-and-frisk, just like that about crime report manipulation, is so overwhelming that one cannot deny the facts.
>
> Scheindlin was doing her job. If the appeals court felt a need to replace this judge, they should at least base their decision on facts. Without doing so, they appear to have been manipulated by the City's whisper campaign. They appear to be three blind mice.
>
> *(Eterno, 2013)*

On October 31, 2013, an Appeals Panel removed Judge Scheindlin, basically for making statements to the press and for some issues of possible bias. However, on November 13, 2013, the Appeals Panel relaxed its critique yet affirmed its disqualification. They did not say she was biased in her ruling. As stated by Kavanaugh (2014, p. 4),

> it reasoned that Judge Scheindlin's comments about the validity of the plaintiff's claim in Daniels, along with her comments to the media about her unfavorable history with the NYPD, taken together, created the appearance of bias such that she should be disqualified.

After Judge Scheindlin was removed, a new judge was assigned to the *Floyd* case to oversee the sanctions: Judge Analisa Torres. A graduate of Harvard University and Columbia Law School, she served as a New York State Supreme Court judge and was recommended for the federal bench by Senator Gillibrand. She was nominated by President Obama and approved by the Senate. She is a third-generation judge (Gregorian, 2019), clearly prepared for the job. Her influence on stop and frisk will be seen in the coming chapters.

Summary

After 9/11, with the NYPD having enormous public support, the City settled the *Daniels* lawsuit. The agreement was generally favorable to the City, allowing practices, for the most part, to continue as they were. Raymond W. Kelly was soon appointed Police Commissioner as Mayor Michael Bloomberg was elected. Mr. Kelly has excellent credentials and was known for his community-oriented policing style. However, he becomes exceedingly aggressive on crime. While crime was already down 60 percent with relatively few stop and frisks, Mr. Kelly, through CompStat, ramps up the practice. Hundreds of thousands of additional stops of mostly minority youth take place. Little effect is seen on decreasing crime, getting guns off the streets, or preventing homicides. Nevertheless, the practice continues to increase. It becomes a numbers game with quotas being enforced. It becomes clear to the *Daniels* litigants that the NYPD has gone astray. A new lawsuit was initiated called *Floyd v. City of New York* (2013). In 2013, the City loses the case, and a monitor is appointed to oversee the stop-and-frisk practices on NYPD. Judge Shira Scheindlin writes a scathing opinion about these unconstitutional and racist practices.

Discussion Questions

1. With all the goodwill of the people toward the police after 9/11, should the police have ramped up stop-and-frisk practices? Why? Why not?
2. Was the stop-and-frisk practice in New York City effective under Mr. Kelly? Explain your answer.
3. Could the crime control aspects of CompStat have been done differently? Explain.
4. List and explain some of the evidence Judge Scheindlin uses to find the NYPD liable in the *Floyd* case.
5. Compare the settlement in *Daniels* with the remedies in *Floyd*.
6. Do you think the decision in *Floyd* was fair? Why? Or why not?
7. Explain the NYPD's use of the media with respect to Judge Scheindlin. Was it fair?

References

Center for Constitutional Rights (CCR). (2025a). *Daniels v. City of New York historic case, at a glance.* https://ccrjustice.org/home/what-we-do/our-cases/daniels-et-al-v-city-new-york#files

Center for Constitutional Rights (CCR). (2025b). *Summary of remedies opinion and order in Floyd v. City of New York, 08-cv-1034 (SAS).* https://ccrjustice.org/files/Remedy%20Decision%20Summary%20-%20Final.pdf

Charney, D. (2016, August 17). *The Daily News admits it was wrong on stop-and-frisk.* Center for Constitutional Rights. https://ccrjustice.org/home/blog/2016/08/17/daily-news-admits-it-was-wrong-stop-and-frisk

City of New York. (n.d.). *Mayor's Office.* Retrieved January 8, 2026, from https://www.nyc.gov/mayors-office

Daniels v. City of New York, 138 F. Supp. 2d 562 (S.D.N.Y. 2001). https://law.justia.com/cases/federal/district-courts/FSupp2/138/562/2462331/

Department of Citywide Administrative Services. (n.d.). *Mayors of the City of New York.* Retrieved January 8, 2026, from https://www.nyc.gov/site/dcas/about/green-book-mayors-of-the-city-of-new-york.page

Eterno, J. A. (2012a, May 18). An examination of stop and frisk policy and practice [Testimony before the New York State Assembly Standing Committee on Codes, Standing Committee on Corrections, and New York State Black, Puerto Rican, Hispanic, and Asian Legislative Caucus Roundtable].

Eterno, J. A. (2012b, June 18). Policing by the numbers. *The New York Times.* https://www.nytimes.com/2012/06/18/opinion/the-nypds-obsession-with-numbers.html

Eterno, J. A. (2013, November 6). *In defense of Judge Scheindlin.* New York Daily News. http://www.nydailynews.com/opinion/defense-judge-scheindlin-article-1.1507911

Eterno, J. A. (2015a). *The New York City Police Department: The impact of its policies and practices.* CRC Press.

Eterno, J. A. (2015b). CompStat: Strengths and weaknesses. *Journal of Police Studies*, *4*(37), 41–55.

Eterno, J. A., & Silverman, E. B. (2005). The New York City Police Department's CompStat: Dream or nightmare? *International Journal of Police Science & Management*, *8*(3), 218–231.

Eterno, J. A., & Silverman, E. B. (2010a). Understanding police management: A typology of the underside of CompStat. *Professional Issues in Criminal Justice*, *5*(2&3), 11–28.

Eterno, J. A., & Silverman, E. B. (2010b). NYPD's CompStat: Compare statistics or compose statistics? *International Journal of Police Science & Management*, *12*(3), 426–449.

Eterno, J. A., & Silverman, E. B. (2012). *The crime numbers game: Management by manipulation.* CRC Press.

Eterno, J. A., & Silverman, E. B. (2013a). Crosstabulations for Eli Silverman testimony in Floyd v. City of New York. United States District Court, Southern District of New York.

Eterno, J. A., & Silverman, E. B. (2013b, September 11). Mike Bloomberg's fact-free defense of stop-and-frisk. *The Guardian.* https://www.theguardian.com/commentisfree/2013/sep/11/stop-and-frisk-michael-bloomberg

Eterno, J. A., Verma, A., & Silverman, E. B. (2016). Police manipulation of crime reports. *Justice Quarterly*, *33*(5), 811–933. https://doi.org/10.1080/07418825.2014.980838

Floyd v. City of New York, 283 F.R.D. 153 (S.D.N.Y. 2012) (pre-trial motion granted)

Floyd v. City of New York, 959 F.Supp.2d 668 (2013)

Gillmore, I. (2011, August 30). *How I got that story: The NYPD tapes.* Association of Alternative Newsmedia. https://archive.altweeklies.com/aan/how-i-got-that-story-the-nypd-tapes/Article?oid=4801034

Gregorian, D. (2019, January 10). *New judge assigned in NYPD stop-and-frisk case, Analisa Torres, has been critical of the police tactic in the past.* Daily News. https://www.nydailynews.com/2013/11/01/new-judge-in-nypd-stop-and-frisk-case-analisa-torres-has-been-critical-of-police-tactic-in-past/

Kavanaugh, J. (2014). Judicial impartiality in recent civil rights victories: An analysis of the disqualification of Judge Shira Scheindlin in *Floyd v. New York City. Journal of Gender, Social Policy & the Law*, *23*(1), 196–229. https://digitalcommons.a.american.edu/cgi/viewcontent.cgi?article=1656&context=jgspl

Levine, H. G., & Siegel, L. (2015). Marijuana madness: The scandal of New York City's racist marijuana arrests. In J. A. Eterno (Ed.), *The New York City Police Department: The impact of its policies and practices* (chap. 6). CRC Press.

Mac Donald, H. (2010, June 26). Fighting crime where the crimes are. *The New York Times*. https://www.nytimes.com/2010/06/26/opinion/26macdonald.html

New York City Law Department, Office of the Corporation Counsel. (2003, September 18). *NYPD announces settlement in Daniels class action "stop-and-frisk" lawsuit* [Press release]. https://www.nyc.gov/html/law/downloads/pdf/pr091803.pdf

New York Civil Liberties Union. (2025, May 27). *Stop-and-Frisk data*. https://www.nyclu.org/data/stop-and-frisk-data

New York State Office of the Attorney General. (1999). *The New York City Police Department's stop-and-frisk practices: A report to the people of the State of New York from the Office of the Attorney General*. https://ur.ag.ny.gov/sites/default/files/reports/stp_frsk.pdf

New York State, Office of the Governor. (2017). *Raymond W. Kelly biography*. https://www.governor.ny.gov/sites/default/files/atoms/files/Raymond_Kelly_Bio_2017.pdf

NYPD Monitor. (n.d.). *About*. https://www.nypdmonitor.org/about/

Rayman, G. (2013). *The NYPD tapes: A shocking story of cops, cover-ups, and courage*. St. Martin's Press.

Roberts, S. (2021, November 10). Peter Zimroth, who oversaw stop-and-frisk reforms, dies at 78. *The New York Times*. https://www.nytimes.com/2021/11/10/nyregion/peter-zimroth-dead.html

Schram, J., & Conley, K. (2013, September 19). Gun crime up after stop-and-frisk ruling. *New York Post*. https://nypost.com/2013/09/19/gunstats/

6

NEW MAYORS, NEW POLICE COMMISSIONERS

Introduction

Bill de Blasio was elected mayor of New York City on a platform of ending the abuse of stop-and-frisk practices of the previous administration. Mr. de Blasio served from January 1, 2014 to December 31, 2021. He chose none other than William Bratton as his police commissioner. Mr. Bratton, who served previously under Mayor Giuliani, was the main architect of the well-known performance management system called CompStat. However, as we have seen, the extreme abuse of stop and frisk never occurred under his tenure. He served his second stint as the New York City Police Department (NYPD) Commissioner from January 1, 2014 to September 16, 2016. Additionally, Mr. Bratton served as the Los Angeles Police Department (LAPD) Chief from October 27, 2002 to October 31, 2009 (New York State, Office of the Governor, 2017). No one else has served as the top commander of both flagship agencies.

In between his first term as NYPD Commissioner and LAPD Chief, Bratton did some consulting work, some of which was associated with the Manhattan Institute, a conservative institute, and some of which was with South American countries, including Brazil and Venezuela. One study suggests some level of controversy with these contracts, but there appears to be no hard evidence of this (Seigel, 2012). It seems to me to be mostly failed attempts to bring his CompStat style of policing to these countries. Basically, it seems that funding disappeared with new political powers. This is not unusual, and also seems to have occurred with Mr. Giuliani, who consulted in Mexico. Mr. Giuliani attempted to do the same sort of consulting, trying to bring the New York City style of policing to another country. This, too, was not without controversy and did not last long (Solomon & Mosk, 2007).

At the LAPD, Mr. Bratton oversaw many issues, but, most related to this chapter is that he was Chief when the LAPD was under a consent decree for unconstitutional and systematic misconduct. Bratton's leadership was instrumental in having the decree removed in 2009.

I have already covered Bratton's leadership in New York City under Mayor Giuliani. There was some controversy, but he clearly did not abuse his authority. We saw an increase in pressures on officers but, at the same time, there was an increase in pressures to obey

DOI: 10.4324/9781003593256-6

the law. In an interview with *60 Minutes* (Streeter, 2003), Bratton talks to officers in the Los Angeles Police Department. He warned them that there are "three kisses of death on this department: corruption, racism, and brutality." Bratton is portrayed as a no-nonsense leader who expects work from everyone under him. He goes on to talk about the importance of obeying the law while enforcing it. He is one of a select group of inspirational police leaders who not only understands the difficulties of policing in a democracy, but also puts it into practice. In the *60 Minutes* segment, while talking to high-level officers, he says, "You cannot break the law to enforce the law under any circumstances." Mr. Bratton, then, shows himself to be genuinely concerned about the proper balancing of crime control and due process, sometimes missing from police leaders. This balance is especially critical in terms of stop and frisk.

LAPD Police Chief

Mr. Bratton was hired by Mayor James Hahn (2002–2005) in October 2002. Bratton was retained by the next mayor, Antonio Villaraigosa (2005–2009). Mr. Bratton later resigned in August 2009, after what most would say was a successful tenure. As we have seen, when Bratton first came to the LAPD, he brought confidence and a new inspirational leadership to a department that was demoralized. Bratton brought in his CompStat, performance-style management to the LAPD. In 2007, Bratton talks about his aggressive broken windows type of policing: "The one thing I have learned—and now strongly advocate—is that the police, properly resourced and directed, can control behavior to such a degree that we can change behavior" (Stop LAPD Spying Coalition, 2021, p.7). Overall, Bratton's aggressive style was properly balanced with due process reforms. Bratton won over many of those in minority communities, and even more liberal critics, such as Rice (2013, p. 31), a known critic of the LAPD:

> Mr. Bratton slowly broke down the hostility from the Black community and, once crime began dropping, he won its backing and eventual admiration. By 2009, Mr. Bratton had an approval rating of 66 percent; the police department was even higher, including among Latinos and African Americans.

At first, there was predictable resistance to Mr. Bratton's style, and some concerns still remain. Initially, he had to contend with a department that was reeling from the Rampart scandal, the Rodney King beating, low race and community relations, and a demoralized police force. Critics were quick to attack him. For example, the Stop LAPD Spying Coalition criticizes Bratton's reforms in using technology to create a climate of privacy concerns. This is not unusual for Bratton as the New York Civil Liberties Union and the Center for Constitutional Rights had similar concerns. However, as we have seen in previous chapters, those concerns were not nearly as worrisome as the work of other police commissioners in New York City, especially Mr. Kelly, who ramped up stop and frisk to incredulous levels.

Perhaps Mr. Bratton's most successful legacy from his time in Los Angeles was getting the consent decree on the LAPD lifted. The decree was lifted on May 16, 2013. The decree was placed on the LAPD after the Rampart scandal. In general, the scandal involved a series of events spanning 1997 through 1998. These events seem similar to what occurred in New York City in the 75th Precinct just a few short years earlier. In this case, Officer Michael

Dowd and many in the precinct were taking money from drug dealers in return for police protection, stealing found drug money, and using illegal drugs. While Dowd was the ringleader, his partner Kenny Eurell was also deeply involved. Eventually, many in the precinct either turned the other way or somehow participated (Russell, 2014).

Similarly, in the Rampart scandal, officer Rafael Perez was the apparent ringleader of corruption. He stole and fabricated evidence, and took drug money and illegal drugs. This officer and one of his partners, David Mack, bonded in their illegal acts. They were part of the anti-gang CRASH (Community Resources Against Street Hoodlums) unit. Perez feels that he was influenced by another corrupt colleague, Nino Durden. Durden, however, suggests it was the other way around. In one event, for example, they were involved in the shooting and framing of a gang member who was left paralyzed. They planted a gun on the suspect, who was sentenced to 23 years (Frontline, 2001; Young, n.d.).

There were many illegal activities similar to the 75-corruption scandal in New York City. Both of these large-scale corruption affairs have similar circumstances. They stem from a negative subculture, which, interestingly enough, is comparable to criminal gangs. A previous corruption scandal was investigated by the well-known Knapp Commission in the 1970s in New York City. In that Commission, they suggest that there are "meat-eaters" and "grass-eaters." The meat eaters are the ones who are very involved in illegal acts, while grass-eaters will take advantage of opportunities and turn the other way. The Knapp Commission (1972) advised that the root of the problem is not the meat-eaters but the grass-eaters who refuse to expose the problem. Similarly, the Mollen Commission (City of New York Commission to Investigate Allegations of Police Corruption and the Anti-Corruption Procedures of the Police Department [Mollen Commission], 1994), which investigated the 75 scandal, also talks about the problem of the police culture, which attempts to protect officers from outsiders. That is, officers will not "rat-out" fellow officers. This is a strict informal rule. It develops from the dangerousness of the work environment, where officers must rely on one another for help. In these scandals, the meat-eaters take advantage of this, knowing full well that other officers are likely to protect them by not speaking out.

Going back to Bratton in Los Angeles, as a result of the Rampart corruption scandal, the LAPD was placed under a court-ordered consent decree. A United States Federal judge, Gary Feess, oversaw this decree. A task force was appointed to gauge LAPD's compliance. The main reasons for the consent decree were patterns of excessive force, false arrest, and unreasonable search and seizures (United States v. City of Los Angeles, Consent Decree, 2001). Due in part to Bratton's leadership, the LAPD enters into a transition agreement in July, 2009. Just before the transition agreement is signed, Bratton is quoted as saying, "We are arguing if you continue the consent decree, symbolically that basically is a slap in the face of the department. The polling by the *L.A. Times* shows that a majority of the people in this city feel this department is really doing a good job" (Los Angeles Police Protective League, 2009).

Bratton was to end the consent decree by collaborating with communities, establishing a Consent Decree Compliance Unit, creating liaisons with the most vocal critics of the department, and promoting a new generation of leaders, among other reforms (Luzer, 2013). The District Court judge who ended the consent decree was also very positive about the current state of the agency: "The LAPD has become the national and international policing standard for activities that range from audits to handling of the mentally ill to many aspects of training to risk assessment of police officers and more" (Halle, Beveridge, & Beveridge, 2013). The piece goes on with additional applause:

> The LAPD has entered into new partnerships with various community organizations, and in recent polls nearly eight[y] percent of LA residents expressed strong approval for the performance of the department. Remarkably, this included 76 percent and 68 percent of the Black and Latino respondents, respectively.
>
> *(Halle et al., 2013)*

In 2009, when Bratton was about to leave, now former mayor James Hahn stated, "Crime is down, the consent decree has been lifted, morale has been improved, and I think the relationship between the communities and their police officers has never been better" (Lloyd, 2009). The mayor at the time of Bratton leaving also had praise for him. Mayor Antonio Villaraigosa stated that the LAPD, "didn't just comply with the decree but took it to heart" (Bryan, 2013).

However, there are some critiques of Bratton's work as well. One of the more salient and powerful pieces discusses three key issues with the LAPD. The first is the sheer number of stops that the LAPD does. The number of stops compared with the population is very high. It is comparable to the NYPD's number when they were in the middle of abusing stops during Mr. Kelly's and Mayor Bloomberg's time in office. Second, similar to the NYPD, is the high number of minorities being stopped. In the LAPD, there was an attempt to improve the quality of investigations of racial profiling. However, at the same time, a program to place cameras in patrol cars did not happen. Third, and perhaps of most concern, is when the monitor was removed, the LAPD stopped collecting data on stops. Without that data, it will be difficult, if not impossible, to be proactive in addressing issues related to stops before they occur. For example, tracking problematic officers will be far more difficult without data. Bratton is known for what gets measured, and gets done. If these statistics are not collected, it is far less likely, if at all, that issues will be monitored. Collecting the data at the NYPD was, and is, a critical aspect of monitoring and determining issues. For example, the New York State Office of the Attorney General's report (1999) was one of the first to raise a red flag. This was based on the computerization of stop-and-frisk reports from previous years (Benigno, 2013). With the caveat of these concerns, Bratton's record of stressing that officers obey the law and Constitutional rights, of not wildly increasing the number of stops, and getting the monitor removed at LAPD, are laudable and generally healthy for democratic policing.

Bratton as NYPD Police Commissioner II

Bratton's return to New York City as Police Commissioner commenced on January 1, 2014. He served for nearly three years, until September 16, 2016. His previous success and reputation made him the ideal choice. However, Mayor de Blasio was essentially elected on a wave of police reform. The stop-and-frisk *Floyd v. City of New York* (2013) District Court case was lost by the City. The City was appealing, but after Mayor de Blasio was elected, the appeal was stopped. The holding of the District Court was essentially that the NYPD was liable for unconstitutional and racist stop practices through "a policy of indirect racial profiling." One of the most important aspects of the case was placing a federal court monitor on the department. The court-appointed monitor was Peter Zimroth, who was appointed by Judge

Shira Scheindlin on August 12, 2013, and later continued under Judge Angelina Torres, who succeeded Judge Scheindlin after some controversy. Mr. Zimroth died in November 2021 (Roberts, 2021).

Peter Zimroth and Consent Decree Under Bratton

Zimroth had an outstanding career, including former prosecutor (local and United States Attorney) and corporate lawyer. He also served as Corporation Counsel (New York City's highest lawyer) from 1987 to 1989. His work as a monitor of the NYPD on stop and frisk was critically important and laid the foundation for what continues to this day. There were three reports by the monitor under Bratton's tenure. They focused on training, changes to NYPD policy (the Patrol Guide), auditing of stops, improved supervision, and instituting body-worn cameras. During this time, the focus of the monitor was on what needs to be done in the future. Today, body-worn cameras are a staple of police work, but they were innovative at the time (Zimroth, 2015, 2016a, 2016b).

Bratton's Focus

Under Bratton, numerous commanders were transferred in a complete shifting of priorities. Essentially, Bratton was focusing on crime control and satisfying citizens' concerns. His aim was to develop community partnerships. In terms of stop and frisk, there were both accolades and issues. In terms of positive development, the Heritage Foundation felt that stop-and-frisk practices were effective in reducing crime and that Bratton endorses the practice (Larkin, 2014).

However, the racial divide between police and minorities has historically been wide. Many who want reform see Bratton as part of the problem. His style seemed overly aggressive. CompStat, his masterpiece, seems like an anachronism. His staunch support for broken windows type policing seems out of place in a city looking for reform. The chokehold death of Mr. Eric Garner on July 17, 2014, for selling "loosie cigarettes" did not seem to be a good sign for Bratton. Indeed, this seemed like an ominous harbinger of things to come. Bratton felt that he was ahead of the curve in terms of race relations. Bratton's crime control philosophy morphed as issues among minorities increased. Bratton felt that a "peace dividend" was called for as crime declined enormously (Baker & Goodman, 2016). At this point, Bratton was looking to increase community relations.

Bratton's new focus in his second term was on "precision in going after the people, places, and things driving crime; strategies for preventing crime and the evolving threat of terrorism; and, neighborhood policing, with officers assigned to small areas to address local concerns of crime and disorder" (Baker & Goodman, 2016, p. A1). On December 20, 2014, two officers were killed in the line of duty, Rafael Ramos and Wenjian Liu. The incident happened about a year into his second term and indicates only some of the challenges Bratton was faced with. Some critics, such as Norman Siegel, the former Executive Director of the New York Civil Liberties Union, were skeptical of Bratton. He felt that the peace dividend that Bratton was in favor of, indicated that a war with communities did indeed take place (Baker & Goodman, 2016). Nevertheless, Bratton was very concerned about implicit bias and the need to open officers' minds to other viewpoints (Baker & Goodman, 2016). Bratton was confident that he had many others who would continue supporting his policies and solidify his legacy.

Trends in Stop and Frisk Under Bratton II

The decreasing trend of stop-and-frisk statistics by the NYPD under Bratton is interesting. If Bratton were to continue in the vein of his last stint in New York City, we would expect large increases. Just the opposite occurred. This is possibly due to the difficulties of racial relations at the time in the larger society. For example, the Black Lives Matter movement and the Defund the Police Movement (to be discussed in the next chapter) could have a negative influence of police behavior uncontrollable by police leadership. In 2014, there were 45,787 stops; in 2015, there were 22,563 stops; and in 2016, 20,404 (New York Civil Liberties Union, 2025). Additionally, the percentage of stops that resulted in arrests or summonses did not drastically change, ranging from 15 to 20 percent. Since the sheer number of stops were decreasing, the number of arrests based on stops also correspondingly decreased. While these only include stops recorded by the police, the trend is clear. The era of aggressive stop and frisk based on heavy-handed quotas under the previous administration is unquestionably over. There was also no appreciable increase in crime as suggested by some critics such as Heather MacDonald (Cullen, 2016) and Peter Vallone, Jr. (Richard French Live, 2013). The suggestion that fewer stops would lead to the Wild West in New York City was simply and conclusively wrong. While one cannot rule out the importance of stop and frisk as an important tactic, the substantial abuses based on quota pressures were not only uncalled for but likely caused a backlash that police are still trying to recover from. Indeed, the abuses of the past may very likely be responsible for movements that led to anti-police protest. The NYPD engaged in outlandish increases in stop and frisk, in mostly minority communities, that had little to no impact whatsoever on crime. If anything, the backlash against such abuse was a healthy response leading to rightful correction.

James O'Neill and Dermot Shea

James O'Neill

James O'Neill was appointed Police Commissioner after Bratton in September 2016. He spent three years in this role, resigning in November 2019. He was Bratton's protégé. Both were very committed to maintaining low levels of crime and respecting people's rights. O'Neill felt that stop and frisk is a "constitutionally tested tool…[that] helps to keep the city safe" (McCarthy, 2019). In addition, he agreed with Bratton that the rights of all need to be respected while conducting stops.

The number of recorded stops under O'Neill is fairly low and consistent: 2017, 11,628; 2018, 11,008; and 2019, 13,469. The sheer number of stops compared with Bratton's last two years was roughly half as many. The percentage of stops that led to an arrest or summons in those same years ranged from 30 to 34 percent. Thus, the hit rate—the percentage of stops leading to an arrest/summons—is about double compared with the previous three years under Bratton. Although there is a little fluctuation in the number of homicides, they did not appreciably increase or decrease during these years (Stebbins, 2024). This is especially important when we compare that with the high in 1990 of 2,262 (New York City Police Department, 2025).

The reports of the court monitor during James O'Neill's tenure began to address specific issues. The first report, dated November 18, 2016, outlines intentions to amend in-service training courses. The report also indicated amending the Patrol Guide to comport better with the *De Bour* case (the New York State case on police stops previously discussed). A new stop report was piloted in five precincts with some changes indicated on the form (Zimroth, 2016). The second report from the monitor under O'Neill was dated May 30, 2017. Stop-and-frisk data were analyzed, showing fewer stops, but disparities continued. The monitor felt no conclusions could be made from these reports to determine compliance (Zimroth, 2017a). The third report under O'Neill, dated June 29, 2017, advised that the new body-worn camera program would be piloted as a randomized control trial. This was accomplished in 40 police precincts with thousands of officers participating. This will be discussed later as detailed results of this trial are contained in a peer-reviewed article that is not part of the monitor's report. The monitor's report does suggest that civilian complaints, community surveys, and data from the cameras will be used to assess the program (Zimroth, 2017b). The fourth report under O'Neill (the seventh

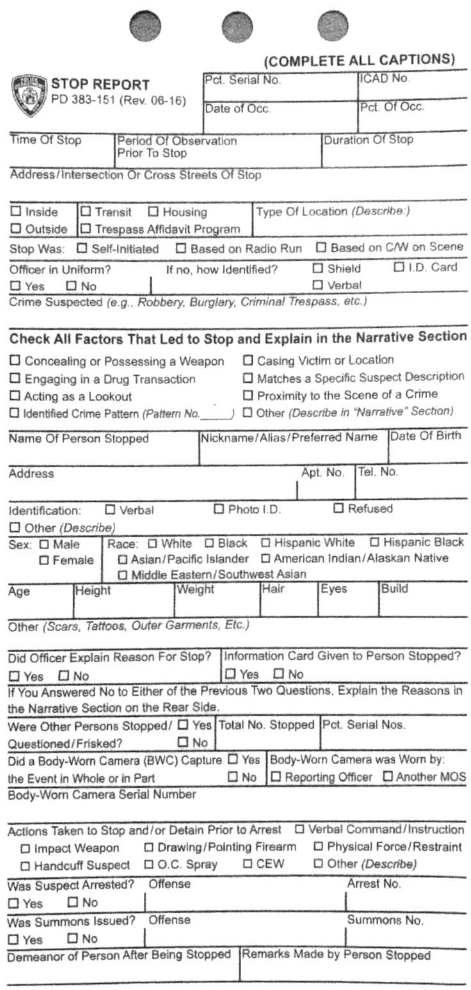
(COMPLETE ALL CAPTIONS)
STOP REPORT
PD 383-151 (Rev. 06-16)
Pct. Serial No. | ICAD No.
Date of Occ. | Pct. Of Occ.
Time Of Stop | Period Of Observation Prior To Stop | Duration Of Stop
Address/Intersection Or Cross Streets Of Stop
☐ Inside ☐ Outside | ☐ Transit ☐ Housing ☐ Trespass Affidavit Program | Type Of Location (Describe:)
Stop Was: ☐ Self-Initiated ☐ Based on Radio Run ☐ Based on C/W on Scene
Officer in Uniform? ☐ Yes ☐ No | If no, how Identified? ☐ Shield ☐ I.D. Card ☐ Verbal
Crime Suspected (e.g., Robbery, Burglary, Criminal Trespass, etc.)
Check All Factors That Led to Stop and Explain in the Narrative Section
☐ Concealing or Possessing a Weapon ☐ Casing Victim or Location
☐ Engaging in a Drug Transaction ☐ Matches a Specific Suspect Description
☐ Acting as a Lookout ☐ Proximity to the Scene of a Crime
☐ Identified Crime Pattern (Pattern No.____) ☐ Other (Describe in "Narrative" Section)
Name Of Person Stopped | Nickname/Alias/Preferred Name | Date Of Birth
Address | Apt. No. | Tel. No.
Identification: ☐ Verbal ☐ Photo I.D. ☐ Refused ☐ Other (Describe)
Sex: ☐ Male ☐ Female | Race: ☐ White ☐ Black ☐ Hispanic White ☐ Hispanic Black ☐ Asian/Pacific Islander ☐ American Indian/Alaskan Native ☐ Middle Eastern/Southwest Asian
Age | Height | Weight | Hair | Eyes | Build
Other (Scars, Tattoos, Outer Garments, Etc.)
Did Officer Explain Reason For Stop? ☐ Yes ☐ No | Information Card Given to Person Stopped? ☐ Yes ☐ No
If You Answered No to Either of the Previous Two Questions, Explain the Reasons in the Narrative Section on the Rear Side.
Were Other Persons Stopped/Questioned/Frisked? ☐ Yes ☐ No | Total No. Stopped | Pct. Serial Nos.
Did a Body-Worn Camera (BWC) Capture the Event in Whole or in Part ☐ Yes ☐ No | Body-Worn Camera was Worn by: ☐ Reporting Officer ☐ Another MOS
Body-Worn Camera Serial Number
Actions Taken to Stop and/or Detain Prior to Arrest ☐ Verbal Command/Instruction ☐ Impact Weapon ☐ Drawing/Pointing Firearm ☐ Physical Force/Restraint ☐ Handcuff Suspect ☐ O.C. Spray ☐ CEW ☐ Other (Describe)
Was Suspect Arrested? ☐ Yes ☐ No | Offense | Arrest No.
Was Summons Issued? ☐ Yes ☐ No | Offense | Summons No.
Demeanor of Person After Being Stopped | Remarks Made by Person Stopped

FIGURE 6.1a NYPD Stop Report.

Narrative *(Describe the Circumstances That Led to the Stop)*:

Was Person Frisked? ☐ Yes ☐ No **IF YES, INDICATE BASIS FOR FRISK:** ☐ Object Observed Suspected of Being a Weapon
☐ Statement by Suspect ☐ Suspect Known to Carry Weapons ☐ Violent Crime ☐ Other *(Describe Below)*
Was Person Searched? ☐ Yes ☐ No **IF YES, INDICATE BASIS FOR SEARCH:** ☐ Hard Object Resembling Weapon ☐ Consent to Search
☐ Admission Of Weapons Possession ☐ Outline of Weapon ☐ Search Incident to an Arrest ☐ Other *(Describe Below)*

Was Weapon Found? ☐ Yes ☐ No | If Yes, Specify: ☐ Firearm ☐ Knife/Cutting Instrument ☐ Other *(Describe)* | Was Other Contraband Found? ☐ Yes ☐ No | If Yes, Describe Contraband and Location

Narrative *(Describe the Circumstances That Led to the Frisk and/or Search, if Conducted. Include Area Searched)*:

Reporting MOS *(Rank, Name Printed)*	Signature	Tax No.	Command	Date

Supervisory Action *(Must Complete)*: Supervisor on Scene During Stop? ..... ☐ Yes ☐ No
Encounter Reviewed With Officer? ... ☐ Yes ☐ No
Report Accurate and Complete? ..... ☐ Yes ☐ No
Corresponding Activity Log Entry Reviewed? ☐ Yes ☐ No
Sufficient Basis for Stop? ...... ☐ Yes ☐ No
Sufficient Basis for Frisk? ...... ☐ Yes ☐ No ☐ N/A
Sufficient Basis for Search? .... ☐ Yes ☐ No ☐ N/A

Follow-Up Action *(If Appropriate)*:
Report Corrected .. ☐ Training .... ☐
Instruction .... ☐ Disciplinary Action . ☐

Reviewing Supervisor *(Rank, Name Printed)*		Tax No.	Command
Signature	Pct. Serial No.	Date	Time

FIGURE 6.1b (Continued)

total) dated December 13, 2017, indicated that the pilot was initiated with over 1,000 officers currently participating from 20 precincts (Zimroth, 2017c). A performance evaluation system was initiated that removed the sheer number of stops as an evaluative tool. With respect to trespass arrests, some additional guidelines were implemented. Another new electronic stop report was initiated during this time period as well (see Figures 6.1a and b). The fifth report under O'Neill (eighth report in total) dated July 27, 2018, goes into more detail on the research design, especially related to Police Housing Service Areas (PSA). They use a quasi-experimental design, which will be discussed in more detail with the peer-reviewed article. This will include nine PSAs. The monitor will use audits to evaluate the program (Zimroth, 2018). In the last report under O'Neill (ninth total report and sixth under O'Neill), the monitor states that there are problems with underreporting of stops, and supervisors are failing to deal with that issue, as well as the poor quality of the stop reports. Due to a new "Right to Know Law" (Local laws 54 and 56), officers must now give out a business card as part of the stop, explain reasons for the stop, and inform citizens of the possibility of refusing to be searched in certain cases (especially consent cases) (Zimroth, 2019).

Dermot Shea

After James O'Neill, Dermot Shea worked as Police Commissioner from December 1, 2019 to December 31, 2021. Under his leadership, there were some criticisms. Most notable were suggestions that the Department was using false and misleading statements, and excessive force, and failing to stop gun violence (Khurshid & Max, 2020). One example of this is with stop and frisk.

> Dermot Shea called out—the once pervasive NYPD practice of "stop and frisk," vowing he would not return to days when thousands of New Yorkers—most Black or Hispanic—were targeted by cops with little or no justification … [however] during his rise to the head of the nation's largest police force, Shea was twice involved in stops that included tactics since labeled unconstitutional.
>
> *(Smith, 2021)*

It should be noted that Shea served in exceedingly difficult times as COVID-19 was at its peak. Also, he served for two years in the role of Commissioner. He was unable, as were others, to remove the monitor from the NYPD.

In the brief period he was Commissioner, there were no fewer than six reports by the *Floyd* monitor. The essence of the first report, dated January 7, 2020, was that the body-worn cameras went citywide, violent crime was down, and stops were quite low compared with the past. On a need for improvement note, the NYPD needed to address that lack of documentation (Zimroth, 2020a). The second report under Shea (eleventh report overall) dated October 28, 2020 (Zimroth, 2020b), focused on COVID-19 and post-Floyd death in custody incidents. The report generally notes a new disciplinary matrix for officers, a law against chokeholds, another law that police must provide medical/mental help to citizens, and many other similar changes in both state and local laws. On November 30, 2020 (Zimroth, 2020c), a third monitor's report under Shea indicated the results of the data on body-worn cameras. Most notably, the report stated there was a 21.1 percent decrease in the number of civilian complaints and a 38.8 percent increase in the number of stops reported. It also noted a few changes in citizen perceptions of police behavior. The fourth report under Shea (thirteenth report overall), dated September 1, 2021, basically stated that racial disparities still exist in stops (Zimroth, 2021a). The fifth report, dated October 12, 2021, under Shea indicated that the NYPD was not complying well with COVID-19 stop guidelines (Zimroth, 2021b). The department did not manage masking and other state guidelines in a manner acceptable to the monitor. There were unexplained disparities in police behavior. However, body-worn camera footage indicated that the police were generally following the law. The sixth and final report by the monitor under Shea, dated December 14, 2021, indicated the passing of Peter Zimroth. Deputy Monitor Richard Jerome issued this report. The Deputy Monitor noted a decline in racial disparities related to trespass enforcement (Jerome, 2021).

Mayor Eric Adams

Mayor Eric Adams won the election on a platform of crime reduction. As such, the expectations were high that the city would be safer. He began serving on January 1, 2022, and served until December 31, 2025. He is the second Black mayor (Mayor Dinkins discussed earlier was the first). His administration was filled with allegations of corruption. He was indicted by the United States Attorney for the Southern District of New York for abusing his power by obtaining personal benefits and illegal campaign contributions from foreign nations. Additionally, many who served under him were left under a scandal, such as Phil Banks, David Banks, Ingrid Lewis, and others (Smith, 2025). The case against Adams, however, was eventually dismissed by the federal government under a cloud of controversy with claims that Adams got a deal from the Trump administration after he allowed Immigration and Customs Enforcement (ICE) to operate in New York City (Marcelo, 2025). The mayor's first police commissioner is Keechant Sewell. As Police Commissioner, unlike the administration in general, she left an outstanding legacy, especially of respect and integrity: "she won the respect of the city's cops and praise from the police union for trying to make officers' lives better. She left a stellar record of integrity" (Schulz, 2023).

Keechant Sewell

Sewell was the first female police commissioner in New York City. Previously, she was the Chief of Detectives in the Nassau County Police Department, a highly respected officer.

Her choice was seen as very enlightened and beneficial to the NYPD. Informally, the detectives I know from Nassau County felt she was the consummate professional and an excellent leader. Sewell served from January 1, 2022 to June 30, 2023. She supported higher education for officers and maintaining high standards. There appeared to be a public rift between the administration and her on this and other issues. Sewell left under a cloud of apparent lack of support from the mayor (McCarthy & Marsh, 2023). It should be noted that Sewell has received numerous accolades, including the meritorious police award, numerous community awards, 2021 Person of the Year from the Nassau Detectives Association, and many others (Concordia, 2022).

There were four monitor's reports under Sewell's tenure. The first is dated May 6, 2022, and is the first with the new monitor appointed by the Court, Mylan L. Denerstein. She is a Partner for Gibson, Dunn, and Crutcher LLP. This report essentially addresses underreporting, the weakness of supervision, training, performance evaluations, and disparities in stops (Denerstein, 2022a). The second report (and seventeenth total for the monitor) under Sewell is October 17, 2022. This report deals with body-worn cameras and generally finds favorable results. However, while stop reports increased, arrests and summonses were way down (Denerstein, 2022b). The third report under Sewell, dated March 3, 2023, indicated that a controversial Trespass Affidavit Program had ended. The report was about the monitoring of the end of the program. There were still some issues with stop-and-frisk compliance even though the program had ended. The monitor recommended additional training to help terminate these issues (Denerstein, 2023a). The fourth and last report under Sewell is dated June 5, 2023. A new Neighborhood Safety Teams initiative was formed to target gun violence and high-crime areas. The monitor found there were serious issues with this program in violation of legal criteria, especially biased policing and underreporting of stops. A plan was initiated to attempt to bring the NYPD into compliance (Denerstein, 2023b).

Edward Caban

Caban served from July 1, 2023 to September 13, 2024. He was the first Hispanic police commissioner in New York City. It was reported that he was downgrading discipline for NYPD misconduct (Umansky, 2024). He resigned under a controversy of alleged bribery and fraud. His phone was seized as part of a federal court investigation. His twin brother James was also alleged to be involved. The scandal appeared to revolve around taking payments in exchange for favors to nightclubs (Cramer, 2024). As of February 2025, Caban and his brother have not been charged. Additionally, the case against the mayor was dropped (Hong, 2025). After the resignation of Caban, the next police commissioner, Thomas Donlon, lasted only two months, from September 13, 2024 to November 25, 2024. Donlon was the temporary head of the police department when he resigned. At the time, a search warrant was issued for his home, and material was seized (Mena, 2024). This led to the next police commissioner under Mayor Adams.

There were two monitor's reports under Caban. The first is the monitor's twentieth report overall. The monitor noted that stop reports decreased enormously; however, there is still a wide disparity between minorities and Whites who were stopped. They also noted that the disparities were most pronounced for frisks and searches. Additionally, they advise that underreporting is still a major issue, with an estimated 31.4 percent not documented. This report analyzed data from 2013 to 2022 (Denerstein, 2024a). The second report under Caban was nearly at the end of his tenure, dated September 4, 2024. A new system of accountability called ComplianceStat was developed to oversee officers' behaviors with respect to adherence to the Constitution. According to the report, there were 9,544 stops in 2020. In 2021, the number slightly decreased to 8,947. In 2022, the number of stops increased significantly to 15,102. Lastly, in 2023, the number increased again to 16,971 stops. This could be due to increased reporting by officers. Furthermore, many of these additional stops were due to self-initiated activity by officers (self-initiated stops 2020 = 19 percent and 2023 = 46 percent [at the time of this report]). It should be noted that unlawful searches increased during this period as well. In 2021, the rate was 20.4 percent, and in the first half of 2023, the rate increased to 33 percent (Denerstein, 2024b). This is, of course, very concerning. There was one report under Donlon dated October 7, 2024, indicating that data from body-worn cameras showed that only 59 percent of stops were being properly documented (Denerstein, 2024c).

Jessica Tisch

On November 25, 2024, Jessica Tisch was appointed Police Commissioner by Mayor Adams. Her career began at the NYPD in 2008. In this same year, Ms. Tisch completed both her law degree and MBA as a dual degree student at Harvard University. In 2011, she was admitted to the New York State Bar. She was an Intelligence Research Specialist. She had increasing responsibilities in the department. When Bratton became Police Commissioner in 2014, she was appointed Deputy Commissioner of Information Technology. She was in charge of new and emerging technologies and many of the NYPD databases. In November 2019, she was appointed Commissioner of the Citywide Department of Information Technology and Telecommunication, where she controlled the city's technology infrastructure. In April 2022, she was appointed by Mayor Adams as the Commissioner of Sanitation. That was the last position she held before becoming Police Commissioner (City of New York, 2025). It should be noted that Commissioner Tisch's family's net worth is approximately $10 billion (Barkan, 2024).

There were several reports by the court monitor regarding stop-and-frisk practices. The first is dated February 3, 2025. This is the twenty-third report overall by the monitor. The report is quite negative about the NYPD, essentially stating that they are not constitutionally compliant with the court and have not improved since the 2022 audit. Stops initiated by officers were less likely to be lawful than those based on radio calls. The monitor states they are looking for an 85 to 90 percent compliance rate by December 2025 (Denerstein, 2025a).

The second report under Tisch is dated May 21, 2025. The report advises "an increase in compliance over the first three-quarters of 2024 with 91% of stops, 79% of frisks, and 78% of searches being lawful in the third quarter of 2024." However, for self-initiated stops only, the percentages were a bit lower at 79 percent for stops, 60 percent for frisks, and 66 percent for searches. Underreporting and lack of proper supervision are still issues. At this point, many commands do not meet the criteria set by the monitor (Denerstein, 2025b).

The third report by the monitor is dated June 3, 2025 (Denerstein, 2025c). A Community Response Team (CRT) is now being used to help with quality-of-life issues. They are assigned to patrol boroughs. The main mission in the past has been illegal motorcycles/mopeds, demonstrations, and supporting the New York City Sheriffs' enforcement of illegal smoke shops. Of the stops by the CRT, 85 percent were lawful, 64 percent of frisks were lawful, and 59 percent of searches were found to be lawful. For patrol, 92 percent of stops were lawful, 89 percent of the frisks were lawful, and 77 percent of searches were lawful. Clearly, there are significant issues with the CRT. The monitor also found issues with underreporting and minorities being targeted too often.

The fourth report by the monitor under Commissioner Tisch is dated October 14, 2025 (Denerstein, 2025d). It details findings of a 2023 to 2024 audit of stop-and-frisk reports. This report shows similar concerns to the past ones. The fifth monitor's report is dated October 22, 2025, and this is the twenty-seventh report overall (Denerstein, 2025e). Largely, for the entire NYPD, the visual snapshot of the stop-and-frisk reports indicated that compliance rates were 89 percent for stops, 71 percent for frisks, and 73 percent for searches. While close, their numbers do not appear to be going in the right direction in terms of compliance. Self-initiated stops still appear to be a large problem. Unlawful conduct does not appear to be flagged by supervisors. The Comptroller's report repeats what was found in the monitor's report, indicating that supervisors found 98 percent compliance by officers, while the federal monitor found 11 to 14 percent being lawful. Body-worn camera footage indicated problems with reporting. However, this is already known (Office of the New York City Comptroller, 2025).

Based on available data (not the monitor's report), the sheer number of reported stops essentially remains low: although there has been some increase in recent years: 2017 = 11,628; 2018 = 11,008; 2019 = 13,459; 2020 = 9,554; 2021 = 8,947; 2022 = 15,102; 2023 = 16,971; 2024 = 25,386. The percentage of stops leading to arrests or summonses falls between 30 and 40 percent. Compared with earlier years, the percentage of stops leading to an arrest or summons is up approximately 20 to 30 percent (New York Civil Liberties Union, 2025). It would appear that the NYPD is more successful at identifying suspects who are doing something illegal. This improvement is certainly good, with the caveat that there are still issues with reporting. The monitor's final two reports—the sixth and seventh reports (Denerstein, 2026a, 2026b)—indicate some improvement in the execution of lawful Terry stops, frisks, and searches, including progress in self-initiated stops and the frisks and searches conducted during those stops.

Body-Worn Camera Studies in New York City

While the monitor's reports provide some summaries, they do not go into great detail about the body-worn camera study. For example, they do not explain a complete methodology and sophisticated analyses. There are peer-reviewed articles written by the monitors themselves that explain far more detail compared with the report summaries. For the remainder of this chapter, I will explain that information.

One of the most important is published in the well-respected journal *Criminology* (Braga, MacDonald, & McCabe, 2022). In this article, the authors use a cluster randomized controlled trial with 40 precincts—20 were treatment that used body-worn cameras, and 20 were control. These were selected randomly and matched on numerous criteria. There were 3,889 officers involved in the study with 1,991 being in the treatment group. The methodology was very well thought out and clearly administered. There is no doubt this study is statistically sound. The authors report that their main results are that the body-worn cameras increased the number of stop-and-frisk reports and also reduced the number of civilian complaints (Braga et al., 2022). Generally, there was a 38.8 percent increase in the number of stop reports and a 21.1 percent decrease in CCRB complaints (Braga et al., 2022). BWC officers appear to be complying better with policies to prepare stop-and-frisk reports (Braga et al.,

2022, p. 147). Additionally, the authors advise that the use of body-worn cameras (BWCs) can be used to help supervisors (Braga et al., 2022). However, within the article, there are some other curious results. They advise that there are no statistical differences between those using BWCs and those not for the following criteria: number of arrests, use of force arrests, number of summonses, domestic incident reports, and crime complaints.

While these results are important, there were some concerns with the results that should be highlighted. Those wearing BWCs were less likely to be reporting lawful stops.

> This study further suggests that the NYPD still has problems with unconstitutional stops of citizens made by its officers. Indeed, only 68.2 percent of stops made by BWC treatment officers and 81.3 percent of stops made by control officers met Fourth Amendment lawfulness standards.
>
> *(Braga et al., 2022, p. 148)*

This is also translated into increased levels of frisk and searches for those wearing BWCs. While BWCs may allow additional supervision, this does not seem to translate into increased legal behaviors on the street by officers. A previous study, prior to *Floyd*, showed only about 15 percent of NYPD officers were flagrantly illegal in their Fourth Amendment behaviors (Eterno, 2003). Another area of concern with this study is the lack of explanatory power in the multivariate models predicting whether the officer frisked, whether the officer searched, whether the officer arrested/summonsed, whether the officer did a lawful stop, and whether the officer did a lawful frisk/search (Pseudo R^2 =.201,.044,.059,.052,.092, respectively). What this means is that this set of variables does not explain the dependent variable well. A major concern is that there is no variable measuring management pressures. This probably would likely increase explanatory power, making their model more parsimonious and predictive. Indeed, previous studies were mentioned by the authors themselves suggesting the importance of management (Rivera & Ba, 2019; Mummolo, 2018). The *Floyd* court decision itself cites research with far more explanatory power (see, for example, table 5.1 with gamma =.461, testimony by Eli Silverman in the court case). Also, while not exactly the same comparison, but important, in explaining crime report manipulation by New York City officers, Eterno, Verma, and Silverman (2016) have far more explanatory power with one of the key independent variables being management style (R^2 =.390). Importantly, however, another study had about the same modest explanatory power as the most powerful model in the Braga et al. (2022) study (see Eterno, Barrow, & Silverman, 2017). This lack of explanatory power likely means another explanatory variable is not in the model. Other than management pressure, there are other possible independent variables missing from the analyses. For example, the demeanor of the suspect (Worden & Shepard, 1996; Lundman, 1994), as well as the law (with demeanor). That is, the law could be included as an independent variable, as opposed to a dependent variable, predicting the stop, search, and/or frisk (as the dependent variable) (Klinger, 1996).

There were two other peer-reviewed articles published by the monitor (Braga, MacDonald, & McCabe, 2024; Braga, MacDonald, & Barao, 2021). They basically provide similar ideas. In one article, they talk more about Housing officers (Braga et al., 2024), and in the other, they talk more about trust between communities and police, suggesting body-worn cameras do not assist with that but are good with accountability and transparency (Braga et al., 2021). In the end, BWCs appear to be a reasonable technological advance. However, they are clearly not a panacea completely solving stop-and-frisk issues. As a concluding point, it would be helpful for the monitor to be more transparent by publicly suggesting very specifically defined targets that the NYPD would have to meet, such that the monitor will be completely satisfied. This should be discussed in each and every report. That is, they could write something like, "the NYPD is nearly at its target and simply needs to do the following to satisfy the monitor." While the judge will make the final decision to remove the monitor, the more specificity, the better. It has been more than ten years, and it seems the NYPD is, for all practical purposes, no closer to having the monitor removed than when it was first placed on them by the court. This is despite the enormous decrease in stops from hundreds of thousands to tens of thousands, body-worn cameras, extensive and new oversight agencies (e.g., the monitor, an Inspector General), new mayors, new police commissioners, new forms, new training, and more.

Summary

As new mayors are elected, new police commissioners are chosen. Each mayor is elected on a platform. For example, Mayor de Blasio was elected on a platform of ending the stop-and-frisk abuse of the previous administration. William Bratton, a highly respected police professional, was selected by Mayor de Blasio. Bratton had respect for the rank and file. However, during this time, and under the time of two other commissioners chosen by de Blasio, the monitor overseeing NYPD under the *Floyd* case remained critical of the NYPD. Mayor Eric Adams was then elected on a platform of controlling crime. He selected Keechant Sewell, who was also highly respected in the field. Again, the monitor remained extremely critical of the NYPD during this period despite a lower number of stops, a higher hit rate, and the addition of body-worn cameras. The monitor also changed from Peter Zimroth to Mylan Denerstein. Even after over ten years of oversight, the NYPD still seems to be a long way from satisfying the court.

Discussion Questions

1. If you were mayor, who would you select as police commissioner?
2. Are the monitor's reports fair and balanced?
3. Does the monitor give good direction to the NYPD?
4. What criteria would you use to remove the NYPD from the monitor?
5. When Bratton was at the LAPD, the consent decree was removed. Was this justified?
6. Do you think body-worn cameras are beneficial or harmful? Why?
7. Do you think there is an appropriate number of stops that should be done by the police?
8. If you were the monitor, what specific targets would you enact to allow the NYPD to manage itself?

References

Baker, A., & Goodman, D. J. (2016, July 26). Bratton, who shaped an era in policing, tries to navigate a racial divide. *The New York Times*. https://www.nytimes.com/2016/07/26/nyregion/william-bratton-new-york-city-police-commissioner.html

Barkan, R. (2024, December 30). *The billionaire in charge of the cops*. Political Currents by Ross Barkan. https://rosselliotbarkan.com/p/the-billionaire-in-charge-of-the-cops

Benigno, M. (2013, December 17). *Bratton shouldn't bring LAPD's stop model back to NY*. ACLU Southern California. https://www.aclusocal.org/en/news/bratton-shouldnt-bring-lapds-stop-model-back-ny

Braga, A. A., MacDonald, J. M., & Barao, L. M. (2021). Do body-worn cameras improve community perceptions of the police? Results from a controlled experimental evaluation. *Journal of Experimental Criminology*, *19*(2), 461–484. https://doi.org/10.1007/s11292-021-09476-9

Braga, A. A., MacDonald, J. M., & McCabe, J. E. (2022). Body-worn cameras, lawful police stops, and NYPD officer compliance: A cluster randomized controlled trial. *Criminology*, *60*(1), 124–158. https://doi.org/10.1111/1745-9125.12293

Braga, A. A., MacDonald, J. M., & McCabe, J. E. (2024). Police reform in public housing contexts: Body-worn cameras, surveillance, and harm reduction in New York City Housing Authority developments. *Criminology & Public Policy*, *23*(3), 515–544. https://doi.org/10.1111/1745-9133.12644

Bryan, D. (2013, May 16). *Civil rights consent decree over LAPD lifted after almost 12 years*. CBS News. https://www.cbsnews.com/losangeles/news/civil-rights-consent-decree-over-lapd-lifted-after-almost-12-years/

City of New York. (2025). *Police commissioner*. New York City Police Department. https://www.nyc.gov/site/nypd/about/leadership/commissioner.page

City of New York Commission to Investigate Allegations of Police Corruption and the Anti-Corruption Procedures of the Police Department [Mollen Commission]. (1994). *Commission report*. City of New York.

Concordia. (2022, September 13). *Commissioner Keechant Sewell*. https://www.concordia.net/community/commissioner-keechant-sewell/

Cramer, M. (2024, September 25). Investigators trace former police commissioner's ties to night-clubs. *The New York Times*. https://www.nytimes.com/2024/09/25/nyregion/nypd-commissioner-night-clubs.html

Cullen, J. (2016). *Ending New York's stop-and-frisk did not increase crime*. Brennan Center for Justice. https://www.brennancenter.org/our-work/analysis-opinion/ending-new-yorks-stop-and-frisk-did-not-increase-crime

Denerstein, M. L. (2022a, May 6). *Sixteenth report of the independent monitor*. NYPD Monitor. https://www.nypdmonitor.org/wp-content/uploads/2022/09/16-Sixteenth-Report-.pdf

Denerstein, M. L. (2022b, October 17). *Seventeenth report of the independent monitor: The deployment of body-worn cameras on NYPD housing bureau officers assigned to police service areas: A quasi-experimental evaluation measuring effects on the civility of police-citizen encounters, policing activities, and police lawfulness*. NYPD Monitor. https://www.nypdmonitor.org/wp-content/uploads/2022/10/2022.10.17-Dkt.-894-Seventeenth-Report-of-the-Independent-Monitor.pdf

Denerstein, M. L. (2023a, March 3). *Eighteenth report of the independent monitor: Monitor's audit of the trespass affidavit program*. NYPD Monitor. https://www.nypdmonitor.org/wp-content/uploads/2023/03/NYPD-Monitors-18th-Report-re-TAP.pdf

Denerstein, M. L. (2023b, June 5). *Nineteenth report of the independent monitor: Monitor's audit of the neighborhood safety teams*. NYPD Monitor. https://www.nypdmonitor.org/wp-content/uploads/2023/06/NST-Report.pdf

Denerstein, M. L. (2024a, April 11). *Twentieth report of the independent monitor: Racial disparities in NYPD stop, question, and frisk practices: An analysis of 2013 to 2022 stop reports*. NYPD Monitor. https://www.nypdmonitor.org/wp-content/uploads/2024/04/2024.04.11-927-1-Twentieth-Report.pdf

Denerstein, M. L. (2024b, September 4). *Twenty-first report of the independent monitor: Monitor's compliance report*. NYPD Monitor. https://www.nypdmonitor.org/wp-content/uploads/2024/09/21st-Monitor-Report-General-Compliance-Report_Stamped.pdf

Denerstein, M. L. (2024c, October 7). *Twenty-second report of the independent monitor: Underreporting of Terry stops by the NYPD*. NYPD Monitor. https://www.nypdmonitor.org/wp-content/uploads/2024/10/2024.10.07-937-1-NYPD-Underreporting-of-Terry-Stops-Report.pdf

Denerstein, M. L. (2025a, February 3). *Twenty-third report of the independent monitor: The NYPD's NST and PST units' stop, frisk, and search practices*. NYPD Monitor. https://www.nypdmonitor.org/wp-content/uploads/2025/02/2025.02.03-Floyd-Dkt.-952-1-Monitors-23rd-Report.pdf

Denerstein, M. L. (2025b, May 21). *Twenty-fourth report of the independent monitor: Compliance snapshot of NYPD's stop, frisk, and search practices.* NYPD Monitor. https://www.nypdmonitor.org/wp-content/uploads/2025/05/2025.05.21-960-Monitors-Twenty-Fourth-Report.pdf

Denerstein, M. L. (2025c, June 3). *Twenty-fifth report of the independent monitor: The NYPD's Community Response team's stop, frisk, and search practices.* NYPD Monitor. https://www.nypdmonitor.org/wp-content/uploads/2025/06/963-Twenty-Fifth-Report-of-the-Independent-Monitor.pdf

Denerstein, M. L. (2025d, October 14). *Twenty-sixth report of the independent monitor: The NYPD's accountability efforts.* NYPD Monitor. https://www.nypdmonitor.org/wp-content/uploads/2025/10/2025.10.14-As-filed-Floyd-26th-Monitor-Report.pdf

Denerstein, M. L. (2025e, October 22). *Twenty-seventh report of the independent monitor: Compliance snapshot of NYPD's stop, frisk, and search practices.* NYPD Monitor. https://www.nypdmonitor.org/wp-content/uploads/2025/11/2025.11.19-971-1-Exhibit-1-Monitors-Twenty-Seventh-Report-Corrected.pdf

Denerstein, M. L. (2026a, January 20). *Twenty-eighth report of the independent monitor: Compliance snapshot of NYPD's stop, frisk, and search practices.* NYPD Monitor. https://www.nypdmonitor.org/wp-content/uploads/2026/02/2026.01.20-974-Monitors-Twenty-Eighth-Report.pdf

Denerstein, M. L. (2026b, February 26). *Twenty-ninth report of the independent monitor: Compliance snapshot of NYPD's stop, frisk, and search practices.* NYPD Monitor. https://www.nypdmonitor.org/wp-content/uploads/2026/02/2026.02.26-979-Monitors-Twenty-Ninth-Report.pdf

Eterno, J. A. (2003). *Policing within the law: A case study of the New York City Police Department* (1st ed.). Praeger.

Eterno, J. A., Barrow, C. S., & Silverman, E. B. (2017). Forcible stops: Police and citizens speak out. *Public Administration Review*, *77*(2), 181–192. https://doi.org/10.1111/puar.12637

Eterno, J. A., Verma, A., & Silverman, E. B. (2016). Police manipulations of crime reporting: Insiders' revelations. *Justice Quarterly*, *33*(5), 811–835. https://doi.org/10.1080/07418825.2014.980838

Floyd v. City of New York, 959 F.Supp.2d 540 (2013)

Frontline. (2001, May 15). LAPD blues [Television series episode]. PBS. https://www.pbs.org/wgbh/pages/frontline/shows/lapd/

Halle, D., Beveridge, A., & Beveridge, S. (2013, December 24). *Bill Bratton on both coasts: New York and Los Angeles: The uncertain future.* Oxford University Press Blog. https://blog.oup.com/2013/12/new-york-los-angeles-police-departments/

Hong, N. (2025, February 10). If Adams is cleared, other inquiries in his orbit would face uncertainty. *The New York Times.* https://www.nytimes.com/2025/02/10/nyregion/nyc-city-hall-investigations-future.html

Jerome, R. (2021, December 14). *Fifteenth report of the independent monitor: Analysis of New York City Police Department (NYPD) trespass enforcement activity in and around New York City Housing Authority (NYCHA) buildings: Trends and patterns in racial disparities and numbers of NYPD trespass arrests, trespass summonses, and trespass stops, 2013–2019.* NYPD Monitor. https://www.nypdmonitor.org/wp-content/uploads/2022/09/15-Fifteenth-Report.pdf

Khurshid, S., & Max, B. (2020, December 8). Dermot Shea's rocky first year as NYPD commissioner. *Gotham Gazette.* https://www.gothamgazette.com/city/9952-dermot-shea-rocky-first-year-nypd-commissioner-de-blasio

Klinger, D. A. (1996). More on demeanor and arrest in Dade County. *Criminology*, *34*(1), 61–82. https://doi.org/10.1111/j.1745-9125.1996.tb01196.x

Knapp Commission. (1972). *The Knapp Commission report on police corruption.* George Braziller.

Lloyd, J. (2009, August 5). *Bratton: It is the right time.* NBC News. https://www.nbclosangeles.com/news/local/bratton-to-step-down-report/1844338/

Larkin, P. J. (2014, March 24). Reviewing the rationale for stop-and-frisk. *The Heritage Foundation.*

Los Angeles Police Protective League. (2009). *Bratton says LAPD is improved, wants consent decree lifted.* https://lapd.com/article/bratton-says-lapd-improved-wants-consent-decree-lifted

Lundman, R. J. (1994). Demeanor or crime? The Midwest city police-citizen encounters study. *Criminology*, *32*(4), 631–656. https://doi.org/10.1111/j.1745-9125.1994.tb01166.x

Luzer, D. (2013, December 9). William Bratton is the right man for the job. Really. *Governing*. https://www.governing.com/archive/gov-william-bratton-nypd-police-chief.html

Marcelo, P. (2025, February 11). *What to know about the Trump administration moving to drop corruption charges against NYC mayor*. AP News. https://apnews.com/article/nyc-mayor-eric-adams-corruption-dropped-trump-93c95b8d1aba9a7adc6ee01a7674442e

McCarthy, C. (2019, November 19). O'Neill defends stop and frisk after Bloomberg apology. *New York Post*. https://nypost.com/2019/11/19/oneill-defends-stop-and-frisk-after-bloomberg-apology/

McCarthy, C., & Marsh, J. (2023, June 13). NYPD head Keechant Sewell was pushed to "breaking point" by City Hall, including NYC Mayor Eric Adams: sources. *New York Post*. https://nypost.com/2023/06/13/nypd-head-keechant-sewell-was-pushed-to-breaking-point-by-city-hall-including-nyc-mayor-eric-adams-sources/

Mena, K. (2024, October 11). *Adams continues to deny reports Tom Donlon is resigning*. NY1. https://ny1.com/nyc/all-boroughs/politics/2024/10/11/mayor-adams-tom-donlon-not-resigning-ny1.com

Mummolo, J. (2018). Modern police tactics, police-citizen interactions, and the prospects for reform. *The Journal of Politics*, *80*(1), 1–15. https://doi.org/10.1086/694393

New York City Police Department. (2025). *Police Department historical statistics*. https://www.nyc.gov/assets/nypd/downloads/pdf/crime_statistics/cs-en-us-city.pdf

New York Civil Liberties Union. (2025). *Stop and frisk data*. https://www.nyclu.org/data/stop-and-frisk-data

New York State, Office of the Governor. (2017). *Raymond W. Kelly biography*. https://www.governor.ny.gov/sites/default/files/atoms/files/Raymond_Kelly_Bio_2017.pdf

New York State Office of the Attorney General. (1999). *The New York City Police Department's "stop & frisk" practices: A report to the people of the State of New York from the Office of the Attorney General*. New York State Office of the Attorney General. https://ur.ag.ny.gov/sites/default/files/reports/stp_frsk.pdf

Office of the New York City Comptroller. (2025, October 31). *Review of the New York City Police Department's body-worn camera program*. https://comptroller.nyc.gov/reports/review-of-the-new-york-city-police-departments-body-worn-camera-program/

Rice, C. (2013, December 11). Hail to the police chief: William J. Bratton's record bodes well for New York. *The New York Times*, p. A31. https://www.nytimes.com/2013/12/11/opinion/william-j-brattons-record-bodes-well-for-new-york.html

Richard French Live. (2013, January 16). *What would you do about guns? NY passes tough new gun laws* [Video]. YouTube. https://www.youtube.com/watch?v=IH-1vBUR8vY

Rivera, R., & Ba, B. (2019). *The effect of police oversight on crime and allegations of misconduct: Evidence from Chicago* [Unpublished working paper]. University of Pennsylvania Law School.

Roberts, S. (2021, November 10). Peter L. Zimroth, who oversaw stop-and-frisk, dies at 78. *The New York Times*. https://www.nytimes.com/2021/11/10/nyregion/peter-zimroth-dead.html

Russell, T. (Director). (2014). *The seven five* [Film]. All3Media America; Belfor Entertainment; Waltz International Pictures.

Schulz, D. M. (2023, June 13). Dignity and integrity: Commissioner Keechant Sewell's resignation is a loss for the NYPD and the city. *City Journal*. https://www.city-journal.org/article/keechant-sewells-dignity-and-integrity

Seigel, M. (2012). William Bratton in the other L.A. In J. M. Loyd, M. Mitchelson, & A. Burridge (Eds.), *Beyond walls and cages: Prisons, borders, and global crisis* (pp. 122–140). University of Georgia Press.

Smith, G. B. (2021, March 22). Misconduct complaints trailed NYPD Commissioner Shea and other police brass' rise to the top. *THE CITY*. https://www.thecity.nyc/2021/03/22/nypd-misconduct-complaints-trailed-shea-police-brass/

Smith, G. B. (2025, August 18). Banks brothers investigation Eric Adams. *THE CITY*. https://www.thecity.nyc/2025/08/18/banks-brothers-investigation-eric-adams/

Solomon, J., & Mosk, M. (2007, May 13). *Giuliani's road to private sector wealth.* NBC News. https://www.nbcnews.com/id/wbna18636813

Stebbins, S. (2024, January 25). *How New York's crime rate has changed since the 1990s.* 24/7 Wall Street. https://247wallst.com/special-report/2024/01/25/how-new-yorks-crime-rate-has-changed-since-the-1990s

Stop LAPD Spying Coalition. (2021). *Automating banishment: The surveillance and policing of looted land.* https://automatingbanishment.org/index.html

Streeter, R. (Producer). (2003, February 20). Top cop, William Bratton [Television series episode]. In J. Hewitt (Executive Producer), *60 Minutes.* CBS.

Umansky, E. (2024, September 11). NYPD tossed out hundreds of police misconduct discipline cases under Commissioner Edward Caban. *ProPublica.* https://www.propublica.org/article/nypd-tossed-out-police-misconduct-discipline-cases-edward-caban

United States v. City of Los Angeles, Consent Decree (C.D. Cal. 2001). https://library.csun.edu/virtual-exhibit/LAFR/documents/Part3_Training_1.pdf

Worden, R. E., & Shepard, R. L. (1996). Demeanor, crime, and police behavior: A reexamination of the police services study data. *Criminology, 34*(1), 83–105. https://doi.org/10.1111/j.1745-9125.1996.tb01197.x

Young, R. (n.d.). *Rafael Perez: In the eye of the storm.* PBS Frontline. https://www.pbs.org/wgbh/pages/frontline/shows/lapd/scandal/eyeofstorm.html

Zimroth, P. L. (2015, July 9). *First report of the independent monitor.* NYPD Monitor. https://www.nypdmonitor.org/wp-content/uploads/2022/09/01-MonitorsFirstReport-AsFiledInFloydDocket.pdf

Zimroth, P. L. (2016a, February 16). *Second report of the independent monitor.* NYPD Monitor. https://www.nypdmonitor.org/wp-content/uploads/2022/09/02-2016-02-16FloydvCityofNY-MonitorsSecondStatusReport.pdf

Zimroth, P. L. (2016b, August 9). *Third report of the independent monitor: Interim briefing on body-worn camera pilot program.* NYPD Monitor. https://www.nypdmonitor.org/wp-content/uploads/2022/09/03-2016-08-09MonitorsLtrtoJudgeTorresencl3rdReportInterim-Brief.pdf

Zimroth, P. L. (2016c, November 18). *Fourth report of the independent monitor.* NYPD Monitor. https://www.nypdmonitor.org/wp-content/uploads/2022/09/04-2016-11-18FourthReportoftheIndependentMonitor-1.pdf

Zimroth, P. L. (2017a, May 30). *Fifth report of the independent monitor: Analysis of NYPD stops reported, 2013–2015.* NYPD Monitor. https://www.nypdmonitor.org/wp-content/uploads/2022/09/05-2017-05-30-MonitorsFifthReport-AnalysisofNYPDStopsReported2013-2015-Asfiled.pdf

Zimroth, P. L. (2017b, June 29). *Sixth report of the independent monitor: The NYPD's body-worn camera pilot: Research and evaluation plan.* NYPD Monitor. https://www.nypdmonitor.org/wp-content/uploads/2022/09/06-2017-06-29-MonitorsSixthReport.pdf

Zimroth, P. L. (2017c, December 13). *Seventh report of the independent monitor.* NYPD Monitor. https://www.nypdmonitor.org/wp-content/uploads/2022/09/07-2017-12-13-FloydLigonDavis-Monitor-Seventh-Report_EAST_80301353_1.pdf

Zimroth, P. L. (2018, July 27). *Eighth report of the independent monitor: Evaluation of NYPD body-worn camera implementation in NYCHA housing developments.* NYPD Monitor. https://www.nypdmonitor.org/wp-content/uploads/2022/09/08-2018-07-27-Monitors-Eighth-Report-Evaluation-of-NYPD-BWC-Implementation-in-NYCHA-Housing-Developments.pdf

Zimroth, P. L. (2019, January 11). *Ninth report of the independent monitor.* NYPD Monitor. https://www.nypdmonitor.org/wp-content/uploads/2022/09/09-2019-01-11-Combined-Ninth-Report-4.pdf

Zimroth, P. L. (2020a, January 7). *Tenth report of the independent monitor.* NYPD Monitor. https://www.nypdmonitor.org/wp-content/uploads/2022/09/10-Monitors-Corrected-Tenth-Report.pdf

Zimroth, P. L. (2020b, October 28). *Eleventh report of the independent monitor*. NYPD Monitor. https://www.nypdmonitor.org/wp-content/uploads/2022/09/11th-Report-Submission-2.pdf

Zimroth, P. L. (2020c, November 30). *Twelfth report of the independent monitor: The deployment of body-worn cameras on New York City Police Department (NYPD) officers*. NYPD Monitor. https://www.nypdmonitor.org/wp-content/uploads/2022/09/12th-Report.pdf

Zimroth, P. L. (2021a, September 1). *Thirteenth report of the independent monitor: Racial disparities in NYPD stop, question, and frisk practices: An analysis of 2013 to 2019 stop reports*. NYPD Monitor. https://www.nypdmonitor.org/wp-content/uploads/2023/09/13th-Report-and-Submission-Letter.pdf

Zimroth, P. L. (2021b, October 12). *Fourteenth report of the independent monitor: NYPD social distancing enforcement, 2020*. NYPD Monitor. https://www.nypdmonitor.org/wp-content/uploads/2022/09/14-Fourteenth-Report.as-filed.pdf

7

WORLDWIDE INFLUENCE OF THE NYPD

An International Movement Against Police

Introduction

New York City (NYC) is a cornucopia of diversity. With 8.4 million people from numerous backgrounds, nearly everyone is represented. In terms of race, NYC is 36 percent White, 23 percent Black, 16 percent other, 15 percent Asian, and 10 percent two or more races (World Population Review, 2025). The population of the city is trending down about.77 percent annually and is down 3.755 percent since the last census in 2020. The poverty rate in the city is 17.6 percent (World Population Review, 2025). Approximately 37 percent of the population is foreign born (New York City, Department of Planning, 2025).

Nearly every type of situation can be observed somewhere in the large metropolis. The police department is the largest metropolitan police agency in the world. The breadth and scope of the agency's reach should never be underestimated. Due to their excellent training and experiences, its former managers, supervisors, and officers of every rank and specialty can be found throughout the United States and even the world. Police departments in Philadelphia, Los Angeles, Chicago, Baltimore, New Orleans, and Newark, just to name a few, were commanded by previous New York City Police Department (NYPD) high-ranking officials. They bring with them a vast array of talents but also spread the NYPD way of doing police work. The NYPD also, with funding from the federal government, hosted meetings that countless national and international police leaders visited to learn NYPD methods—especially, but not exclusively, CompStat (Silverman, 1999; Eterno & Silverman, 2012).

In previous chapters, we see an outline of what has occurred at the NYPD and in New York City. Generally, we see community policing in the 1980s and early 1990s. Then, in the mid-1990s, the beginning stages of aggressive policing. In the early 2000s, this style drastically increases with its peak just before the *Floyd* verdict in 2013. After this, we see a tempered aggressiveness and even some reduction in standards, including physical and educational qualifications to get on the NYPD. With the NYPD diaspora of leaders, as well as its forceful methods, there appears to be a corresponding backlash by the public against police. The pattern of the aggressive NYPD broken windows policing seems, at least in part, to be responsible for the establishment of movements against police. Crime control has become

DOI: 10.4324/9781003593256-7

the mantra of this aggressiveness. As with the forcefulness of the NYPD, similar claims are made about the need for extremely aggressive tactics to protect the public. Furthermore, the primacy of the crime control philosophy has also been used to expand, in more recent years, the use of the military. Their use in contemporary policing has been, to some extent, normalized. In general, troops were rarely used. We have seen them after 9/11, during the civil rights movement, and at some other assorted events. Describing some of these events and their history is important. Today, the use of the military has become more routine. To that end, this chapter will give an overview of these events that are extremely critical of police for their actions or inactions.

Black Lives Matter

Black Lives Matter (BLM) began in 2013. This is the exact time the *Floyd* case was decided, and at the peak of aggressive policing. The organization advises that their existence commenced with the shooting of Trayvon Martin (a Black youth) by a former neighborhood watch captain, George Zimmerman. This movement was clearly a backlash to forceful crime-control policies. While Zimmerman claimed self-defense and was acquitted, the event is still seen as a focal point of racial animosity (CNN, 2013). They cite their own mission as "Black Lives Matter is working inside and outside of the system to heal the past, reimagine the present, and invest in the future of Black lives through policy change, investment in our communities, and a commitment to arts and culture" (Black Lives Matter, n.d.).

There were numerous other incidents that inspired the BLM to increase its presence and make it resilient and popular. The two most notable involve Eric Garner and George Floyd (Black Lives Matter, n.d.).

Eric Garner

Although discussed earlier in this book, it is important to further explain the chokehold death of Mr. Eric Garner in New York City, since he was a flashpoint of the beginning of BLM. Mr. Garner was subjected to a chokehold by Officer Daniel Pantaleo while resisting arrest. Mr. Garner was committing a very minor violation by selling "loosie cigarettes" on the streets (i.e., opening a pack and selling one at a time; selling untaxed cigarettes). Although a very minor violation, the officers were working under what is known as a "precinct condition." That is, it was flagged as an important issue by higher-ups. During the arrest, Mr. Garner stated, "I can't breathe," audibly 11 times. The officers waited for backup before arresting Mr. Garner. Once backup officers arrived, they immediately pounced without giving another warning. Additionally, after making the arrest, there was no obvious attempt to assist Mr. Garner. The medical examiner found blood in four layers of skin in Mr. Garner's neck. While the law of New York State permitted chokeholds by police officers at that time, the NYPD policy was very clear in prohibiting chokeholds or any pressure about the neck. Ultimately, the officer was not charged by either the Staten Island District Attorney or the United States Attorney for the Southern District of New York. However, Officer Pantaleo was given a department trial and fired for not following police policy (Eterno & Verma, 2024). Most other officers did not face penalties other than their initial punishments of suspension and desk duty (Durkin, 2019). However, the sergeant on the scene was hit with a penalty of 20 days' vacation (Kashiwagi, 2019).

George Floyd

In an incident with the Minneapolis Police Department, police officer Derek Chauvin murdered Mr. George Floyd. The circumstances of this case are horrible.

Mr. Floyd was approached by Officer Chauvin and two other officers, whom he was training, as they responded to a radio call of using a counterfeit $20 bill. They arrive at the scene, investigate, and decide to place Mr. Floyd under arrest. They find Mr. Floyd nearby in a car. Then, one of the officers pulls his gun because Mr. Floyd is not completely obeying verbal commands such as putting his hands on his head (Slisco, 2020). After, Mr. Floyd is arrested. There was a bit of a struggle in arresting Mr. Floyd as he was reluctant to get out of the car he was sitting in when initially approached by the officers. He is then taken to a police car that he refuses to get into. This is because he apparently felt claustrophobic. At that point, Mr. Floyd found himself in the car, but he was placed face down, causing him to resist. He manages to get out and purposely falls to the ground. Officer Chauvin then placed his knee on the neck of the suspect. Mr. Floyd continues to announce audibly that he cannot breathe. He is heard calling for his mother. Over the span of a few minutes, Mr. Floyd goes silent. Passersby are heard complaining to the officers to stop using force. The officers do not comply. Eventually an ambulance arrives, and Mr. Floyd is placed on a gurney. Mr. Chauvin is placed into the ambulance and brought to a local hospital (YouTube, 2021). Mr. Floyd stopped moving at approximately 8.24 p.m. He is declared dead about an hour later at the hospital after numerous attempts to revive him (Linder, n.d.).

Officer Chauvin has a trial and is found guilty of third-degree murder and second-degree manslaughter. He is sentenced to 22½ years in prison. He pled guilty to federal civil rights charges and was sentenced to 20 years. He is currently serving the federal charges as they take precedence over the state charges. There were three other officers on the scene. Two of them were rookies. All three were jointly convicted of civil rights violations in federal court. The most culpable had the most experience. Tou Thao received 3½ years for second-degree manslaughter in state court and was convicted on federal civil rights violations. He served the time concurrently. He was recently released. One of the rookie officers got 36 months for failing to give medical aid, and the other received 30 months for the same offense (U.S. Department of Justice, Office of Public Affairs, 2022; WCCO Staff, 2025).

Other Aspects of BLM

There are numerous other incidents involving Blacks and police. Some of these include Daunte Wright, Tyre Nichols, Breonna Taylor, Sonya Massey, Michael Brown, Jr., Jacob Blake, Freddie Gray, Jr., and many others. Regardless of the merits of these cases, they have become rallying events that catalyzed BLM. Another organization, related to BLM, tallies police violence events. This organization is called Mapping Police Violence. The details of each of the above events are available to the reader on their website (Mapping Police Violence, 2025). Among the many statistics this organization supplies, the following are pertinent to this discussion. First, 95 percent of major city police kill Blacks at higher rates than Whites. However, it should be noted that Blacks do commit more crimes than Whites. This has been a staple of the NYPD argument; namely, that stopping Blacks more than Whites may be due to their committing more crimes (*Floyd v. City of New York*, 2013). Second, three of these killings started with an alleged violent crime. Third, between 2016 and 2024, police killings increased in Red (Republican) states and reduced in Blue (Democratic) states (increase in Red states: 2016, 3.8 per million versus 2024, 4.7 per million; reduction in Blue states: 2016, 3.0 per million versus 2024, 2.7 per million) (Mapping Police Violence, 2025). It should be noted here as well that these numbers are exceedingly small and likely not statistically significant. Nevertheless, the organization does find this to be a key point. Another important statistic cited by the organization is that Blacks involved in these incidents are more likely to be unarmed (Blacks are 1.3 times as likely to be unarmed as Whites) (Mapping Police Violence, 2025). While one can question the interpretation of these data, those who follow BLM would argue that these are exceedingly vital facts.

Importantly, there are six pillars of BLM: policy, arts, healing justice, front-line organizing, research and education, and culture. They are critical to understanding the organization. When BLM speaks of policy, they are talking about the basic staples of life for Blacks, such as clean water, housing, education, food, and the like. With respect to the Arts, the movement means preserving Art with respect to Black liberation and activity. The next pillar, healing justice, means supporting Black communities that are impacted by discrimination. The fourth pillar is frontline organizing, which means working with organizations to focus on ending discrimination and building a strong Black culture. The fifth pillar is research and education. Under this pillar, building curricula on Black identity and ending racism are paramount. The last pillar is culture, which means helping the Black community thrive (Black Lives Matter, n.d.).

Defund the Police

Contemporaneously with the BLM movement, a defund the police groundswell was occurring. One of the key themes of defunding the police is the use of social workers to respond to emergency calls of overdosing or similar. In Durham, North Carolina, the government attempted to put into practice such ideas.

> In 2022, Durham created unarmed emergency response teams called Holistic Empathetic Assistance Response Teams (HEART). Rather than following traditional procedures of sending police officers to deal with nonviolent situations, this program: embeds mental health clinicians in Durham's 911 center; dispatches unarmed three-person teams to nonviolent calls for service; follow[s] up with those in crisis after the response to help them connect with proper service providers; pairs mental health clinicians with police officers in calls with higher safety concerns.
>
> *(Mollenkamp, 2025)*

Based on their statistics, the program was successful. For example, community response teams and co-response teams resolved 56.81 percent and 57.06 percent of their calls, respectively, with less than 3 percent of calls being redirected to the police (Mollenkamp, 2025).

While this appears to work well in Durham for very innocuous calls, New York City did not have a similar experience. In 2023, I interviewed NYPD Chief of Interagency Operations, Theresa Tobin (Eterno, 2023). She advised, "I really wish they had not used the words, 'Defund the police.' Better is 'reallocating' because what really happened was not taking away a billion dollars, but it was actually reallocated" (Eterno, 2023, p. 29). The NYPD gave money to numerous agencies to respond as experts, such as the Department of Homeless Services and the Department of Health and Mental Hygiene. Unfortunately, in

New York City, such reallocation was not nearly as successful. As Chief Tobin stated, "People don't want to do the job without some police presence" (Eterno, 2023, p. 29).

In sum, it appears that these movements are more complicated than simply defunding. Indeed, defunding is a misnomer. These are complicated social issues that generally do not have simple answers. Police are generally called in when all else fails. Overall, simply taking money from the police to solve problems can lead to additional problems unless properly implemented. Some cities, like Durham, may have a positive experience without police in very innocuous calls. However, in New York City, the experience was less successful. In the end, there needs to be serious consideration of the roles of each agency. The safety of all parties needs to be a top priority. Removing the police, especially from more dangerous situations, did not even occur in Durham. Some police presence would seem obvious, such that defunding is way too simplistic and dangerous. Excellent training, recruitment, use and purchase of non-lethal devices, appropriate pay for professional officers, collecting and analyzing data, developing plans, rules, regulations, and much more costs money. Simply defunding will have serious consequences. Thoughtful changes based on experience and research require time, effort, and money. Overly simplistic solutions can be more ineffective, if not outright harmful.

Cities in Peril

In 2020, the dissatisfaction with the police was at its zenith. Riots occurred in 140 United States cities. Many were peaceful, but in some the police essentially lost control. Insurance estimates for damage during this period range from $1 billion to $2 billion, making these the most expensive violent demonstrations in recent history (Kingson, 2020). Below is an overview of the loss of control in three cities in the United States: Minneapolis, Minnesota; Seattle, Washington; and Kenosha, Wisconsin.

Minneapolis

After the death of George Floyd (discussed earlier) on May 28, 2020, people in Minneapolis took to the streets. This quickly escalated to the point where the 3rd Precinct on Minnehaha Avenue was rushed. Officers soon abandoned the precinct as hundreds of people stormed the area. People broke through the windows and started fires. They also broke into police cars where weapons were stored. At that point, police were authorized to use rubber bullets and tear gas (Fung, 2020). Eventually, the police took their police cars and fled the scene, leaving the precinct to the mob. As the police left, the mob set off fireworks and threw materials at the fleeing officers. Local stores in the area were also ransacked. The National Guard was called out, but order was not fully restored for days (Bakst, 2020). In total, at least two people were killed, 604 were arrested, $500 million in property damage resulted, 1,500 property locations were destroyed, and 164 structure fires occurred due to arson (FOX 9, 2020; St. Anthony, 2021). It should also be noted that five years later, the precinct remains uninhabited and boarded up. A new area for the police is scheduled to open soon (Blume, 2025).

Seattle

Similar protests over the murder of George Floyd by police occurred in other cities. In Seattle, the riots began in earnest on May 26. From the 29th to the 31st, "protests over Floyd's killing begin in Seattle and continue throughout the weekend. Concentrated in downtown, the protests result in broken windows, car fires, dozens of arrests, a citywide 5 p.m. curfew, and a statewide activation of the national guard" (Takahama, 2020). The police used similar tactics, such as tear gas. Eventually, an area of the city is taken over by protesters. The area is known as Capitol Hill Occupied Protest (CHOP), also called Capitol Hill Autonomous Zone. This essentially begins on June 12, 2020. For approximately a month, the police have not been in charge of the area, which appears self-governed by the protesters. The police precinct was taken over for a time. Some orders were restored in early July. There were also fires and other issues in the area throughout the time period. Overall, 261 arrests were made, but only about half were prosecuted. Shattered windows, fire damage, looting, and graffiti were common during this time (Markovich, 2020). In the end, Seattle settled with those who claimed injuries for $10 million (Radil, 2024) and those who claimed property damage for $3.6 million (Spiegelman, 2023).

Kenosha

Around the same time as the George Floyd riots, on August 23, 2020, police in Kenosha, Wisconsin, shot and seriously injured Jacob Blake. He was shot in the back while trying to enter his car with three of his children in the back seat (Biscontini, 2023). It was alleged that Mr. Blake had a knife and that police did attempt to use their taser first (Good Morning America, 2021). The police were there on a domestic call, where it was alleged that the victim was violating a restraining order. He was left partially paralyzed (Biscontini, 2023). A video of the shooting circulated widely on the internet (Good Morning America, 2021). As a result, riots occurred, leading to significant property damage and violence (McAdams, 2020). A secondary incident occurred involving Kyle Rittenhouse who shoots and kills two individuals and injures another. Rittenhouse is armed with an AR 15 to protect himself from the rioters. One of the individuals who was killed, Joseph Rosenbaum, was trying to wrestle Rittenhouse's rifle from him. After the shooting, he runs to the police. Others in the crowd begin to chase him, including Anthony Huber and Gaige Gross Kreutz. Huber struck Rittenhouse with a skateboard. Gross Kreutz admits to aiming a pistol at Rittenhouse. Rittenhouse shoots both and is acquitted of all charges (Sullivan, 2021). This incident goes viral on the internet and spurs on additional violent protests in Kenosha (NBC Chicago, 2020).

Thus, on the evening of August 23, protests against what occurred with Mr. Blake begin. The typical clash with officers in riot gear takes place as well as property damage in the area. Tensions continue to grow as government officials try to ease the situation. The National Guard is called out at this time. A curfew on the 24th is issued for 8 p.m. and expires at 7 a.m. Near the courthouse, protesters continued after the curfew. Protests then spread throughout the country. It becomes clear that the initial incident where Mr. Blake is shot will lead to significant bodily harm. Curfews continue as do the number of National Guard troops involved. Tensions continue to rise despite the attempt by authorities to defuse the situation. Some protests continue through August 27 (NBC Chicago, 2020). In the end, at least three people were shot by Rittenhouse and two die without prosecution. Property damage due to this unrest was estimated to be up to $50 million by Kenosha Area Business Alliance (McAdams, 2020). The initial police officers who responded to the domestic call were never prosecuted due to insufficient evidence (Lozano & The Associated Press, 2021).

During 2020, after George Floyd was murdered, such protests were commonplace. This can be attributed, in part, to aggressive police tactics. The Floyd murder was simply the catalyst for the events. Tension was building, especially in minority communities, well before this. Police and minority community relationships have had a well-known problematic relationship.

Issues of Militarization, Military, and Police

The police in the United States are generally armed with guns and various other weapons. They have a paramilitary structure and obey orders. However, generally speaking, they are trained in law enforcement, service, and similar duties. Their training is generally for six months in a Police Academy setting followed by a varied period of field training. Typically, in the United States, policing is controlled by state authorities. To that end, all states have peace officer's standards, and training (POST). Thus, states control the minimum standards of police.

With respect to the training, officers learn to follow and obey the law and the Constitution. Prospective officers generally go through a battery of tests before they are hired. These include character background, psychological, physical, and medical tests. Academy training will include studies on law, police science, social science, physical and self-defense. Officers are also taught how and when to shoot and drive safely. Officers are specifically trained for the rigors of law enforcement in a democratic society.

The military, on the other hand, are trained for the rigors of war. Although there may be components of dealing with civilians, they are generally not prepared for police work. While some specific units such as military police have more training in this area, their training is not generally focused on policing in the streets of the United States. This is one of the reasons for the posse comitatus act (formally known as Use of Army, Navy, Marine Corps, Air Force, and Space Force as Posse Comitatus, 2021). The key portion of the Posse Comitatus Act reads:

> Whoever, except in cases and under circumstances expressly authorized by the Constitution or Act of Congress, willfully uses any part of the Army, the Navy, the Marine Corps, the Air Force, or the Space Force as a posse comitatus or otherwise to execute the laws shall be fined under this title or imprisoned not more than two years, or both.
>
> *(Use of Army, Navy, Marine Corps, Air Force, and Space Force as Posse Comitatus, 2021)*

There are exceptions to this Act, which can also be used to enforce federal law when state authorities are unable or unwilling to do so (Elsea, 2018). First, the Insurrection Act, which allows the President of the United States to deploy troops domestically to suppress an insurrection, rebellion, or other forms of violence within the United States. Second, there is an emergency exception. The federal military can also be used in civil disturbances, disasters, calamities, and so forth (Elsea, 2018).

Militarization of Police

In the United States there have been some efforts at advancing some of the military training and hardware for use within the states. There is, of course, some need for these materials and training. For example, Special Weapons and Tactics (SWAT), bomb disposal, protection from terrorist type attacks, active shooters, and other associated events. However, it seems to have become a focus in recent years. This trend appears after the community policing era. In the mid-1990s there is an ethos change from "service and the beat cop to crime and commanding officers" (Eterno, 2003; Eterno & Silverman, 2012). Police work generally involves collaborating with communities, traffic control, and so forth. Nevertheless, this movement has been well documented.

The trend toward the use of special units such as SWAT PPUs (police paramilitary units) has grown exponentially (Campbell & Campbell, 2010; Kraska & Kappeler, 1997). Some argue that problem-solving policing is a more significant trend. Regardless, the trend with police missions and leaders in recent times is essentially focused on crime control: "The expanding use of these PPUs in mainstream police work is a major alteration in crime-fighting orientation and arguable represents 'revolution' in policing" (Campbell & Campbell, 2010, p. 329). Thus, the essence of the beat cop working with communities seems an anachronism.

One important concept often forgotten with the crime control ethos is that police working with communities could be a staple of crime control as well. As officers develop relationships with communities, they are more likely to garner intelligence to weed out crime. William Bratton stands out as an advocate of this strategy in New York during the de Blasio administration. This method of policing could better lead to the police being seen as legitimate by all communities. However, what was set in motion under the previous administration during the peak of stop and frisk, extremely aggressive stop behavior by officers, had momentum that continues to this day. The backlash against police as seen in this chapter should not be underestimated. In New York City in November 2025, for example, the citizenry elected a far-left mayor (Zohran Mamdani) who, based on his rhetoric, may weaken the NYPD as an institution.

Nevertheless, the overly aggressive militarization of the police can be problematic. It can alienate communities, especially minorities, and lead to police being seen as enemies of the public (Eterno & Silverman, 2012). Even the police who find such aggressiveness ineffective will still accept the use of the tactics:

> These commanders noted that the community often objects to these show-of-force initiatives and finds them offensive. Nonetheless, even commanders who recognize that these role activities are problematic reluctantly endorse the behaviors they question, observing that the PPU is an elite unit with members who simply want to be distinguishable.
>
> *(Campbell & Campbell, 2010, p. 335)*

The police acting in a militaristic manner can become an ethos within the agency. The police culture often stresses the danger of the work environment (Drummond, 1976; Crank, 2014). In an article that examines police and military convergence, the authors suggest that culture change will take place in both organizations. For example, Campbell and Campbell (2010, p. 346) write, "These changes portend a substantial alteration in the organizational cultures of both professions, as each profession adjusts to new orientations, new norms, and new values surrounding its core purpose." As such, the aggressive crime-control strategies help create an "us versus them" philosophy. That is, police versus outsiders. This, in turn, will damage the legitimacy of police. This means that the law-abiding public will be less likely to turn to the police with information and perhaps even for help. That is, people, in general, will try to limit their encounters with police. Additionally, police will limit their time on anything not associated with crime control. Thus, encounters with police will be decidedly negative. Ironically, this may actually reduce the effectiveness of crime control because the police will have limited contact and get minimal intelligence.

ICE/Use of Troops

Just as concerning is that the role of the military is increasing in domestic affairs. We have seen this with immigration, civil unrest, and crime control. Again, some of this may be necessary, such as after 9/11; however, such expanded use is genuinely concerning. As Campbell and Campbell (2010, p. 331) write, "This evolution has also been evidenced by the increasing use of the military to address domestic issues, such as internal disaster relief or involvement in immigration control and the war on drugs."

The use of troops to defend operations by immigration within the United States is one area of controversy. If the troops are used to help enforce federal law, it is likely completely legal. However, such use of troops has proven very unpopular, especially in very Democratic-run cities. While there has been exaggeration and hyperbole by the media, this does not take away the concern. Under the more recent Trump administration, for example, two-thirds of aliens deported have criminal histories (Arthur, 2025). Removing criminal aliens is what Mr. Trump said he would do during the election. This, in fact, is generally acceptable to the people. However, more controversial is the use of troops. Some argue that the use of troops to protect ICE agents in doing their jobs is illegal. Nunn (2025), in one of its papers, focuses on a lower federal court ruling, which argues that the use of troops in Los Angeles violates the Posse Comitatus Act. However, on appeal it is likely that the courts will overturn this decision, assuming that troops are assisting in enforcing federal law.

A more recent local court decision on the use of police in city streets occurred on November 20, 2025. Judge Jia Cobb, appointed by former President Biden, issued a ruling that seems to be a more reasonable opinion. This case occurred in Washington D.C., where troops were deployed on the premise of fighting crime. The Administration's rationale for the use of troops on domestic soil seems less based on an exception to the Posse Comitatus Act, which was discussed earlier in this chapter. "The Court finds that the district's exercise of sovereign powers within its jurisdiction is irreparably harmed by defendants' actions in deploying the Guards," wrote Cobb (Kim, 2025). In another case, a federal judge in Los Angeles also found that the Trump Administration went too far in sending the National Guard to Los Angeles because there was no rebellion. The Los Angeles case may be weaker since the troops arguably were deployed to help ICE enforce federal immigration law. In the Washington D.C. case, conversely, the troops were deployed on the reasoning of reducing crime—a weaker argument for troops to be deployed domestically.

As we have seen, ultimately, the use of troops is permitted under certain circumstances. However, if crime control is the only reason for deployment, this seems to be a very weak rationale. Crime is always occurring, and local authorities should handle that. This is, of course, unless they are completely overwhelmed and perhaps also asking for help. With respect to ICE, deployment of federal troops may be on more solid ground, assuming the rationale is to enforce federal immigration law. President Trump claims that he needs the troops, especially in Democratic cities. The Administration argues that, "his use of the troops is necessary to quell violence ... crack down on crime and *support his deportation initiatives*" (Epstein, 2025; emphasis added). Based on my previous discussion, once again, the troops helping to enforce federal immigration law seems to be a more reasoned argument. Thus, the crime-control argument seems weak and may not withstand judicial scrutiny without more extensive supporting evidence.

It seems logical that protecting ICE agents, protecting federal property, and helping enforce federal law are more solid grounds for using troops. However, some experts argue that the aforementioned reasons, as well as the crime control rationale, are weak.

> Trump has deployed the National Guard in five Democratic-led cities so far—often over the objections of state and local leaders—claiming troops are needed to control crime and lawlessness, although data show that violent crime in many of those places has decreased in recent years .... But legal experts say there's a clear connection developing between Trump's use of the troops and his immigration enforcement tactics. "We see these as deeply intertwined," says Benjamin Farley, special counsel at the National Immigration Law Center, which advocates for immigrant rights. "The Trump administration is using an increasingly aggressive, increasingly brutal approach to immigration enforcement, which, unsurprisingly, inspires protests. And then the protests themselves serve as a pretext or an excuse for the Trump administration to deploy the National Guard and the Armed Forces of the United States," he says.
>
> *(Lonsdorf & Martínez-Beltrán, 2025)*

In the United States these are deeply divisive issues. The backlash to aggressive crime-control policies is unmistakable. Police stop practices and the surrounding events have created a chasm between left and right. In democratic societies around the world, similar results are observed. The remaining part of this chapter will discuss police stop policies in other countries as well as issues related to them.

Other Democratic Countries

Recently, while I was in Brazil in the summer of 2025, at an international conference on policing in the Amazon, I had the opportunity to lecture and discuss with active officers' issues with respect to stop and frisk in New York City. One officer got up and asked me about *Floyd*. He then talked about how the case has been used by politicians in Brazil to weaken their powers to stop suspects. This is simply one example of the wide reach of NYPD.

Numerous other democratic countries have stop practices. Most have some similarities to United States police training and programs. For the remainder of this chapter, I will compare and contrast the practices of other countries with the United States.

England and Wales

The law on police stops in England and Wales is similar to that in the United States, and for New York State in particular. Person stops are based on reasonable suspicion that a crime has occurred, is occurring, or will occur. The officer must be able to articulate how he/she developed reasonable suspicion. A search may occur if the person is suspected of having a weapon or evidence on them. Reasonable force may be used, if necessary, to obtain these items (Lennon, Himanen, Marks, & Mouhanna, 2024). "Police stops in England and Wales primarily serve to allow an officer to allay or confirm the suspicion of wrongdoing and are justified for the investigation or detection of crime" (Lennon et al., 2024, p. 26). The type of offense can significantly broaden the authority of the officer. For example, for murder, officers have wider latitude than minor crimes. The police cannot compel people stopped to provide identity as part of the stop. Annually, there are approximately 800,000 stops in England and Wales (Lennon et al., 2024, p. 26). Officers can be held accountable for their actions with respect to stops. For example, the stop can be deemed inadmissible, officers can be liable for false imprisonment, and/or assault and battery.

Data are collected by agencies on stops. These data are critically important to holding officers accountable and determining patterns that help oversight authorities. For example, "Black people are nine times more likely to be stopped and searched by police than white people, official figures for England and Wales show" (Dodd, 2020). The authorities that oversee the police use these data to make sure that police are properly using their powers. For example, "HMICFRS [His Majesty's Inspectorate of Constabulary and Fire & Rescue Services] determined that, of the records it reviewed, 14% failed to provide reasonable suspicion, while an additional 22% provided weak grounds" (Lennon et al., 2024, p. 30).

Studies show that police stops are correlated with some issues with citizens. Youth that are stopped, for example, are more likely to have issues with education. Jackson, Testa, Semenza, Skinner, and Vaughn (2022, n.p.) write, "The findings indicate that being stopped by the police was related to diminished educational expectations among youth concerning the continuation of secondary and post-secondary education." Another study indicates that there is a weak correlation, at best, between crime decreases and police stops (Tiratelli, Quinton, & Bradford, 2018).

Finland

In Finland there is not an exact program emulating police stops, as outlined in New York, the United States, and England and Wales. However, there is some equivalent, albeit not exact. Police stops can include pedestrian stops, although they generally refer to car stops. With pedestrians there is no specific police practice of "stops" but a generalized police power "that all police officers have and [that] can be used in multiple contexts including criminal investigations" (Lennon et al., 2024, p. 31). The police can require someone to obtain a person's name, personal identity code, or, if this does not exist, date of birth and nationality, and information concerning a place where the person can be reached. If a person refuses to comply, the officer may establish identity or conduct a search (Lennon et al., 2024). When conducting their work in the field, officers usually use this power for investigation and prevention of crime, internal domestic control, and public order (Lennon et al., 2024). Police have additional powers with aliens and foreigners where they must show some identification. More intrusive types of encounters, such as search and frisk, are generally reserved for criminal activity. Finland does not have to post statistics with respect to police stops (Lennon et al., 2024). Because of this, oversight is exceedingly difficult, at best.

Due to the lack of data, there is not in-depth, peer-reviewed research like that in the United States and England and Wales. However, there are some studies on the topic of racial profiling and the police. Nordic research generally shows some evidence of racial profiling. For example, one study shows that police are singling out Roma people (Europe's largest minority group consisting of people who migrated to Europe from Northern India from the ninth century onward, also known as "Gypsies" [Hewitt & Vihan, 2025]) and non-Whites for stops. This research is based on interviews with officers (Schclarek-Mulinari & Keskinen, 2022).

Slovenia

The most pertinent aspects of the laws on police stops in Slovenia are contained in Articles 5, 40, 41, and 42 (G. Mesko, personal communication, November 21, 2025). Determining the identity of a person is one area of importance for police to stop people. Anyone who presents a danger, goes to a prohibited area, displays suspicious behavior, and so forth is subject to having their identity checked (Republic of Slovenia, 2013, Article 40). To determine the identity of these individuals, police of Slovenia may require a person to uncover his/her mask, interview the person, get assistance from others, use official records and documents, and, if necessary, officers may take the person to a police station and further investigate. Fingerprints, palm prints, DNA, and other methods of identification may be used (Republic of Slovenia, 2013, Articles 41 and 42). Because these laws are somewhat vague, officers in Slovenia, like in many countries, have a certain level of discretion with respect to police stops. While I was in Slovenia on a Fulbright scholarship in September 2025, I was invited to the Police Academy, and I learned how officers were trained on stops. The training, as it appeared to me, was very professional and equivalent to that of the police in the United States. Not only did I speak and learn from the key Academy instructor, but I also spoke with the Academy commanders. Their curriculum and training were some of the best I have seen—very professional and respectful of the public. Reviewing some select peer-reviewed studies on stops in Slovenia offers more insight.

Milenkov and Modic's (2024) survey, conducted in July 2021, asked Slovenian police and their superiors about their perspectives on stops. Results indicated that most felt that the attitude of the suspect influenced their own behaviors toward the accused. The respondents also strongly felt that, regardless of the manner of the suspect, they worked within legal parameters. There are several studies in the United States also suggesting that police are influenced by suspect demeanor. These studies, in some ways, contradict one another. Worden and Shepard (1996), as well as Lundman (1994), found that officers were likely to violate legal restrictions when suspects had negative behavioral attitudes with the police. Conversely, Klinger (1996) found that while suspect demeanor did influence officers, such demeanor did not overcome legal parameters. The latter study agrees with the findings of Milenkov and Modic (2024). However, it should be noted that five of the respondents in this study from an urban area indicated that they did focus attention on Roma and migrants, and that these groups were more suspicious than others. Seven respondents also indicated their additional focus on young people and foreigners (Milenkov & Modic, 2024).

A report issued by the non-governmental body European Network Against Racism (Tefera, 2010) does indicate some issues with discrimination in Slovenia. While not mentioning the police directly, the report does talk about the government. It points out that there is extraordinarily little data, official or otherwise, on bias in Slovenia. It must be noted that this report is not a peer-reviewed scientific article but a monitoring report from outside the government. It highlights publicly available information and concludes that there are serious issues in the country.

> This report is concerned about: Roma communities and settlement issues, the problem of erased people and their legal limbo, hate speech and freedom of speech, the political discourse of Muslim communities and Islam in the media, and third country nationals (TSN) in employment.
>
> *(Tefera, 2010, p. 9)*

However, since this is not an official report based on scientific methods, while concerning, it should be read with some skepticism.

France

France is similar to other countries regarding reasons for police stops, such as identity checks and searches with a flagrant offense. While these stops are talked about separately, they are not necessarily mutually exclusive. All stops must be made by authorized enforcement officers. Identity checks can only be done for a justifiable reason (Lilley, 2025). The purpose of the identity check is to stop or prevent an offense or root out suspects. These checks compel the person stopped to show an identity card, passport, driver's license, family record book, or social security card. Absent of this, a witness statement may be accepted or the person can be taken to the local police station, and a family member summoned to prove the person's identity (Lennon et al., 2024). Similarly, the purpose of stops for flagrant offense is to "prevent a breach of public order and, in particular, to ensure the safety of people or property" (Lennon et al., 2024, p. 37). The police in France are known for doing security checks as well. As the United States Department of State writes, "The French police and military often patrol public spaces. You should expect security inspections. This includes inspection of purses, bags, and backpacks at the entrance of large public places and businesses" (U.S. Department of State, 2025).

The French police, like many countries, uses its authority expansively. For example, "Despite some nominal controls on police stops, broad discretion is evident and the French police often play with the rules" (Lennon et al., 2024, p. 37). The French do not publish statistics on stop practices so it is difficult to oversee, especially for non-governmental groups. Police in France, like many countries, seem to target minorities. As stated by Lennon et al. (2024), "In 2021, a class action suit (still pending as of June 2023) was lodged against the French government by NGOs to stop ethnic profiling in police stops" (Open Society, 2021, as cited in Lennon et al., 2024, p. 38). Although there has been limited input by the courts in relation to searches at demonstrations, it seems that the public prosecutors knowingly permit the police to act outside the law because they think that fighting crime is more important than limiting police officers' power (Mouhanna, 2011, as cited in Lennon et al., 2024, p. 38).

India

In India, like most democracies, there are laws that govern police stops. One of the initial codes defining this is based on the Criminal Procedure Code (CrPC). This empowers the police to detain and search a person based on reasonable suspicion of committing a crime. This has more recently been updated by a new law called Bharatiya Nagarik Suraksha Sanhita (BNSS). While similar to the past law, there is now a new requirement for the police to record such stops via audio-visual technology. There are also countless local laws that influence these police behaviors. Also, the Supreme Court of India has prescribed specific guidelines on how police should behave at these encounters. Some of the issues the Court is examining are: the level of respect that officers must have for individual rights, when officers can request documentation, the requisite level of proof officers need to make a legal stop (reasonable suspicion), how stops must be done (non-arbitrary), among others (D. Suri, personal communication, December 3, 2025).

India is an exceptionally large country with various states and laws. Scholars and others have been critical of law enforcement. It is clear that the country is attempting to address issues such as discrimination, but based on literature it is a slow process with minimal success. Human Rights Watch (2007) did a report on how police act during stops. They found some alarming discriminatory behavior, especially toward lower castes. The report documented how lower castes are regularly subjected to police abuse, discriminatory forces, and even torture. As the report states, "police continue to detain, torture, and extort money … without fear of punishment" (Human Rights Watch, 2007). While it is a watchdog group reporting on India, this is not a scientific peer-reviewed article and could be subject to some hyperbole.

One peer-reviewed study that examines police accountability and custodial violence in India indicates clear issues with police misconduct. For example, the researchers cite Supreme Court writing, "in various judgements has conceded criticism against police torture and viciousness on prisoners, under-trials and accused persons" (Lamba & Jain, 2023, p. 1). They also advise that police misuse interrogation tactics. In another study on crime reporting in India, Verma and Arun (2023), in discussing the crime-reporting system, also indicate issues with the police. They point out, however, how the system is trying to change for the better. One example is using special areas where lower castes who have traditionally been denied human rights can at least have a hope of reporting crimes. Nevertheless, they report key problems: "However, the police officers commonly refuse to believe or accept certain types of complaints such as domestic violence or discrimination based upon caste" (Verma & Arun, 2023, p. 49). They also point out that a large number of laws against discrimination are being passed, but their impact is not fully understood yet.

Brazil

In Brazil, officers have similar powers to those of American officers. While not the same, the law is remarkably close to that of the United States. A noted South American scholar summarizes Brazilian law in this way:

> The Brazilian Supreme Court (STF) has reaffirmed that police stops must comply with objective criteria, and mere "suspicious behavior" or nervousness is not enough to justify a search. Recent rulings, such as in Agravo Regimental no RE 1.485.279 and HC 208.240, established that evidence obtained without probable cause can be annulled. Furthermore, the Court prohibited discriminatory practices based on race, gender, or physical appearance, ensuring that personal searches are grounded in concrete indications. This guidance reinforces fundamental rights such as freedom of movement and

> presumption of innocence. Another relevant point is the recognition of police intuition, accepted as a factor for stops, provided it is accompanied by objective criteria and technical training. The STF is also discussing the need to inform people of the right to remain silent at the moment of the stop, which may affect the validity of informal confessions.
>
> *(V. Riccio, personal communication, November 26, 2025)*

Thus, Brazilian law requires some objective reason to stop someone. While not the same as reasonable suspicion in the United States, it is clearly similar. Further, stops cannot be based solely on race, gender, or physical appearance. This is similar to racial profiling, which is also not allowed in the United States. Lastly, evidence improperly obtained is "annulled" in Brazil. This, too, is similar to the exclusionary rule in the United States. This is when courts do not allow the use of evidence attained illegally by police, such as evidence obtained as a result of frisking someone without reason during a stop (see Chapter 1).

Two peer-reviewed articles on stops in Brazil suggest some issues, especially racism and using too much force. One study was a survey of residents in São Paulo. "The distribution of police stops at gunpoint is not homogeneous across the city and is mainly concentrated in disadvantaged and racially diverse neighborhoods" (Oliveira, 2022, p. 102). However, the author also reports that a quarter of wealthy White residents indicated the police pointed their firearms during stops. Over half of the residents who reported stops stated that the firearm was used (Oliveira, 2022).

A second peer-reviewed article indicates similar issues. The study examines issues in Northeastern Brazil with young Blacks. It is a qualitative study in three cities: Salvador, Recife, and Fortaleza. A typical interaction between police and Black youth is cited:

> Even with a school uniform here, with a backpack on my back and a book in my hand, if the man (the police) crosses paths with me it's a sure thing: I know I am going to be stopped. I get frisked, my backpack is opened and they keep looking for shit inside, like drugs, weapons, or stolen stuff.
>
> *(Anunciação, Trad, & Ferreira, 2020, p. 6)*

The authors clearly state the issue: "Young blacks who are poor and inhabit favelas are a prime target for police control actions such as the stop-and-frisk" (Anunciação et al., 2020, p. 1). The authors go further, directly stating, "the police, like the rest of society, sees them [Black and poor] as prime suspects in the world of crime" (Anunciação et al., 2020, p. 8).

Taiwan

The Laws and Regulations Database of the Republic of China (Taiwan) and Police Power Exercise Act (PPEA) (2003a) discuss identity checks, which is similar to stops in the United States. There are four requirements to make a lawful stop. These include reasonable suspicion, police must identify themselves, police must state the legal reason for the stop, and police must also state the purpose for the stop (Laws & Regulations … PPEA Articles 6–9, 2003a). With respect to this power, pat-downs are generally not allowed without a warrant. If there is enough evidence to make an arrest, or if there is a risk of danger, warrantless body-searches are permitted. Pat-downs may only be done by members of the same gender (Laws & Regulations Database of the Republic of China [Taiwan], Code of Criminal Procedure, Article 1310, 2003b).

With respect to recent peer-reviewed literature on stops in Taiwan, a convenience sample of 688 college students across the country was surveyed (Lai, 2016). The results of this study indicated that a sizable number of students experienced involuntary police stops (23.8%). Another 22.5 percent experienced voluntary contacts, and the remainder had no contact at all with the police. Of those who had contact, due to the Taiwanese culture of respect for public servants, many of those who had contact were satisfied with the encounter ($M = 3.25$ on a scale of 1 to 5) (Lai, 2016). Taiwanese society as a whole is very homogeneous, and such positive feelings for the police are not surprising.

Another article studied perceptions of disorder in Taiwan (Yang & Pao, 2015). This study included 120 police officers and 241 students. It was noted that lower-class foreign groups were most likely to be perceived as disorderly by police and students. "Images of physical disorder that featured foreign social actors in casual outfits led to the highest disorder ratings" (Yang & Pao, 2015, p. 549). When traits of physical disorder, race, and social class appear together, perceptions of disorder are even stronger (Yang & Pao, 2015). Again, such results are not surprising given the homogeneity of society.

Summary

New York City is an exceptionally large metropolis that impacts the rest of the nation and even the world. Previous chapters covered the NYPD's aggressive policing. This chapter covered the backlash of this aggressive policing method. One of the consequences, at least in part, of the NYPD is the Black Lives Matter movement. Examples of problematic policing incidents, such as those involving Eric Garner and George Floyd, were discussed. The chapter also discussed the Defund the Police movement and cities revolting against aggressive police behavior. This chapter also points out how police have been militarized as opposed to working with communities. The issue of using troops in the United States was also covered. Lastly, the chapter overviewed seven democratic countries and their use of police stops: England and Wales, Finland, Slovenia, France, India, Brazil, and Taiwan.

Discussion Questions

1. Explain the impact of the NYPD's aggressive policing policies. Give specific examples.
2. What is the Black Lives Matter movement?
3. Discuss what happened in various cities in the United States. What do you think were some of the causes of this unrest?
4. Does the militarization/use of troops of the police help or hurt issues of civil unrest? Explain your answer.
5. Compare and contrast the various countries' police practices discussed in the chapter.

References

Anunciação, D., Trad, L. A. B., & Ferreira, T. (2020). "Mão na cabeça!": abordagem policial, racismo e violência estrutural entre jovens negros de três capitais do Nordeste. *Saúde e Sociedade*, *29*(1). https://doi.org/10.1590/s0104-12902020190271

Arthur, A. R. (2025, September 8). *Trump vs. Biden on ICE arrests, removals*. Center for Immigration Studies. https://cis.org/Arthur/Trump-vs-Biden-ICE-Arrests-Removals

Bakst, B. (2020, July 10). *Guard mobilized quickly, adjusted on fly for Floyd unrest*. MPR News. https://www.mprnews.org/story/2020/07/10/guard-mobilized-quickly-adjusted-on-fly-for-floyd-unrest

Biscontini, T. (2023). *Shooting of Jacob Blake*. EBSCO Research Starters. https://www.ebsco.com/research-starters/law/shooting-jacob-blake

Black Lives Matter. (n.d.). *About Black Lives Matter*. Retrieved December 11, 2025, from https://blacklivesmatter.com/about/

Black Lives Matter Global Network Foundation. (n.d.). *About—Our history*. Retrieved November 7, 2025, from https://blacklivesmatter.com/about/#our-history

Blume, P. (2025, May 28). *Minneapolis' 3rd Police Precinct burned 5 years ago. This is what it looks like now*. FOX 9 Minneapolis-St. Paul. https://www.fox9.com/news/minneapolis-3rd-police-precinct-burned-5-years-ago-is-what-looks-like-now

Campbell, D. J., & Campbell, K. M. (2010). Soldiers as police officers/Police officers as soldiers: Role evolution and revolution in the United States. *American Behavioral Scientist*, *53*(10), 1545–1565. https://doi.org/10.1177/0002764209356250

CNN. (2013, June 5). *Trayvon Martin shooting: Fast facts*. CNN. https://www.cnn.com/2013/06/05/us/trayvon-martin-shooting-fast-facts

Crank, J. P. (2014). *Understanding police culture* (2nd ed.). Routledge.

Dodd, V. (2020, October 27). Black people nine times more likely to face stop and search than white people. *The Guardian*. https://www.theguardian.com/uk-news/2020/oct/27/black-people-nine-times-more-likely-to-face-stop-and-search-than-white-people

Drummond, D. S. (1976). *Police culture*. Sage Publications.

Durkin, E. (2019, August 20). *NYPD faces calls to discipline more officers in Eric Garner case*. POLITICO. https://www.politico.com/states/new-york/albany/story/2019/08/20/nypd-faces-calls-to-discipline-more-officers-in-eric-garner-case-1148231

Elsea, J. K. (2018, November 6). *The Posse Comitatus Act and related matters: The use of the military to execute civilian law* (Report No. R42659). Congressional Research Service. https://www.congress.gov/crs-product/R42659

Epstein, K. (2025, November 27). *Why is Trump trying to deploy the National Guard to US cities?* BBC News. https://www.bbc.com/news/articles/cwy9z7yg2n7o

Eterno, J. A. (2003). *Policing within the law*. Bloomsbury.

Eterno, J. A. (2023). Police leaders as thinkers: Interview with Chief Theresa Tobin, Chief of Interagency Operations, NYPD. In A. Verma & D. K. Das (Eds.), *Police leaders as thinkers* (pp. 21–34). Springer.

Eterno, J. A., & Silverman, E. B. (2012). *The crime numbers game: Management by manipulation* (1st ed.). Routledge. https://doi.org/10.1201/b11477

Eterno, J. A., & Verma, A. (2024). Does educating students influence their views about a sensational criminal justice event? An experiment on the chokehold death of Mr. Eric Garner. *Journal of Criminal Justice Education*, *35*(4), 1–19. https://doi.org/10.1080/10511253.2024.2418571

Floyd v. City of New York, 959 F.Supp.2d 668 (2013)

FOX 9. (2020, June 17). *Map shows approximately 700 buildings damaged in Minneapolis riots*. FOX 9 Minneapolis-St. Paul. https://www.fox9.com/news/map-shows-approximately-700-buildings-damaged-in-minneapolis-riots

Fung, K. (2020, May 27). Police fire rubber bullets, protesters break precinct windows amid demonstrations over George Floyd's death. *Newsweek*. https://www.newsweek.com/police-fire-rubber-bullets-protesters-break-precinct-windows-amid-demonstrations-over-george-1506932

Good Morning America. (2021, January 6). *No charges filed against officers in shooting of Jacob Blake* [Video]. YouTube. https://www.youtube.com/watch?v=vB-IxAFapNI

Hewitt, C., & Vihan, H. (2025). *Europe's overlooked Roma people*. Rick Steves' Europe. https://www.ricksteves.com/watch-read-listen/read/articles/roma-people

Human Rights Watch. (2007). *Hidden apartheid: Caste discrimination against India's "untouchables"*. Human Rights Watch. https://www.hrw.org/report/2007/02/12/hidden-apartheid/caste-discrimination-against-indias-untouchables

Jackson, D. B., Testa, A., Semenza, D. C., Skinner, R., & Vaughn, M. G. (2022). Police stops and youths' educational expectations: Findings from the UK Millennium Cohort Study. *Journal of Criminal Justice*, *82*, Article 102012.

Kashiwagi, S. (2019, August 21). *Sgt. Kizzy Adonis pleads guilty to NYPD charges, loses 20 vacation days for role in Garner case*. SI Live. https://www.silive.com/news/2019/08/sgt-kizzy-adonis-pleads-guilty-to-nypd-charges-loses-20-vacation-days-for-role-in-garner-case.html

Kim, J. (2025, November 20). *Judge orders an end to Trump's troop deployment in D.C., calling it "unlawful"*. WUFT. https://www.wuft.org/2025-11-20/judge-orders-an-end-to-trumps-troop-deployment-in-d-c-calling-it-unlawful

Kingson, J. A. (2020, September 16). *Exclusive: $1 billion-plus riot damage is most expensive in insurance history*. Axios. https://www.axios.com/2020/09/16/riots-cost-property-damage

Klinger, D. A. (1996). More on demeanor and arrest in Dade County. *Criminology*, *34*(1), 61–82. https://doi.org/10.1111/j.1745-9125.1996.tb01195.x

Kraska, P. B., & Kappeler, V. E. (1997). Militarizing American police: The rise and normalization of paramilitary units. *Social Problems*, *44*(1), 1–18. https://doi.org/10.2307/3096870

Lai, Y. L. (2016). College students' satisfaction with police services in Taiwan. *Asian Criminology*, *11*(3), 207–229. https://doi.org/10.1007/s11417-015-9227-9

Lamba, J., & Jain, E. (2023). A study on police accountability and custodial violence in India. *Curie Journal*, *5*(1), 1–8. https://researth.iars.info/index.php/curie/article/view/227

Laws & Regulations Database of the Republic of China (Taiwan). (2003a). *Police Power Exercise Act*. Laws & Regulations Database of the Republic of China (Taiwan). https://www.law.moj.gov.tw/LawClass/LawAll.aspx?pcode=D0080145

Laws & Regulations Database of the Republic of China (Taiwan). (2003b). *Code of Criminal Procedure*. https://law.moj.gov.tw/ENG/LawClass/LawAll.aspx?pcode=C0010001

Lennon, G., Himanen, M., Marks, E., & Mouhanna, C. (2024). Stop in the name of the law: The legal regulation of police stops in Europe. In E. Aston, S. De Kimpe, J. Fazekas, G. Lennon, & M. Rowe (Eds.), *Governing police stops across Europe* (pp. 19–52). Palgrave Macmillan.

Lilley, Z. (2025, June 24). *More identity checks and less police trust outlined in report: When can you be stopped in France?* The Connexion. https://www.connexionfrance.com/news/more-identity-checks-and-less-police-trust-outlined-in-report-when-can-you-be-stopped-in-france/731288

Linder, D. O. (n.d.). *Timeline of the arrest of George Floyd*. UMKC School of Law, Famous Trials. Retrieved November 11, 2025, from https://www.famous-trials.com/george-floyd/2647-timeline-of-the-arrest-of-george-floyd

Lonsdorf, K., & Martínez-Beltrán, S. (2025, October 17). *Trump ties crime with immigration, blurring the lines with Guard deployment*. KUOW. https://www.kuow.org/stories/trump-ties-crime-with-immigration-blurring-the-lines-with-guard-deployment

Lozano, A. V. & The Associated Press (2021, October 8). *Officer who shot Jacob Blake won't face federal civil rights charges, DOJ says*. NBC News. https://www.nbcnews.com/news/us-news/officer-who-shot-jacob-blake-won-t-face-federal-civil-n1281149

Lundman, R. J. (1994). Demeanor or crime? The Midwest City police-citizen encounters study. *Criminology*, *32*(4), 631–656. https://doi.org/10.1111/j.1745-9125.1994.tb01168.x

Mapping Police Violence. (2025, October 31). *Mapping police violence*. Retrieved December 11, 2025, from https://mappingpoliceviolence.us/

Markovich, M. (2020, December 11). *City attorney: Charges brought in 8 out of 261 protest-related arrests in Seattle*. KOMO News. https://komonews.com/news/local/city-attorney-charges-brought-in-8-out-of-261-protest-related-arrests-in-seattle

McAdams, A. (2020, September 3). *Kenosha unrest damages more than 100 buildings, at least 40 destroyed, alliance says. ABC7 Chicago*. https://abc7chicago.com/post/more-than-100-buildings-damaged-at-least-40-destroyed-in-kenosha-unrest/6402998/

Milenkov, M., & Modic, M. (2024). "Stop and search": Slovenian police officers' perspective. *Varstvoslovje: Journal of Criminal Justice and Security*, *24*(4), 326–351.

Mollenkamp, D. T. (2025, February 4). *Defund the police: Definition, history, where it is now*. Investopedia. https://www.investopedia.com/defund-the-police-5112601

NBC Chicago. (2020, August 27). *Timeline: The Jacob Blake shooting and the unrest that followed*. NBC Chicago. https://www.nbcchicago.com/news/local/timeline-the-jacob-blake-shooting-and-the-unrest-that-followed/2329811/

New York City, Department of Planning (2025). *Population*. https://www.nyc.gov/content/planning/pages/planning/population

Nunn, J. (2025). *Court finds Trump's use of soldiers in Los Angeles illegal*. Brennan Center for Justice. https://www.brennancenter.org/our-work/analysis-opinion/court-finds-trumps-use-soldiers-los-angeles-illegal

Oliveira, T. R. (2022). Aggressive policing and undermined legitimacy: Assessing the impact of police stops at gunpoint on perceptions of police in São Paulo, Brazil. *Journal of Experimental Criminology*, *20*, 83–121. https://doi.org/10.1007/s11292-022-09527-9

Radil, A. (2024, January 25). *Seattle doles out $10 million to settle 2020 protest injury claims*. KUOW. https://www.kuow.org/stories/seattle-settles-injury-claims-from-2020-protests-for-10-million

Republic of Slovenia. (2013). Constitution of the Republic of Slovenia (Article 40). *Official Gazette of the Republic of Slovenia*. https://pisrs.si/pregledPredpisa?id=ZAKO6314

Schclarek-Mulinari, L., & Keskinen, S. (2022). Racial profiling in the racial welfare state: Examining the order of policing in the Nordic region. *Theoretical Criminology*, *26*(3), 377–395. https://doi.org/10.1177/1362480620914914

Silverman, E. B. (1999). *NYPD battles crime: Innovative strategies in policing*. Northeastern University Press.

Slisco, A. (2020, July 15). Bodycam footage in George Floyd case shows officer Lane pulled gun first. *Newsweek*. https://www.newsweek.com/bodycam-footage-george-floyd-case-shows-officer-lane-pulled-gun-first-1518132

Spiegelman, S. (2023, March 20). *The Hill: Seattle pays the price for CHAZ*. Pacific Legal Foundation. https://pacificlegal.org/the-hill-seattle-pays-the-price-for-chaz/

St. Anthony, N. (2021, May 18). Minneapolis Foundation raising $20 million for riot-hurt small businesses. *Star Tribune*. https://www.startribune.com/minneapolis-foundation-raising-20-million-to-rebuild-small-businesses-hurt-in-2020-riots/600058520

Sullivan, B. (2021, November 19). *Kyle Rittenhouse is acquitted of all charges in the trial over killing 2 in Kenosha*. NPR. https://www.npr.org/2021/11/19/1057288807/kyle-rittenhouse-acquitted-all-charges-verdict

Takahama, E. (2020). Timeline of Seattle's 2020 protests. *The Seattle Times*. https://projects.seattletimes.com/2020/local/protest-timeline/?jwsource=cl#:~:text=Scenes%20from%20Seattle%20protests%20sparked%20by%20George%20Floyd's%20death&text=Protests%20over%20Floyd's%20killing%20begin,activation%20of%20the%20National%20Guard.

Tefera, E. (2010). *ENAR Shadow Report 2009/2010: Racism and discrimination in Slovenia*. European Network Against Racism. https://www.enar-eu.org/wp-content/uploads/slovenia-3.pdf

Tiratelli, M., Quinton, P., & Bradford, B. (2018). *Does stop and search deter crime? Evidence from ten years of London-wide data* (Working Paper). UCL. https://discovery.ucl.ac.uk/id/eprint/10050843/1/Stop%20and%20search%20and%20crime.pdf

U.S. Department of Justice, Office of Public Affairs. (2022, July 27). *Former Minneapolis police officers Tou Thao and J. Alexander Kueng sentenced to prison for depriving George Floyd of his constitutional rights* [Press release]. https://www.justice.gov/archives/opa/pr/former-minneapolis-police-officers-tou-thao-and-j-alexander-kueng-sentenced-prison-depriving

U.S. Department of State. (2025, May 28). *France travel advisory*. Travel.State.gov. https://travel.state.gov/en/international-travel/travel-advisories/france.html#safetysecurity

Use of Army, Navy, Marine Corps, Air Force, and Space Force as Posse Comitatus, 18 U.S.C. § 1385 (2021).

Verma, A., & Arun, A. (2023). Counting crime: An exercise in police discretion—Report from India. In J. A. Eterno, A. Verma, & E. B. Silverman (Eds.), *How countries count crime: An exercise in police discretion*. Routledge. https://www.routledge.com/How-Countries-Count-Crime-An-Exercise-in-Police-Discretion/Eterno-Verma-Silverman/p/book/9780367489625

WCCO Staff. (2025, November 3). *Tou Thao released from prison after serving time for role in George Floyd's killing*. CBS Minnesota. https://www.cbsnews.com/minnesota/news/tou-thao-scheduled-prison-release/

Worden, R. E., & Shepard, R. L. (1996). Demeanor, crime, and police behavior: A reexamination of the Police Services Study data. *Criminology*, *34*(1), 83–105. https://doi.org/10.1111/j.1745-9125.1996.tb01196.x

World Population Review (2025). *New York City*. https://worldpopulationreview.com/us-cities/new-york/new-york

Yang, S. M., & Pao, C. C. (2015). Do we "see" the same thing? An experimental look into the black box of disorder perception. *Journal of Research in Crime and Delinquency*, *52*(4), 534–566. https://doi.org/10.1177/0022427815580167

YouTube. (2021, May 31). *Full body-cam footage of George Floyd arrest* [Video]. YouTube. https://www.youtube.com/watch?v=XkEGGLu_fNU

8

IMPLICATIONS FOR THE FUTURE

Introduction

It is a complicated world that police in democracies must work in. Nearly every country has some legal process for police to conduct stops. Various policing methods have been attempted over the years, such as community policing, performance management, aggressive quota-driven policing, and intelligence-led policing. The aggressive style of policing led to an enormous backlash, marked by many movements: Black Lives Matter, Defund the Police, and similar movements. This book reviews a select group of countries around the world. In this chapter, key themes or patterns revealed earlier in the book are examined. These themes will be supported with relevant materials, including peer-reviewed literature. The chapter concludes with specific recommendations on how police stops can be accomplished in a democratic society. Ultimately, the intricate and difficult balance between crime control and due process requires constant review and assessment.

Regardless of what we call them—police stops, forcible stops, stop and frisk, stop, question, and frisk, or numerous other names— this practice is a difficult task to undertake and to study. This chapter begins by analyzing and revealing patterns unveiled through study on police stops. First, the patterns and trends within the literature covering New York City—the heart of democratic policing—will be reviewed. The book has already discussed in detail the history of police stops in New York City, reviewed some global issues, and talked about legal and other issues; I will now focus on patterns or commonalities observed in this previous work. I will use some more recent studies from 2013 to 2025 to support these ideas. While the *Floyd* case is a focal point, its holding is controversial. Recall, the de Blasio administration refused to continue an appeal that the Bloomberg administration was going forward with. *Floyd*, rather than settling the issue, provides fodder for further debate and discussion among academics, practitioners, lawyers, and laypeople. To that end, I now turn to unveiling key patterns and supporting them with relevant materials, including recent scientific literature.

Unveiling Key Themes in Police Stops

This book has covered a variety of materials on police stops, locally, nationally, and internationally. It has examined the New York City Police Department (NYPD) in detail, reviewed

DOI: 10.4324/9781003593256-8

some literature and cases on the topic, and reviewed other countries' stop practices. We have learned that many emulate the NYPD and that researchers have used the NYPD and similar databases to study the topic. In this section, I expose key themes in the research and support those themes with relevant materials. Racial and ethnic disparity is one of the most common themes seen in many countries and studies, including New York City.

Racial and Ethnic Disparity

Many studies throughout the world (see Chapter 7) and in the United States show some level of racial and ethnic disparity. The *Floyd v. City of New York* (2013) case developed this theme in New York City. Other consent decrees and court orders now or in the recent past show this theme is nearly ubiquitous: Pittsburgh, Pennsylvania; Los Angeles, California; Suffolk County, New York; Newark, New Jersey; Portland, Oregon; Ferguson, Missouri; Cleveland, Ohio; Seattle, Washington; Albuquerque, New Mexico; New Orleans, Louisiana; Baltimore, Maryland; Louisville, Kentucky; Minneapolis, Minnesota, to name a few (NAACP Legal Defense and Educational Fund, 2025). Some argue that these focus on just a few officers. Jeff Sessions, former attorney general under Donald Trump, strictly limited the use of these decrees just before being fired by President Trump. He felt that overzealous civil rights lawyers, especially under President Obama, were focusing too much on local law enforcement (Benner, 2018). However, one issue is clear: disparity in race and ethnicity with respect to police stops is nearly pervasive. This does not mean that individual officers are racist or violating rights, at least consciously.

With respect to the other countries studied in this book, there is also ample evidence of some level of racial and ethnic disparities. Nearly every country studied shows at least some evidence for this (see Chapter 7). Additionally, peer-reviewed research also indicates that racial and ethnic disparity is a common theme with respect to police stops.

Avdija (2014), in a study, examines why police officers initiate stop and frisk in New York City. The study analyzes the factors that lead officers to frisk suspects, using the well-known stop-and-frisk data collected by the NYPD. These are stop-and-frisk reports filled out by officers in the field. The study prioritizes which factors are most used to conduct a frisk. Race has a statistically significant influence regardless of other factors. Decisions appear to be more subjectively based rather than objective (Avdija, 2014). It should be noted that this study was conducted during the height of the quota-driven, top-down management style that ultimately resulted in the NYPD being placed under a court monitor by the *Floyd* judge.

A study by Chen, Christensen, John, Owens, and Zhuo (2022), using an innovative research method, looks at police presence in 21 cities in the United States. Using GPS data from a cell phone, the study tracks officers' locations. Results indicate that officers spend significantly more time in Black areas, even after controlling for variables likely to influence police patrol time, such as population density, socioeconomic status, crime, and measures of social capital (Chen et al., 2022). The study also shows that departments with more diverse supervision have fewer disparities in police presence in neighborhoods (Chen et al., 2022).

Another study done in New York City shows how supervision can influence racial disparity. Coviello and Persico (2015) develop a model testing whether individual officers or the system are causing racial disparity. They use the same stop-and-frisk data supplied by the NYPD. It is found that for stops, individual officers are not biased against the people they are stopping – they are not racially profiling. However, in frisk decisions, there is some evidence of bias. Ultimately, it is argued that managerial decisions on where to place officers are most responsible for disparity (Coviello & Persico, 2015). This study, however, fails to emphasize the quota-driven system that the NYPD engaged in during the period of study.

Khan et al. (2021) study non-heterosexual males in New York City between 2014 and 2019. The study uses self-report data to demonstrate and examine disparities in police behavior. Of the 665 participants, 43 percent were stop and frisked. Of them, 47 percent were Black, 45 percent Hispanic, and 38 percent White, indicating a racial disparity. Such disparities persisted throughout the study.

Another study showing racial disparity among police was conducted by Lehrer and Lepage (2018). The study also uses stop-and-frisk data from New York City, and was also conducted during the peak period of top-down management in New York City. The researchers find that stops of Black suspects are less likely to lead to arrest compared with White suspects. They suggest that Blacks are being stopped with less suspicion compared with Whites (Lehrer & Lepage, 2018).

The last study explored was a nationwide study of state patrol traffic stops. It included 20 states (Pierson et al., 2017). After controlling for typical variables such as age, gender, location, and year, the researchers found that Black drivers are stopped about 1.4 times as often as White drivers. Blacks and Hispanics are more likely to be searched, ticketed, and arrested compared with White drivers. The racial disparity remains even after controlling for typical variables. The study demonstrates racial disparities in a national sample of traffic stops (Pierson et al., 2017). It should be noted that police agencies have also been placed under consent decrees for traffic stops, such as the New Jersey State Troopers.

The *Floyd* monitor assigned to the NYPD has also documented consistent disparities over time in the stop-and-frisk reports. Even the most recent reports are documenting the disparities (see Chapter 6). Based on a multitude of evidence, it is clear that a theme for police is some level of disparity against minorities with respect to police stops.

The police mirror the culture they are from. The police do not change the culture but ultimately represent and enforce the laws of the culture in which they exist. Ethnocentrism and xenophobia are concerns for any society, but especially for the police. As has been stated, we have seen evidence of racism in nearly every country we have studied. While the groups change from society to society, their presence is universal. Police, then, need to be particularly careful not to act on such feelings or adopt those biases. Rather, they must focus on legal evidence. To that end, police need to be well trained on processes that may lead to brutality or other behaviors that may reflect a societal norm but not protect equal protection under the law. Justice is supposed to be blind. With respect to racism, there is a five-step process that can ultimately lead to harrowing consequences. All officers should be trained on this process. One of the first steps in racism is stereotyping. Training officers on this danger is paramount: when society starts placing everyone in a group into a category, sometimes based on exaggerations, fears, or half-truths. For example, all Muslims are terrorists or all minorities are criminals. Such stereotyping is the first step in a spiraling and dangerous process. Officers need to be aware of this, not participate in it, and do their best to rebuke such ideas. Stereotyping, as it continues, leads to prejudice against the targeted group. As prejudice becomes more widespread, it leads to hatred. Anger and animosity eventually lead to outright discrimination. The final step is dehumanization. That is, the group being targeted is no longer considered human, but rather a cancer, animal, and so forth. At the point of dehumanization, horrible atrocities can occur, such as genocide.

Police, of course, in a democratic society must be a bulwark against this process. However, because police come from society, they often have these feelings in them and may even notice it as the society itself may not even be aware. To prevent this process, there are laws and safeguards. However, the police must be properly trained to recognize this and act to prevent such feelings. Police must be guided by individualized evidence, not stereotypes, prejudice, or worse. To this end, crime control, while important, is not the only goal of law enforcement. Rather, crime control must be properly balanced by human rights and dignity. The founding fathers of the United States understood this quite well. The Bill of Rights in the United States Constitution has become the blueprint for the Declaration of Human Rights at the United Nations. This must emanate at all ranks and is critically important for police leadership, often mired in the warrior ethos of crime control. I would argue that protecting rights and democracy is actually just as important, if not more important, than crime control. This is a theme that resounds throughout this book.

Training is only one way to handle the issue. Oversight is another. The overseers, however, must have enough power to make a difference. Based on the numerous studies examined in this book, some level of disparity may be inevitable. However, discrimination cannot be tolerated. To that end, individual officers must be screened in and out *before* employment. This means an arduous character background investigation must be done. Additionally, psychological testing must attempt to employ those individuals with the right temperament and attitude. This not only means hiring those who have exhibited legal behaviors such as not being arrested and so forth, but also those who have an understanding of fairness and justice. Bigoted attitudes cannot be tolerated. Once hired, officers must be properly supervised. This means reviewing body-worn camera footage, civilian complaints, peer interactions, and other such behaviors. Signs of stereotyping, at a minimum, must be monitored.

That being said, officers also need to feel confident in doing their work. Officers are entitled to due process and must have a fair process for themselves. Oversight and supervision should not be overly zealous or vindictive but fair and just. New York City has so much oversight that there are some concerns of going too far, for example: sometimes overzealous prosecutors, arrest (the legal system), the committee to combat corruption, an Inspector General, a civilian complaint review board, federal agencies, the *Floyd* monitor, other lawsuits, the City Council, assorted watchdog groups, internal mechanisms such as quality assurance, Integrity Control Officers, Internal Affairs, and more. While any officer exhibiting discriminatory behavior must be properly dealt with (including termination and, or prosecution), there must be a proper balance such that officers are not overly concerned with doing their jobs. While this is easier said than done, illegal behavior on the part of officers including discrimination requires due process. Likewise, just as we require reasonableness for suspects, officers deserve at least the same Constitutional fairness. I suggest an expert panel be formed that could help ascertain how we can best balance all this oversight with the need to allow police the power to properly prevent crime. This is no easy task, especially in New York City. All sides of the political spectrum need to be represented. Yet, a group of no more than six to eight experts, otherwise becoming unwieldy, is recommended. I consider this as something similar to President Obama's *Policing in the 21st Century* initiative (President's Task Force on 21st Century Policing), but at a more local level. Given the political extremes and emotions of this issue, reason and knowledge must be our guides. Since this is one of the more difficult topics of this book, I will discuss this issue in some detail in the conclusion section of this chapter.

Large-Scale, Top-Down Police Management

Another major theme is top-down management. Police generally work in a paramilitary organization. In New York City, from 1994 until the time of this writing, there has been a strong top-down leadership style. The police performance management system (sometimes called CompStat or similar names) is quite popular among many departments (Eterno & Silverman, 2012).

In a review of empirical studies on police stops in the United States, Abrams (2014) uses legal and economic analysis. *Terry v. Ohio* (1968) authorizes police stops based on individualized suspicion. However, in his analysis, Abrams (2014) demonstrates that law enforcement agencies are applying forcible stops as part of a policy rather than based on legal guidelines. That is, department leadership drove officers toward large numbers of stops, emphasizing crime control results rather than individualized reasonable suspicion. Agencies make stop practices a policy that goes beyond officer discretion. Pressures on officers by supervisors led some officers to reduce the legal boundaries required by *Terry*. Abrams (2014) argues that police agency metrics are far too simplistic to capture what is occurring. That is, measures such as counting stops are radically incomplete compared with metrics such as hit rates, difference-in-difference analysis, and other methods.

Ferrandino (2012) studies stop and frisk in New York City from the years 2004 to 2010 during the height of top-down management. In this study, he examines the inputs – number of frisks – and outputs – arrests, weapons, and contraband. The research suggests that some precincts perform more efficiently than others. This suggests management or supervision does make a difference in performance. Performing large numbers of frisks tended to be an inefficient practice. Ultimately, Ferrandino (2012) suggests that training, supervision, and policy make an important difference in practice.

Meares (2014) reviews existing studies on stop and frisk using social science and legal analyses. She describes how stop and frisk changed from a legal doctrine into a routine policing strategy used to prevent crime by police agencies. The organizational culture and policy adoption had an enormous influence on officer behavior. Officer discretion was minimized by agencies adopting top-down policies. How police treat people during stops affects how the police are seen by the public (Meares, 2014). Meares (2014) questions the efficacy of using mass stop and frisk because stops did not lead to many weapons or other contraband, and because of the enormous strain the practice places on community relations, especially in minority neighborhoods.

Another study shows how CompStat is operationalized by police agencies (Willis, 2007). In theory, CompStat is command and control policing, but in practice, it promotes impressions rather than actual change. CompStat is experienced differently at lower levels depending on the command. Thus, it does not promote a uniform change in police behavior. Precinct commanders act as mediators between the upper echelon and the rank and file. The commander's leadership style will influence the level of pressure that officers feel. Organizational change depends heavily on middle-level management. Additionally, CompStat is operationalized differently depending on the agency. One agency may focus on crime numbers and targets, and another on learning and problem-solving. Thus, the agency has a strong influence on practice (Willis, 2007). Willis (2007) does mention how pressures from above can have adverse effects on the agency, such as manipulating crime numbers.

Clearly, there is no consensus on CompStat. Some authors suggest that a data-driven approach similar to that of CompStat is good (Shane, 2008; Henry, 2003). Others argue that CompStat has issues (Weisburd, Willis, Mastrofski, & Greenspan, 2019). Weisburd et al. (2019) argue that top management is responsible for missions' statements and the directions the organization will take. Using data from a Police Foundation study looking at NYPD-like departments, they find that CompStat does very little to change traditional crime-fighting strategies. Thus, the focus of CompStat was not on innovation but on arrests, stops, and traffic enforcement (Weisburd et al., 2019).

Police Legitimacy

When speaking of police legitimacy, this means "the perception of the police by the communities they serve, characterized by trust, respect, and a belief in the officers' authority to maintain order" (Biscontini, 2023, n.p.). Throughout the book, we have seen some level of pushback from the public on over-aggressive stop policies. Black Lives Matter, Defund the Police, and civil unrest were common responses. Clearly, aggressive policing can have strong deleterious effects. Various peer-reviewed articles demonstrate this as well.

Sewell and Jefferson (2016), for example, conducted a study in New York City examining the health effects of invasive police encounters. The authors use 2011 and 2012 data from the Community Health Survey. They demonstrate that the practice of aggressive police stops led to "chronic stressors" for neighborhood residents (Sewell & Jefferson, 2016). There was a climate of fear and psychological strain in residents constantly worried about being stopped by the police. Minorities, in particular, felt that the police were unfair in their treatment during stops. Just living in the neighborhood itself led to negative health effects from the aggressive police activity (Sewell & Jefferson, 2016). Clearly, aggressive stops led to less police legitimacy.

Skogan (2016), using the 2013 Chicago Community Policing survey, studies the effects of police stops in Chicago. Stop-and-frisk led to less community trust of police, especially when no arrest was made. Stops also undermined confidence because they communicate a lack of respect. Skogan (2016), like many others, finds that minorities are more affected by police stops because they experience the aggressive police tactics more often. Stops had a similar negative effect on trust as being arrested, summoned, or being removed to a precinct (Skogan, 2016).

Similar to Skogan (2016) and other studies, Gelman, Fagan, and Kiss (2007) find that minorities experience police stops more often. Their study uses the NYPD stop-and-frisk records from 2003 to 2005. Minority stop levels remained higher even after controlling for local crime. The study suggests that stops lacked individualized, reasonable suspicion. In turn, this likely had a negative influence on minorities, in particular on the police. In a later study, MacDonald, Fagan, and Geller (2016), using updated stop-and-frisk data from NYPD, yielded similar results to those of the previous study. Their study examines high-crime areas called impact zones. They find a high volume of stops is unproductive and leads to numerous negative interactions with police, especially in minority areas. This, in turn, results in less legitimacy. MacDonald et al. (2016) cite other articles finding similar results with respect to legitimacy, especially in minority areas.

Globally, Legal Guidelines Have Striking Similarities for Democratic Police

The previous chapter reviewed other countries' police stop practices. While not exactly the same, there are striking similarities. All countries had some legal criteria required of officers.

All had something like reasonable suspicion (more or less), like the United States. Most countries, however, gave more discretion to police. Indeed, some countries allowed identification checks. That being said, in general, while democratic countries have different cultures, the laws generally protect people from over-aggressive policing but, at the same time, grant police some power to properly do their jobs. While this balance is not easy, it is not meant to be. Indeed, this is the focal point of democracy. Police must have the power to do their jobs but, simultaneously, society must guard against too much police power. As James Madison in *Federalist 51* (1788/2001) states,

> If men were angels, no government would be necessary. If angels were to govern men, neither external nor internal controls on government would be necessary. In framing a government which is to be administered by men over men, the great difficulty lies in this: you must first enable the government to control the governed; and in the next place oblige it to control itself.

Scholars have commented widely on this theme. Quinton (2023), for example, argues that police stops can stop crime but also can have harms. This raises legal and ethical questions for democratic societies. While not a review of laws, this article stresses the need to justify using these broad police powers. Quinton (2023) argues that crime control alone cannot be the sole factor permitting officers to forcibly stop people. It should be based on reasonable suspicion or something like that, protecting individual rights from arbitrary interference by the states. These protections should especially include dignity, proportionality, and non-discrimination (Quinton, 2023). In sum, Quinton (2023) argues that, even if stops can reduce crime, police policy must still align with legal norms that protect civil liberties and avoid discriminatory enforcement.

Weisburd, Groff, and Yang (2021) comment on police stops in various countries. They point out that many countries have similar legal guidelines requiring some level of suspicion to stop someone. However, they also point out that there can be specialized circumstances in some countries allowing the police to stop without suspicion. In some cases, for example, in the UK, police can do stops in high-risk zones. There are controversies surrounding this practice throughout the democratic world. They also find that racial discrimination and fairness have led to litigation and issues in many countries (Weisburd et al., 2021). There are other studies confirming that the legal parameters of the United States are similar to those in other democracies throughout the world (MacDonald et al., 2016). Also, in another study, Vito, Higgins, and Vito (2021) similarly suggest that United States law has similarities in the world, and racial disparities and concerns with human rights are ubiquitous with police stops.

Conclusions

What lessons can be learned from the previous themes? I have already discussed some ideas on what can be done. In this section I bring it all together and also add some specific recommendations based on these materials. As we have learned, the balance between crime control and due process is essential. Those who suggest crime control is the only necessary aspect of police stops fail to grasp the complexity of policing in a democratic society. Racism, for example, is nearly ubiquitous and, at the same time, unacceptable to our ideal vision of the law as blind. At the same time, we must be realistic and not place unreasonable burdens on officers who, after all, are products of the society from which they came. Reason is our guide with the ideal as our hope and what we ultimately strive for. For example, in courts in the United States we must prove "beyond a reasonable doubt" that the suspect is guilty. This burden is not "beyond any doubt," although that is truly what we all hope for. Consequently, a listing of reasonable expectations for law enforcement in democracies is outlined.

Police Need Power to Fight Crime

The balance between crime fighting and protecting rights is a complicated one. This balance ebbs and flows with the times. For example, when society is threatened, such as after 9/11, the power of the executive, and therefore the police, expand. Over time, this reverts back to a more limited structure in which police are less powerful. At all times, however, we must allow our police the ability to prevent crime. What is the proper balance?

At its peak, stop and frisk in New York City was at an astounding 685,724 stops. This occurred in 2011. This increase was excessive and likely an abuse of power. There were 515 murders in 2011—a fairly high number ((Eterno & Silverman, 2013).

Since the *Floyd* case in 2013, the number of stops has generally been below 25,000. Furthermore, the number of homicides has not skyrocketed as predicted by some, such as Heather MacDonald (Grawert & Cullen, 2016). This suggests that some level of stops is important but not to the point at which police become abusive. For example, in 2021, the NYPD recorded only 8,947 stops (Denerstein, 2022). In that same year, New York recorded 488 murders (New York Police Department, 2023). Notably, in 2025, the stop numbers moderately increased to a more reasonable level culminating at 26,422 (New York City Police Department, n.d.). Simultaneously, there was a low of 305 murders in 2025 (New York Police Department, 2026a, 2026b). This is a critically important point. With stops slightly increasing (not to the point of hundreds of thousands in a single year), there is also a corresponding decrease in homicide. In addition, my colleague, Dr. Eli Silverman, and I, in 2020, advocated for additional police stops because the number seemed so low. In 2019, there were 13,459 stops (Zimroth, 2021a). In 2020, there were only 9,544 (Denerstein, 2024b). This is a 29 percent decrease. Correspondingly, in 2019 there were 318 murders (New York Police Department, 2020), and in 2020, we see a dramatic increase to 462 murders (New York Police Department, 2021). This represents an astounding and revealing 45 percent increase in murder. A similar correlation between homicides and stops is seen in data from 2015 to 2025 ($r = -.29$; $r_s = .-20$). While these are a correlation and not causation, this likely means some level of police stops is healthy.

Yet another indicator of the importance of some police intervention is when Commissioner Bratton came to the NYPD. In 1994 and 1995, Bratton, with the NYPD, recorded huge decreases in crime (Silverman, 2001). This was done with some aggressiveness by the Department. Eventually, when Mr. Kelly became Police Commissioner under Mayor Bloomberg, crime was already down by a miraculous 60 percent. In 2002, at the time Mr. Kelly took over, there were approximately 100,000 stops per year. He then ramped that up to nearly 700,000. Again, stops, at this point, were generally under 100,000 (Eterno & Silverman, 2013). Thus, Mayor Giuliani and his police commissioners were able to substantially bring crime under control without the corresponding wild increases in police stops.

Based on this, I would suggest that some level of police stops in New York City is important. While numbers will fluctuate depending on conditions, right now I would suggest under 100,000, but not less than 20,000. Again, the number will depend on conditions in the city. These numbers are just a suggestion based on the basic facts. The main point, however, is not the sheer number but giving the police enough power to do their work without abusing it. We can make this case yet again in more recent times. These numbers can vary widely but must be based on local conditions. While not proving causality, we can say that some level of police intervention seems appropriate if not necessary.

In sum, some level of police power is needed to control crime. However, a balance must be struck between fighting crime and due process. While this can be difficult, it is meant to be so, as we live in a democracy. Checks and balances are part of our everyday lives. The police must find legal ways to do their crime-fighting. Getting guns off the streets, for example, can be done by stop and frisk, but this is not the most efficient way to do so. The police need the power to stop individuals, but this should be targeted and legal. Other strategies to remove guns in New York City, for example, include expanding investigations to determine where those arrested with guns got them and then targeting those places and individuals, working with the federal government to prevent gun-running from other states with more access to handguns, obtaining and deploying advanced technology, using federal resources such as gun tracing by the ATF (Bureau of Alcohol, Tobacco, Firearms and Explosives), expanding gun buy-back programs, working with communities to obtain information about guns, working with informants to expose illegal practices and operations to purchase unlawful weapons, and more.

Additional and constant updating of training on police stops is very important. The law is not static, and neither is policing. Learning from scientific studies and academic work on police stops must be accomplished. The NYPD has recently reduced its education requirements for officers. This is a mistake. Officers need to be critical thinkers who understand their important roles in the democratic process (Eterno, 2008). Advanced education should be encouraged and even required, where possible. One way to do this and save countless dollars is to move the basic training of the police academy to colleges (Eterno, Silverman, & Berlin, 2021). We do this with nursing, teaching, lawyers, medical doctors, and many other professions. Officers would have to earn a certificate and then look for openings in law enforcement. In this way, officers would be exposed to various cultures and ideas outside of the police culture, which starts at the academy. While basic tactics, shooting, driving, and other aspects of policing would still remain, prospective officers would at least have a modicum of knowledge about their trade outside of the rigid police academy experience.

Other lawful police tactics with respect to stops include monitoring, patrolling, and stopping those entering public transit facilities. As ruled in *MacWade v. Kelly* (2006), police in New York have the lawful authority to stop and search those in public transit facilities. Given the vulnerability of such systems (see, for example, the London Underground bombings), it is paramount for the police to not only show a presence but also to actively engage the public (New York Civil Liberties Union, 2007). When the police use a random method of searching, they may stop and search riders. This would seem to be a powerful legal tool for police to protect the public. Such legal tactics need to be expanded and encouraged. It should be noted that a recent study of the New York City subway indicated that perceptions of safety do affect ridership, but, at the same time, complaints against officers are higher after implementing a safety plan (Roberts et al., 2024).

Areas of concern also include schools, shopping malls, stadiums, and other large public events. Schools sometimes work closely with police or even have police guarding them. NYPD school safety officers, while not police, guard public schools. Any large gathering of people needs to be protected. In many cases, the police must work closely with private security. Even Disney parks, for example, engage in searches before entering. While this is private security, it is clear that the public must be prepared to surrender some level of privacy to ensure their safety.

There is a growing body of literature showing the importance of private security, sometimes working with the public police. One study in Denmark, for example, shows that private entities were able to control the public even though they had little authority to do so (Kammersgaard, 2019). Private security is sometimes seen as less respected than public police. Yet their roles are increasing (Wakefield, 2008). Public police often have difficulty working with private security and this can be problematic (Perrott & Trites, 2017). Partnerships are absolutely necessary.

Technology is another burgeoning area to advance police crime-fighting efforts. As we have seen, body-worn cameras increase the number of stop reports filed and reduce civilian complaints (Braga, MacDonald, & McCabe, 2022). Another powerful tool for police is using data and surveillance analytics. Directed surveillance involves activities by police with suspicion, and dragnet surveillance is without such suspicion. It has been suggested that technology is far outpacing the law, and there needs to be a review of the law, policies, and practices (Brayne, 2018). It is without a doubt that new technologies hold promise but have the same concerns as police stops. Namely, the balance between crime control and basic rights. Drones, facial recognition, artificial intelligence (AI)-enabled surveillance, surveillance robots, hidden surveillance systems, and other predictive tools are just some of the new technologies that may be causing concern.

Numbers Alone Are Problematic

Data to support extremist positions also seems abused, if not outright manipulated. Key performance indicators (KPIs) are all the rage. A strategic plan with such KPIs is essential to any organization. However, once the KPIs are known, they often become subject to manipulation. For example, once police commanders in New York City knew they were being graded on their crime numbers, suddenly, and steadily, the crime numbers went down. At some level, this is due to purposeful manipulation (Eterno & Silverman, 2012, 2010). This occurs in nearly every situation where the social indicator is known (Campbell, as cited in Eterno & Silverman, 2012, p. 10). Yet we continue to use such numbers as if they were truthful and entirely accurate. They are used to make decisions and support positions, often those that are extremist.

While we should continue to use data, we must use them as one piece of a complex puzzle. Putting the pieces together requires critical thinking and using many other tools. For example, when performance management was not used in policing, community meetings, fighting corruption, morale, training, and many other aspects of policing were critical. After performance management, commanders were obsessively focused on crime numbers. Commanders would count every index crime (crimes used to calculate the crime rate) religiously. Nothing, absolutely nothing, was as critical. Everything else became almost meaningless as the numbers were so absolutely important.

My abundant research and experiences at the NYPD confirm this. Additionally, there have been scandals in the United Kingdom, France, and other countries as they too became embroiled in quotas, targets sometimes attached to officers' pay (Eterno & Silverman, 2012).

In New York City, the quota system for officers was one of the most damaging aspects of its stop-and-frisk activity.

More specifically, stop and frisk became a tool of crime numbers. It was thought to be one key to crime control—again, the myopic and obsessive goal of the police at the time. Officers, especially those assigned to what were known as Impact Zones, were forced to write a certain number of stop-and-frisk reports every shift. Importantly, Impact Zones were in high-crime areas and staffed mostly with new or rookie officers who were still on probation and learning the job. They were most susceptible to the influence of supervisory pressures. These officers, under the top-down pressures of management, were burdened with extreme performance targets. If they did not meet these targets, there were various punishments, such as losing a good post, not getting vacation requests, lower evaluations, and more. Consequently, the officers did exactly as they were told. That is, they wrote stop-and-frisk reports, regardless of quality and even though they were highly illegal, to satisfy the upper echelon. The mechanism for this was performance management or CompStat. Upper management pressured commanders of precincts at CompStat meetings, and, in turn, commanders pressured supervisors. Stop-and-frisk reports became an "activity" that was absolutely required through heavy quotas especially, but not exclusively, at Impact Zones. The reasoning was that these reports by the hundreds of thousands annually would somehow be critical to reducing crime. Even if that were true, which it is not, as demonstrated throughout this book, the police must work within the law to enforce the law. The officers were under such pressure that they did not obey the law but, rather, succumbed to the pressures of supervisors. It is this quota-driven system of management that needs to be addressed. Just as crime targets tied to pay and other incentives were problematic in the UK, France, and other countries, so too are quotas or targets for officers with respect to stop and frisk. It is without a doubt that the numbers game being played by a top-down management system is the culprit. Sheer numbers are not the answer. While I support police stops, officers need to have the discretion to conduct those stops only when they have the legal criteria to do so. Management pressures must not be excessive. Officers, supervisors, and upper-management should work as a team, not as a dictatorship. Lower-level officers should have some say as should the public, especially in a democratic society. Additionally, social scientists who are studying such issues should also be listened to. This does not mean that management must follow the whims of such parties. Rather, they should listen and weigh the evidence judiciously. In the case of stop and frisk in New York City, the rational outcries of numerous parties were simply dismissed. Reason, not a passionate position, needs to rule. When communities, scholars, police unions, and numerous others are all on one page, managers need to heed the warning. In this case, the NYPD dismissed what was clear fact. As a result, they now have a federal monitor on them that has lasted since 2013—a terrible price to pay.

One recent study would seemingly contradict this recommendation on numbers. Piquero and Sherman (2025) have done a highly sophisticated study in London. However, other than the issues previously discussed, London has very specific criteria. Thus, external validity to the United States and other countries may be quite limited. Gun control, for example, is far more expansive, making knives the weapon of choice. The NYPD seems to have been able to keep the number of murders very low without the subsequent immense number of stops suggested by Piquero and Sherman (2025). Indeed, the NYPD has reported the lowest number of murders in decades in 2025: 305. In 1990, there were over 2,000 murders (New York Police Department, 2025). Thus, if we can get the large decreases of the NYPD without the corresponding numerous police stops, it would seem the Department has found a better way. Piquero and Sherman (2025) are unable to parse out officer motivation. While I understand it is police discretion, was it legal criteria, focus on minorities, managerial pressures, or some other unmeasured factor that led to the officers' stop behaviors?

Piquero and Sherman (2025) suggest, however, that large numbers of police stops will reduce knife murders. They suggest that perhaps 10,000 to 40,000 stops per month will lower murder. This is just the opposite of the New York City experience. So, how can this other study be explained? Most importantly, the stops were based on the discretion of the officers, not quotas. The pressures on the officers, based on this study, seemed minimal. Second, it does not seem a legal analysis of the stops themselves was done. That is, if the police are making a large number of illegal stops, it does not matter that murder goes down. Specifically, the police must work within the law to follow the law. Third, as in the current book, the authors bring up the disproportionate stops of minorities by police. They point out the adverse influence of police on minority communities, including weakening legitimacy. At some point, this suggests optimizing police stops such that they are balancing crime reduction with important due process rights considerations. Piquero and Sherman (2025) do suggest hot-spots or focusing police stops on areas of high-intensity crime activity. This, it seems to me, is appropriate, but officers must be working within their legal powers. In New York City, even in less intense management eras, the police were still found to be conducting a large amount of illegal stops (Zimroth, 2015–2021). Thus, the sheer number of stops is not correct. Even the authors of this study recognize that. While they find that a large number of stops does reduce knife murder, which minorities will most benefit from that (since they are victims more often), other factors are just as, if not more, critical. While an "army of occupation" will reduce crime, it is not necessarily the type of society we want to live in. Indeed, in a democracy, we would rather have the guilty go free than have an innocent in prison (thus one is innocent until proven guilty in the United States, and the level for conviction with the burden on the state is high, beyond a reasonable doubt). Legal criteria, minimizing discrimination, maintaining police legitimacy, and fundamental fairness are even more important.

Weisburd, Petersen, and Fay (2023) find very differently from Piquero and Sherman (2025). In a systematic review of empirical studies on stop and frisk, they suggest that stops tend be very inefficient. That is, officers must make many stops to find illegal materials. Further, individuals who are stopped incur significant harm. Minority communities, in particular, are subject to the most harm from such police activity. Ultimately, they argue, as I do, that a large number of police stops is not a palatable crime control strategy.

In sum, numbers alone are not an effective strategy for the police. While police need the power to reduce crime, they need to do so in a more sophisticated way. Numbers alone do not solve the crime control problem and, indeed, may exacerbate numerous other problems—including alienating minority communities, which, in turn, may reduce crime control efforts (lack of information, few informants, less police legitimacy so people do not go to the police ...). Police need the power to conduct stops but must use it judiciously. Quality, not quantity, would seem best. Some level of police stops is necessary, but over-emphasizing numbers will likely lead to more harm than good. In this work I suggest a number in the goldilocks zone. That is, not too many or too few. For each locale this may differ. Regardless, in democracies, police must have the requisite legal criteria to properly stop people.

Transformational Leadership and Police Legitimacy

Leadership in policing needs to recognize that while crime control is important, it is not necessarily the most critical concept of law enforcement. Unfortunately, many leaders and scholars have suggested that crime fighting is paramount (Henry, 2003; Maple & Mitchell, 1999). Those in management positions are essential. They promote change. Kumar (2023, p. 34), for example writes, "Police executive leadership sets the climate for the 'much needed police organizational reform'" (Wakefield and Fleming, 2009, p. 188).

Transformational leaders develop trust, openness, respect, involvement, empowerment, and shared vision. Kumar (2023) suggests a process for police legitimacy to take place. Starting with transformational leadership, police agencies can develop police legitimacy. That is, the public accepting and working with the police voluntarily. People are cooperative and compliant because they recognize police authority. Transformational leadership starts the process of legitimacy. Without such a leader, legitimacy will not occur. Trust, openness, respect, involvement, empowerment, and shared vision "[signify] that a transformational police executive leadership will naturally foster organizational justice and internal legitimacy and therefore procedural justice and external legitimacy of policing" (Kumar, 2023, p. 38). Ultimately, the process of legitimacy starts with leadership, which transforms the organization and, in turn, leads to police being seen as legitimate.

In a systematic review of 101 peer-reviewed studies, Moura, Borges, Morgado, and Ramalho (2022) find that the qualities of transformational leaders, including inspiration, individual consideration, and intellectual stimulation, are widely recognized as key community partnerships and critical thinking. Similarly, Ford, Boles, Plamondon, and White (1999) argue that leadership that engages officers to work as a team is important for police to move toward more community-based approaches. Transformational leadership also supports frontline decision-making (Decker, 2018). In sum, transformational leadership is critical to creating a respected police organization.

Martin Luther King, Jr., John F. Kennedy, and Mahatma Gandhi are all examples of transformational leaders. While they may have created tension, they inspired people to follow them without resorting to fear tactics. Some police managers believe that leadership is best done through fear (Eterno & Silverman, 2012). CompStat, for example, was an excellent innovation that was generally motivated by fear. While initially changing the police culture in New York City likely needed some level of stress, even its founders felt that it should have moderated over time. Bratton, whom I would consider an excellent leader, talked about a peace dividend that should have eased tension among rank and file and communities as crime went down. Indeed, when Bratton returned as police commissioner in 2014, he brought this style with him (Baker, 2015). William Bratton is a good example of a transformational leader in law enforcement. While CompStat was later abused by other leaders following him, his balance of crime control and community policing in his second stint as commissioner shows where he would have gone had he stayed. Keechant Sewell, the first police commissioner under Mayor Adams, was also a transformational leader. She balanced crime-fighting with community relations.

Building community trust is one of the pillars that transformational police leaders need to address. Reducing corruption in the police is a necessary first step. That is, clean up your own house before you work on others. In a survey of European countries, for example, Alalehto and Larsson (2016) show the importance of reducing corruption and conducting individual assessments of fairness. In a meta-analysis of 16 studies, Yesberg, Costi, Chan, and Bradford (2023) find that police community relations help police do their jobs. Thus, corruption, fairness, and working with communities all appear to be critical for police.

Importantly, based on what I have analyzed, minority communities, in particular, have been a concern for police. Therefore, as police develop community partnerships, they need to focus efforts especially on minority communities. Studies show that individual interactions among police and minority groups are critical to developing better relations (Dobson, Dittmann, & Yeager, 2025; Murphy, 2023). It is also important to have good recruitment practices, training, and mechanisms for reporting concerns about police (Olson et al., 2022).

Given that there are many questions with police and minorities, there must be additional work done by police to strengthen relationships with those communities (Eterno, Barrow, & Silverman, 2017). However, at the same time, higher levels of crime in some minority communities should not be dismissed by police (Sherman & Kumar, 2021). Nevertheless, given the overwhelming evidence of issues with police and minority communities, it is essential for police to work more closely with communities of color, treating them with fundamental fairness, dignity, and equality with the majority of individuals. Fairness, respect, and neutrality are critical, especially during police stops (Barber & Tankebe, 2024). Police violence toward minorities can be an issue as well, and also needs to be addressed (Ben-Menachem & Torrats-Espinosa, 2024).

In conclusion, transformational leadership is critical to developing organizational justice and police legitimacy. Police need to build community trust with a special focus on minority communities. Reducing corruption, hiring, training, and focusing on equal protection are all critical to building community trust and legitimacy.

Understand Democratic Policing

Throughout this book, the importance of balance is highlighted. Police in a democracy cannot do as they please. While crime control is important, police must follow the law while enforcing it. Even if police take a "zero tolerance" approach, they must not overstep their authority (Eterno, 2001; Eterno, 2003). With respect to police stops in the United States, this means having reasonable suspicion. For most democratic countries, something like this is also required. What does this mean for police? The burden is on the police (i.e., the government) to demonstrate that it has the authority to conduct the stop legally. Unfortunately, in New York City at least, there have been many reports from the NYPD monitor indicating that police stops do not have the requisite level of proof called reasonable suspicion (Zimroth, 2015–2021). Previous research has shown that in these types of situations, police have some flexibility and, in some cases, do not obey the legal criteria. In my 2003 study, for example, I showed that for basic Fourth Amendment behavior such as stops and searches, police tend to disobey the law in about 15 percent of cases (Eterno, 2003). In this study, police were placed in hypothetical situations and asked to answer a survey as if they were on the streets. The survey was completed with active officers who worked in precincts at the time. The study was done when the NYPD was using a highly crime control-oriented style. One question is, "How much can we expect from officers?" That is, while training in this area is excellent, they still seem to get it wrong about 15 percent of the time (even in a survey). If we are expecting full compliance with the law, this is not likely to happen, especially since officers might err on the side of caution when stopping, questioning, and/or frisking for a gun or other weapon (i.e., the legality of a stop/search is important but not worth one's life). Officers are taught safety first. The saying within the NYPD is "better to be judged by 12 than carried by 6."

The NYPD has had a federal court monitor since 2013. That is over a decade. No department should be strapped with that kind of scrutiny over many years unless they are unable to comply. Bratton managed to get a federal monitor removed from the Los Angeles Police Department (LAPD). A comprehensive report was completed by the Harvard Kennedy School. The findings showed significant improvement in public satisfaction, use of force, governance, and oversight; and, while disparities persisted, there was improvement. Additionally, crime continued to go down, and enforcement activity did not drop (Stone, Foglesong, & Cole, 2009). The report does not indicate perfection. Rather, it shows reasonable improvement such that oversight was no longer necessary. A similar reasonable process to extricate themselves from the *Floyd* monitor should be publicly available. Reading the monitor's reports from *Floyd* did not show clear improvement, but it also did not show a clear pathway for removal. No police agency should have a court-appointed and/or Department of Justice monitor for such a long period of time, unless absolutely necessary.

As we have seen, democratic policing can and should be difficult to practice. For example, Bonner (2019) suggests that a lack of conceptual clarity and various political ideologies make policing difficult, at best. Also, understanding various communities' needs and wants through the social contract is also arduous. Tensions between political accountability and professional autonomy can be particularly strained (Shannon, 2020). A political executive, such as a mayor, may demand something of the police that the police chief or commissioner is unwilling to compromise on. For example, the police chief might be asked to reduce educational and/or physical standards that could compromise professionalism. When the chief is appointed by the executive, this may mean punishment of some sort or even loss of the job. Such tensions are part of democracy. It is recommended that a prospective chief or commissioner be sure to know what they are agreeing to and even make appropriate arrangements before taking the job. Nevertheless, such disagreements are inevitable. The executive should also be cognizant of this issue. Ultimately, however, politicians should allow professional police to do their jobs.

Best Practices

Numerous studies have been conducted on police stops throughout the world. There are some commonalities among them. Notably, officers using fundamental fairness is an essential component to properly conducting stops (Allen, 2017; Fradella & White, 2017; Petersen et al., 2023; Scrase, 2020; Sherman & Kumar, 2021). In a review of court cases, Fradella and White (2017), for example, argue that many departments, including the NYPD, did not follow legal guidelines and abused their authority under the guise of crime control. Fradella and White (2017) specifically argue that stop and frisk should remain a narrow, discretionary tool. In an extensive review of literature, Petersen et al. (2023) suggest targeted stops in high-risk locations and integrating procedural justice into stop practices. Scrase (2020) employs a theoretical review approach, arguing that procedural justice can often not be attained through police stops. Consequently, he argues for targeted and limited stop behavior, addressing fairness issues with the agency, and following legal constraints. Ultimately, these studies are examples of the need for police to be fundamentally fair.

There is also the need to write policies and laws that are based on bright-line rules. In a 2007 study of the NYPD, using the factorial survey method, I argued that the use of clear rules will help police to obey legal guidelines: "These findings suggest that frontline practitioners will be more likely to obey cases with bright-line rules" (Eterno, 2007, p. 721). Allen (2019) argues similarly that clear policies and accountability are necessary steps for police agencies to follow. Hutchins (2013) also argues for clear, structured limitations on *Terry* stop authority. The author suggests that officers should only stop when reasonable suspicion involves more than a minor offense. In this way, a bright-line distinction between what does and does not justify a stop will occur (Hutchins, 2013). Similarly, in conducting a legal analysis, Keenan and Thomas (2014) provide a framework to determine legal versus illegal stops based on the severity of the offense being investigated. Many other legal scholars argue for bright-line rules (Gentithes, 2020).

In a systematic review of police stops, Petersen et al. (2023) argue that police need to shift from quantity to quality of stops. We have seen this in the current book as well. Police in New York City were enamored by using the sheer number of stops as a metric of success for CompStat meetings. Clearly, this was, at least in part, one of the causes of illegal activity by police. If departments engage in more quality stops, this will obviously reduce unlawful stops. Also, the previous suggestion of using bright-line rules, either as police policy or through legal rulings, should diminish non-quality stops. Minimizing unauthorized stops will also help with the mental health of those stopped (Petersen et al., 2023).

Accountability and evaluation are also critically important. Police need to have some oversight, but it should not be overbearing. While court-ordered oversight or Department of Justice consent decrees can be very helpful, it is preferred that other mechanisms such as an Inspector General's office or something similar be available to the public. Police agencies need to be transparent. For example, body-worn camera footage must be made available to the oversight agency as well as written reports and other documentation. Additionally, oversight agencies need subpoena power and the ability to offer immunity in more egregious cases. This means that accurate data and other information need to be collected in the first place (Petersen et al., 2023). High-quality data collection and analytics can help influence police decision-making (Afzal & Panagiotopoulos, 2025). The burgeoning of analysts for police departments and oversight agencies will help establish more comprehensive and proactive methods for policing and reviewing police. To that end, any type of reasonable suspicion stop, including car stops, needs to be accurately recorded.

Police stops may not necessarily be the key to subverting criminal activity. New technologies and other ideas, such as the canine sniff, closed-circuit television, facial recognition, and other assorted innovations, present much promise in this area. Often those being targeted are not even aware of the intrusion. This will markedly reduce the negative mental health effects of police stops. It is highly recommended that such technologies be explored to their fullest. While these also present legal challenges, using these new techniques can be far less intrusive, especially when people are unaware they are being surveilled. Judge Scheindlin, in the *Floyd* case, recommended body-worn cameras, which were, at the time, groundbreaking. Today, with drones and many other devices, police technologies have come a long way. There have been numerous studies on body-worn cameras with varying results. Nevertheless, their use is now ubiquitous and, at a minimum, provides another way of examining a police incident.

Targeted patrols in areas of high crime also seem productive (Fitzpatrick, Gorr, & Neill, 2020; Peterson et al., 2023). Fitzpatrick et al. (2020) did a controlled quasi-experiment in Pittsburgh, where they found that treatment areas reduced violent crime more than non-treatment areas. Treatment areas were more active patrols in identified high-crime areas. The effectiveness of proactive patrols in high-crime areas was demonstrated in this quasi-experiment. Weisburd, Braga, Groff, and Wooditch (2017) similarly found that policing of high-crime or targeted areas had more successful results for police in reducing criminal activity. In another study, foot patrol in high-crime areas also reduced violent crime (Ratcliffe, Taniguchi, Groff, and Wood, 2011).

Increased training is part of any quality program. Police stops need to be a highly trained activity. Additionally, re-training with regular updates is absolutely necessary in this area due to the fluid nature of the law and police policy. As a captain on the police department who was highly involved in stop and frisk at the turn of the century, I trained the entire NYPD with the Legal Bureau. Our training involved recording all reasonable suspicion stops as well as a legal update. A new form was developed and introduced to officers at the time. Training was very comprehensive. However, such training sessions must be conducted on a regular basis to be effective. Studies show the importance of training. For example, Weisburd et al. (2022), in a multi-city study, demonstrate that intensive procedural justice training not only helped reduce crime but also had positive outcomes with the community. Wood, Tyler, and Papachristos (2020), in a study with about 8,500 officers in Chicago, found that procedural justice training helped reduce citizen complaints and use of force. Another study reviewed 35 peer-reviewed articles and found that simulation-based training for police decision-making, de-escalation, threat assessment, and procedural fairness led to better comprehension and competencies for police (Davies, 2024).

Community partnerships are also a necessary bridge for police to gain cooperation from the public. For example, in a study of the New Haven police, non-enforcement interactions between police and the public were important for developing a partnership (Peyton, Sierra-Arevalo, & Rand, 2019). Gill et al. (2014), in another study, review the literature on numerous police departments and find that community policing strategies can improve satisfaction, legitimacy, and perceptions of fairness. Kochel and Weisburd (2019) also examine numerous studies and find that collaborative orientation influences outcomes such as collective efficacy and perceptions of legitimacy. Community partnerships clearly help to establish strong relations between police and the people they serve. This, in turn, will help police better perform their roles. It should be noted that maintaining good relations also means that the police need to obey legal restrictions, such as allowing peaceful protest and not using asymmetric enforcement strategies at these events unless absolutely necessary (Cunningham, 2022).

As stated earlier, experts on police need to be consulted regularly to analyze and make sense of all these issues. There is no "silver bullet" to answer the issues surrounding police stops. Rather, this is a complex issue for a democratic society that will continue for the foreseeable future.

Summary

This book has outlined how the NYPD has been conducting stops, and included a discussion of numerous other countries. This chapter first talked about themes that emerge from this detailed analysis. The themes in this book include: racial/ethnic disparity, large-scale top-down management, police legitimacy, and global similarity of legal guidelines.

These are discussed in some detail with a focus on what they mean and how they influence each other. Specific conclusions were then formulated to guide future research and police agencies. These include: police need to have the power to fight crime, numbers alone are problematic, transformative leadership and legitimacy, understanding democratic policing, and best practices. Under each are various studies and ideas. For example, the need for bright-line rules, collecting and analyzing data, new technologies, and upholding police legitimacy, among many others. Overall, there is a need for continued study and expertise to study police stops.

Discussion Questions

1. How can we ensure that stop-and-frisk policies do not disproportionately target certain communities?
2. How might quotas influence the quality of stops versus the quantity of stops?
3. What actions can police departments take to strengthen community trust?
4. Can too much emphasis on crime fighting compromise ethical policing or community trust?
5. How might transformative leaders address issues like quotas or pressures for high stop numbers while maintaining legitimacy?
6. Why is having accurate and comprehensive data on stop-and-frisk important for assessing whether the practice is lawful and constitutional?
7. Can bright-line rules reduce the likelihood of discriminatory or arbitrary stops? If yes, how? If no, why not?

References

Abrams, D. S. (2014). *The law and economics of stop-and-frisk*. University of Pennsylvania Law School Scholarly Commons. https://scholarship.law.upenn.edu/faculty_scholarship/1592/

Afzal, M., & Panagiotopoulos, P. (2025). Data in policing: An integrative review. *International Journal of Public Administration*, 48(4), 411–430. https://doi.org/10.1080/01900692.2024.2360586

Alalehto, T., & Larsson, D. (2016). *Measuring trust in the police by contextual and individual factors. International Journal of Law, Crime and Justice*, *46*, 31–42. https://doi.org/10.1016/j.ijlcj.2016.01.001

Allen, C. (2017). Stop, question, and frisk: A response via the UK's PREVENT Programme. *Criminology, Criminal Justice, Law & Society*, *18*(3), 65–69.

Avdija, A. S. (2014). Police stop-and-frisk practices: An examination of factors that affect officers' decisions to initiate a stop-and-frisk police procedure. *International Journal of Police Science & Management*, *16*(1), 26–35. https://doi.org/10.1350/ijps.2014.16.1.325

Baker, A. (2015, September 20). Bratton tries a community policing approach on the New York Police. *The New York Times*. https://www.nytimes.com/2015/09/21/nyregion/bratton-tries-a-community-policing-approach-on-the-new-york-police.html

Barber, M., & Tankebe, J. (2024). Tracking procedural justice in stop and search pedestrian encounters with police body-camera records. *Policing: A Journal of Policy and Practice*, 18, article paae074. https://doi.org/10.1093/police/paae074

Ben-Menachem, J., & Torrats-Espinosa, G. (2024). Police violence reduces trust in the police among Black residents. *PLOS One*, *19*(9). https://doi.org/10.7910/DVN/CO404V

Benner, K. (2018, November 8). Sessions, in last-minute act, sharply limits use of consent decrees to curb police abuses. *The New York Times*. https://www.nytimes.com/2018/11/08/us/politics/sessions-limits-consent-decrees.html

Biscontini, T. (2023). *Police legitimacy*. EBSCO.

Bonner, M. D. (2019). What democratic policing is … and is not. *Policing and Society*, *30*(9), 1044–1060. https://doi.org/10.1080/10439463.2019.1649405

Braga, A. A., MacDonald, J. M., & McCabe, J. E. (2022). Body-worn cameras, lawful police stops, and NYPD officer compliance: A cluster randomized controlled trial. *Criminology*, *60*(1), 124–158. https://doi.org/10.1111/1745-9125.12293

Brayne S. (2018). The criminal law and law enforcement implications of big data. *Annual Review of Law and Social Science*, *14*, 293–308. https://doi.org/10.1146/annurev-lawsocsci-101317-030839

Chen, M. K., Christensen, K. L., John, E., Owens, E., & Zhuo, Y. (2022). Smartphone data reveal neighborhood-level racial disparities in police presence. *arXiv*. https://doi.org/10.48550/arXiv.2109.12491

Coviello, D., & Persico, N. (2015). An economic analysis of Black–White disparities in the New York Police Department's stop-and-frisk program. *The Journal of Legal Studies*, *44*(2), 315–360. https://doi.org/10.1086/684292

Cunningham, D. (2022). Policing white supremacy: Asymmetry and inequality in protest control. *Social Problems*, *71*(1), 58–76. https://doi.org/10.1093/socpro/spac010

Davies, A. (2024). How far have we advanced in simulation-based training for policing and law enforcement? A literature review 2014–24. *Policing: A Journal of Policy and Practice*. https://doi.org/10.1093/police/paae116

Decker, J. P. (2018). *A study of transformational leadership practices to police officers' job satisfaction and organizational commitment* (Doctoral dissertation, Seton Hall University). Seton Hall University Dissertations and Theses (ETDs). https://scholarship.shu.edu/cgi/viewcontent.cgi?article=3584&context=dissertations

Denerstein, M. L. (2022, May 6). *Sixteenth report of the independent monitor*. NYPD Monitor. https://www.nypdmonitor.org/wp-content/uploads/2022/09/16-Sixteenth-Report-.pdf

Denerstein, M. L. (2024, September 4). *Twenty-first report of the independent monitor: Monitor's compliance report*. NYPD Monitor. https://www.nypdmonitor.org/wp-content/uploads/2024/09/21st-Monitor-Report-General Compliance-Report_Stamped.pdf

Dobson, K. S. H., Dittmann, A. G., & Yeager, D. S. (2025). A transparency statement improves trust in community-police interactions. *Nature Communications*, *16*, 2285. https://doi.org/10.1038/s41467-024-55709-6

Eterno, J. A. (2001). Zero tolerance policing in democracies: The dilemma of controlling crime without increasing police abuse of authority. *Police Practice and Research: An International Journal*, *2*(3), 189–217.

Eterno, J. A. (2003). *Policing within the Law: A Case Study of the New York City Police Department*. Praeger.

Eterno, J. A. (2007). Understanding the law on the front lines: The need for bright-line rules. *Criminal Law Bulletin*, *43*(5), 706–725.

Eterno, J. A. (2008). Homeland security and the benefits of university education: An exploratory study of the New York City Police Department's cadet corps. *Professional Issues in Criminal Justice*, *3*(2), 1–16.

Eterno, J. A., Barrow, C. S., & Silverman, E. B. (2017). Forcible stops: Police and citizens speak out. *Public Administration Review*, *77*(2), 181–192. https://doi.org/10.1111/puar.12637

Eterno, J. A., & Silverman, E. B. (2010). NYPD's CompStat: Compare statistics or compose statistics? *International Journal of Police Science & Management*, *12*(3), 426–449.

Eterno, J. A., & Silverman, E. B. (2012). *The crime numbers game: Management by manipulation*. CRC Press.

Eterno, J. A., Silverman, E. B., & Berlin, M. (2021). Police of tomorrow: Comprehensive CompStat performance management moving from stagnation to innovation. *Police Practice and Research: An International Journal*, *22*(1), 886–902. https://doi.org/10.1080/15614263.2020.1725273

Ferrandino, J. (2012). The efficiency of frisks in the NYPD, 2004–2010. *Criminal Justice Review*, *38*(2), 149–168. https://doi.org/10.1177/0734016812466570

Fitzpatrick, D. J., Gorr, W. L., & Neill, D. B. (2020). Policing chronic and temporary hot spots of violent crime: A controlled field experiment. *arXiv*: Cornell University. https://doi.org/10.48550/arxiv.2011.06019

Floyd v. City of New York, 959 F. Supp. 2d 540 (S.D.N.Y. 2013). https://casetext.com/case/floyd-v-city-of-new-york-7

Ford, J. K., Boles, J. G., Plamondon, K. E., & White, J. P. (1999). Transformational leadership and community policing: A road map for change. *Police Chief Magazine*, *66*(12), 14–22. https://www.ojp.gov/ncjrs/virtual-library/abstracts/transformational-leadership-and-community-policing-road-map-change

Fradella, H. F., & White, M. D. (2017). Reforming stop-and-frisk. *Criminology, Criminal Justice, Law & Society*, *18*(3), 45–65.

Gelman, A., Fagan, J., & Kiss, A. (2007). *An analysis of the New York City Police Department's "stop-and-frisk" policy in the context of claims of racial bias*. Columbia University, Department of Statistics. https://stat.columbia.edu/~gelman/research/published/frisk9.pdf

Gentithes, M. (2020). Suspicionless witness stops: The new racial profiling. *Harvard Civil Rights–Civil Liberties Law Review*, *55*(2), 491–529.

Gill, C., Weisburd, D., Telep, C. W., Vitter, Z., & Bennett, T. (2014). Community-oriented policing to reduce crime, disorder and fear and increase satisfaction and legitimacy among citizens: A systematic review. *Journal of Experimental Criminology*, *10*(4), 399–428. https://doi.org/10.1007/s11292-014-9210-y

Grawert, A., & Cullen, J. (2016, March 7). *What the data tell us about crime and the "Ferguson effect"*. Brennan Center for Justice. https://www.brennancenter.org/our-work/analysis-opinion/what-data-tell-us-about-crime-and-ferguson-effect

Henry, V. E. (2003). *CompStat paradigm: Management accountability in policing, business and the public sector*. Looseleaf Law Publications.

Hutchins, R. M. (2013). Stop Terry: Reasonable suspicion, race, and a proposal to limit Terry stops. *New York University Journal of Legislation and Public Policy*, *16*, 883–917.

Kammersgaard, T. (2019). Private security guards policing public space: using soft power in place of legal authority. *An International Journal of Research and Policy*, *31*(2). https://doi.org/10.1080/10439463.2019.1688811

Keenan, D., & Thomas, T. M. (2014). An offense-severity model for stop-and-frisks. *Yale Law Journal*, *123*(5), 1118–1625.

Khan, M. R., Kapadia, F., Geller, A., Mazumdar, M., Scheidell, J. D., Krause, K. D., Martino, R. J., Cleland, C. M., Dyer, T. V., Ompad, D. C., & Halkitis, P. N. (2021). Racial and ethnic disparities in stop-and-frisk experience among young sexual minority men in New York City. *PLOS One*, *16*(8), e0256201. https://doi.org/10.1371/journal.pone.0256201

Kochel, T. R., & Weisburd, D. (2019). The impact of hot spots policing on collective efficacy: Findings from a randomized field trial. *Justice Quarterly*, *36*(5), 900–928. https://doi.org/10.1080/07418825.2018.1465579

Kumar, V. (2023). Police executive leadership and police legitimacy. In J. Eterno, A. Verma, A. M. Das, & D. K. Das (Eds.), *Global issues in contemporary policing* (pp. 33–44). Springer.

Lehrer, S. F., & Lepage, L.-P. (2018). Does selective crime reporting influence our ability to detect racial discrimination in the NYPD's stop-and-frisk program? (Working Paper). https://econ.queensu.ca/faculty/lehrer/lpl_disc.pdf

MacDonald, J., Fagan, J., & Geller, A. (2016). The effects of local police surges on crime and arrests in New York City. *PLOS One*, *11*(6), e0157223. https://doi.org/10.1371/journal.pone.0157223

MacWade v. Kelly, 460 F.3d 260 (2d Cir. 2006)

Madison, J. (1788/2001). Federalist No. 51: The structure of the government must furnish the proper checks and balances between the different departments [A. Hamilton, J. Jay, & J. Madison, authors]. In C. Rossiter (Ed.), *The Federalist Papers* (pp. 321–325). New York, NY: Signet Classic.

Maple, J., & Mitchell, C. (1999). *The Crime Fighter: Putting the bad guys out of business*. Doubleday.

Meares, T. L. (2014). The law and social science of stop-and-frisk. *Annual Review of Law and Social Science*, *10*, 335–352. https://doi.org/10.1146/annurev-lawsocsci-102612-134043

Moura, R. C. de, Borges, A., Morgado, S. M. A., & Ramalho, N. C. (2022). Police Leadership 2.0: A comprehensive systematic review of the literature. *Policing*, *17*(1). https://doi.org/10.1093/police/paac068

Murphy, K. (2023). Encouraging minority trust and compliance with police in a procedural justice experiment: How identity and situational context matter. *Group Processes & Intergroup Relations*, *26*(4), 816–832. https://doi.org/10.1177/13684302221119649

NAACP Legal Defense and Educational Fund. (2025). *Consent decrees*. National Police Funding Database. Retrieved December 12, 2025, from https://policefundingdatabase.org/explore-the-database/consent-decrees/

New York Civil Liberties Union. (2007, July 6). *MacWade v. Kelly (Challenging the NYPD's subway bag-search program)*. New York Civil Liberties Union. https://www.nyclu.org/court-cases/macwade-v-kelly-challenging-nypds-subway-bag-search-program

New York Civil Liberties Union. (2025, May 27). *Stop-and-Frisk data*. https://www.nyclu.org/data/stop-and-frisk-data

New York Police Department. (n.d.). *2025 NYPD Stop, Question, and Frisk Data* [Dataset]. New York City Police Department. Retrieved March 30, 2026, from https://www.nyc.gov/site/nypd/stats/reports-analysis/stopfrisk.page

New York Police Department. (2019, January 6). *Overall crime in New York City hits record low in 2019*. https://www.nyc.gov/site/nypd/news/pr0106/overall-crime-new-york-city-hits-record-low-2019

New York Police Department. (2020, January 6). *Overall crime in New York City reaches record low in 2020*. https://www.nyc.gov/site/nypd/news/p0106a/overall-crime-new-york-city-reaches-record-low-2020

New York Police Department. (2023, January 5). *NYPD announces citywide crime statistics for December 2022*. NYC.gov https://www.nyc.gov/site/nypd/news/p00071/nypd-citywide-crime-statistics-december-2022

New York Police Department. (2026a). *Citywide Crime Statistics* (CompStat report). City of New York. https://www.nyc.gov/assets/nypd/downloads/pdf/crime_statistics/cs-en-us-city.pdf

New York Police Department. (2026b, January 6). *NYPD announces safest year ever for gun violence with fewest shooting incidents and shooting victims in recorded history*. NYC.gov https://www.nyc.gov/site/nypd/news/PR001/nypd-safest-year-ever-gun-violence-fewest-shooting-incidents-shooting

Olson, J., Tucker, J., Simi, P., Wrucke, S., & Jordan, C. (2022). Building towards community-oriented policing: Forming an academic-community-police partnership. *Preventive Medicine Reports*, *30*, 102015. https://doi.org/10.1016/j.pmedr.2022.102015

Perrott, S. B., & Trites, K. (2017). On the acceptability of closer public–private policing partnerships: Views from the public side. In J. A. Eterno, A. Verma, A. Mintie Das, & D. K. Das (Eds.), *Global issues in contemporary policing* (pp. 45–62). Routledge.

Petersen, K., Weisburd, D., Fay, S., Eggins, E., & Mazerolle, L. (2023). Police stops to reduce crime: A systematic review and meta-analysis. *Campbell Systematic Reviews*, *19*(1), e1302. https://doi.org/10.1002/cl2.1302

Peyton, K., Sierra-Arévalo, M., & Rand, D. G. (2019). A field experiment on community policing and police legitimacy. *Proceedings of the National Academy of Sciences of the United States of America*, *116*(40), 19894–19898. https://doi.org/10.1073/pnas.1910157116

Pierson, E., Simoiu, C., Overgoor, J., Corbett-Davies, S., Ramachandran, V., Phillips, C., & Goel, S. (2017). A large-scale analysis of racial disparities in police stops across the United States. *arXiv*. https://arxiv.org/abs/1706.05678

Piquero, A. R., & Sherman, L. W. (2025). Did more stop and search by police cause less knife injury in London? Evidence from 2008–2023. *Journal of Quantitative Criminology*, *41*, 459–494. https://doi.org/10.1007/s10940-025-09609-7

Quinton, P. (2023). Striking the right balance? Evidence, ethics and the policing use of stop and search. *Policing: A Journal of Policy and Practice*, *17*. https://doi.org/10.1093/police/paad003

Ratcliffe, J. H., Taniguchi, T., Groff, E. R., & Wood, J. D. (2011). The Philadelphia foot patrol experiment: A randomized controlled trial of police patrol effectiveness in violent crime hotspots. *Criminology*, *49*, 795–831. https://doi.org/10.1111/j.1745-9125.2011.00240.x

Roberts, L. E., Mehranbod, C. A., Bushover, B., Gobaud, A. N., Eschliman, E. L., Fish, C., Zadey, S., Gao, X., & Morrison, C. N. (2024). Trends in police complaints and arrests on New York

City subways, 2018 to 2023: An interrupted time-series analysis. *Injury Epidemiology*, *11*(1), 16. https://doi.org/10.1186/s40621-024-00501-9

Scrase, S. (2020). Re-thinking procedural justice theory through stop and search: Shame, anger, and police legitimacy. *Policing: A Journal of Policy and Practice*, *15*(2), 1476–1490. https://doi.org/10.1093/police/paaa039

Sewell, A. A., & Jefferson, K. A. (2016). Collateral damage: The health effects of invasive police encounters in New York City. *Journal of Urban Health*, *93*(1), 42–57. https://doi.org/10.1007/s11524-015-0016-7

Shane, J. M. (2008). *Developing a performance management model*. Looseleaf Law Publications.

Shannon, I. (2020). Democratic oversight and political direction of chief police officers in England and Wales: Implications for police legitimacy. *Policing: A Journal of Policy and Practice*, *15*(2), 912–926. https://doi.org/10.1093/police/paaa088

Sherman, L. W., & Kumar, S. (2021). Equal protection by race with stop-and-frisk: A Risk-Adjusted Disparity (RAD) index for balanced policing. *Cambridge Journal of Evidence-Based Policing*, *5*, 1–19. https://doi.org/10.1007/s41887-021-00065-4

Silverman, E. B. (2001). *NYPD battles crime: Innovative strategies in policing* (Rev. ed.). Northeastern University Press.

Skogan, W. G. (2016). *Stop-and-frisk and trust in police in Chicago* (IPR Working Paper No. WP-16–08). Institute for Policy Research, Northwestern University. https://www.ipr.northwestern.edu/documents/working-papers/2016/WP-16-08.pdf

Stone, C., Foglesong, T., & Cole, C. M. (2009). *Policing Los Angeles under a consent decree: The dynamics of change at the LAPD* (Harvard Kennedy School Working Paper Series). Harvard Kennedy School. https://www.hks.harvard.edu/publications/policing-los-angeles-under-consent-decree-dynamics-change-lapd

Terry v. Ohio, 392 U.S. 1, 88 S. Ct. 1868, 20 L. Ed. 2d 889 (1968)

Vito, A., Higgins, G., & Vito, R. (2021). Police stop-and-frisk and the impact of race: A focal analysis. *Societies*, *11*(2), 52. https://doi.org/10.3390/soc11020052

Wakefield, A. (2008). Private policing: A view from the mall. *Public Administration*, *86*(3), 659–678. https://doi.org/10.1111/j.1467-9299.2008.00750.x

Wakefield, A., & Fleming, J. (2009). *The Sage dictionary of policing*. Sage.

Weisburd, D., Braga, A. A., Groff, E. R., & Wooditch, A. (2017). Can hot spots policing reduce crime in urban areas? An agent-based simulation. *Criminology*, *55*(1), 137–173. https://doi.org/10.1111/1745-9125.12131

Weisburd, D., Groff, E. R., & Yang, S. M. (2021). Police stops to reduce crime: A systematic review and protocol. *Systematic Reviews*, *10*(1), 59.

Weisburd, D., Petersen, K., & Fay, S. (2023). Does scientific evidence support the widespread use of SQFs as a proactive policing strategy? *Policing: A Journal of Policy and Practice*, *17*, paac098. https://doi.org/10.1093/police/paac098

Weisburd, D., Telep, C. W., Vovak, H., Zastrow, T., Braga, A. A., & Turchan, B. (2022). Reforming the police through procedural justice training: A multicity randomized trial at crime hot spots. *Proceedings of the National Academy of Sciences of the United States of America*, *119*(14), e2118780119. https://doi.org/10.1073/pnas.2118780119

Weisburd, D., Willis, J. J., Mastrofski, S. D., & Greenspan, R. (2019). Changing everything so that everything can remain the same: CompStat and American policing. In D. Weisburd & A. A. Braga (Eds.), *Police innovation: Contrasting perspectives* (2nd ed., pp. 417–439). Cambridge University Press.

Willis, J. J. (2007). Making sense of CompStat: A theory-based analysis of organizational change in three police departments. *Law & Society Review*, *41*(1), 147–188. https://doi.org/10.1111/j.1540-5893.2007.00311.x

Wood, G., Tyler, T. R., & Papachristos, A. V. (2020). Procedural justice training reduces police use of force and complaints against officers. *Proceedings of the National Academy of Sciences of the United States of America*, *117*(18), 9815–9821. https://doi.org/10.1073/pnas.1920671117

Yesberg, J. A., Costi, F., Chan, A., & Bradford, B. (2024). A systematic review and meta-analysis of the relationship between policing and collective efficacy. *Journal of Experimental Criminology*, *20*, 1147–1173. https://doi.org/10.1007/s11292-023-09580-y

Zimroth, P. L. (2015, July 9). *First report of the independent monitor*. NYPD Monitor. https://www.nypdmonitor.org/wp-content/uploads/2022/09/01-MonitorsFirstReport-AsFiledInFloydDocket.pdf

Zimroth, P. L. (2016a, February 16). *Second report of the independent monitor*. NYPD Monitor. https://www.nypdmonitor.org/wp-content/uploads/2022/09/02-2016-02-16FloydvCityofNY-MonitorsSecondStatusReport.pdf

Zimroth, P. L. (2016b, August 9). *Third report of the independent monitor: Interim briefing on body-worn camera pilot program*. NYPD Monitor. https://www.nypdmonitor.org/wp-content/uploads/2022/09/03-2016-08-09MonitorsLtrtoJudgeTorresencl3rdReportInterim-Brief.pdf

Zimroth, P. L. (2016c, November 18). *Fourth report of the independent monitor*. NYPD Monitor. https://www.nypdmonitor.org/wp-content/uploads/2022/09/04-2016-11-18FourthReportoftheIndependentMonitor-1.pdf

Zimroth, P. L. (2017a, May 30). *Fifth report of the independent monitor: Analysis of NYPD stops reported, 2013–2015*. NYPD Monitor. https://www.nypdmonitor.org/wp-content/uploads/2022/09/05-2017-05-30-MonitorsFifthReport-AnalysisofNYPDStopsReported2013-2015-Asfiled.pdf

Zimroth, P. L. (2017b, June 29). *Sixth report of the independent monitor: The NYPD's body-worn camera pilot: Research and evaluation plan*. NYPD Monitor. https://www.nypdmonitor.org/wp-content/uploads/2022/09/06-2017-06-29-MonitorsSixthReport.pdf

Zimroth, P. L. (2017c, December 13). *Seventh report of the independent monitor*. NYPD Monitor. https://www.nypdmonitor.org/wp-content/uploads/2022/09/07-2017-12-13-FloydLigonDavis-Monitor-Seventh-Report_EAST_80301353_1.pdf

Zimroth, P. L. (2018, July 27). *Eighth report of the independent monitor: Evaluation of NYPD body-worn camera implementation in NYCHA housing developments*. NYPD Monitor. https://www.nypdmonitor.org/wp-content/uploads/2022/09/08-2018-07-27-Monitors-Eighth-Report-Evaluation-of-NYPD-BWC-Implementation-in-NYCHA-Housing-Developments.pdf

Zimroth, P. L. (2019, January 11). *Ninth report of the independent monitor*. NYPD Monitor. https://www.nypdmonitor.org/wp-content/uploads/2022/09/09-2019-01-11-Combined-Ninth-Report-4.pdf

Zimroth, P. L. (2020a, January 7). *Tenth report of the independent monitor*. NYPD Monitor. https://www.nypdmonitor.org/wp-content/uploads/2022/09/10-Monitors-Corrected-Tenth-Report.pdf

Zimroth, P. L. (2020b, October 28). *Eleventh report of the independent monitor*. NYPD Monitor. https://www.nypdmonitor.org/wp-content/uploads/2022/09/11th-Report-Submission-2.pdf

Zimroth, P. L. (2020c, November 30). *Twelfth report of the independent monitor: The deployment of body-worn cameras on New York City Police Department (NYPD) officers*. NYPD Monitor. https://www.nypdmonitor.org/wp-content/uploads/2022/09/12th-Report.pdf

Zimroth, P. L. (2021a, September 1). *Thirteenth report of the independent monitor: Racial disparities in NYPD stop, question, and frisk practices: An analysis of 2013 to 2019 stop reports*. NYPD Monitor. https://www.nypdmonitor.org/wp-content/uploads/2023/09/13th-Report-and-Submission-Letter.pdf

Zimroth, P. L. (2021b, October 12). *Fourteenth report of the independent monitor: NYPD social distancing enforcement, 2020*. NYPD Monitor. https://www.nypdmonitor.org/wp-content/uploads/2022/09/14-Fourteenth-Report.as-filed.pdf

INDEX

Page numbers in *italics* denote figures, those in bold denote tables.

For Product Safety Concerns and Information please contact our EU
representative GPSR@taylorandfrancis.com
Taylor & Francis Verlag GmbH, Kaufingerstraße 24, 80331 München, Germany

www.ingramcontent.com/pod-product-compliance
Ingram Content Group UK Ltd.
Pitfield, Milton Keynes, MK11 3LW, UK
UKHW050235200926
475702UK00020B/3037
9781032973272